Detroit Free Press Cookbook

A collection of the best loved recipes
from the Free Press Tower Kitchen

Jeremy Iggers
Nettie Duffield

•

Illustrated by Jon Buechel

Detroit Free Press
1984

Published by the Detroit Free Press
321 W. Lafayette
Detroit, Michigan 48231

Library of Congress Catalog Card Number: 84-70736
Manufactured in the United States of America.

ISBN 0-9605692-2-7

Authors' note

When we first sifted through our files of recipes to include in this book, we chose our personal favorites, and those recipes that got a strong response from readers.

After our first time around, we had some 600 recipes on our list — far more than we could fit. So we went through the list a second time and a third time, painfully culling out favorites. The recipes that survived represent the creme de la creme, more than 280 of the very best recipes that have appeared in our food section.

We've included a broad range of dishes, from gourmet delights that require more painstaking preparation to quick and economical fare.

Although recipes are designated with three degrees of difficulty, there are no recipes in this book that one familiar with kitchen practices cannot do with ease.

Jeremy Iggers

Nettie Duffield

Jeremy Iggers has been Free Press food editor since 1980. He previously wrote a restaurant column for the Minneapolis Star. He is also co-author of another cookbook, "The Joy of Cheesecake."

Nettie Duffield has been in the Free Press food department since 1979. She has taught cooking courses in the Grosse Pointe public schools' adult education program. She has performed cooking demonstrations throughout the Detroit area.

Credits:

Recipe selection: JEREMY IGGERS, NETTIE DUFFIELD

Illustrations: JON BUECHEL

Copy editing: SUE CHEVALIER, BILL DIEM

Book design: P.S. ABRAMS, ANNIE LAZUREK,
HANK SZERLAG

Cover photograph: ROBERT STEWART

Editorial Assistant: NANCY BARNETT

Keylines: P.S. ABRAMS

Project coordinator: JON PEPPER

Contents

Abbreviations:

c	cup
t	teaspoon
T	tablespoon
pkg	package
lb	pound
oz	ounce
qt	quart

Symbols:

Quick and easy

Takes a bit more time

 Time-consuming, but worth the effort

APPETIZERS

MAKES 3 CUPS

Brandade de Morue (Salt Cod with Garlic)

      1 lb salt cod, soaked In several changes of cold water for 12
         hours and drained
      1 to 2 cloves garlic, crushed and mashed to a paste
    ½ c olive oil
    ½ c heavy cream

Place the drained cod in saucepan, cover with fresh cold water and cook over medium heat 15 minutes, until fish is tender. Drain and remove any skin and bones. Place fish in large bowl and mash to a pulp with potato masher, or process in food processor. Put pulp in deep saucepan; add mashed garlic. Over low heat, with wooden spoon, beat in olive oil and cream by alternate spoonfuls. (This step also may be done in a food processor and the paste heated later.) The finished paste should be white, creamy and very smooth. Serve warm or cold with crackers or crusty bread. Makes about three cups of spread.

MAKES 48 PUFFS

Broccoli Puffs

      1 pkg (10 oz) frozen cut broccoli In cheese sauce
    1½ c yellow cornmeal
    ½ c flour
      2 T sugar
    1½ t garlic salt
    1¼ t baking powder
      1 t salt
    ¾ c milk
      1 egg
         Oil for deep frying

Place plastic pouch with broccoli and sauce in boiling water; bring water to a second vigorous boil and cook broccoli, uncovered, 18 minutes. Empty contents of pouch into small bowl and cut broccoli, using two knives, into ½-inch pieces; set aside.

In medium bowl, combine cornmeal, flour, sugar, garlic salt, baking powder and salt. Stir in prepared broccoli and cheese sauce, milk and egg; stir until well mixed. Let batter stand five to 10 minutes.

Meanwhile, in deep fat fryer or heavy saucepan, heat 2 inches of oil to 375 degrees. Drop batter by teaspoonfuls into oil and fry until golden brown, turning once. Drain on paper towels and serve with or without a favorite dipping sauce. Makes about 48 appetizers.

MAKES 30 TARTS

Caviar Tarts

1 c butter, softened, divided
1 pkg (3 oz) cream cheese, softened
1 c flour
3 hard cooked eggs, coarsely chopped
½ c sour cream
2 T mayonnaise
4 large scallions
1 jar (3½ oz) lumpfish caviar
Fresh lemon juice

In medium bowl, cream ½ cup softened butter with cream cheese until thoroughly combined. Slowly mix in flour until a medium-stiff dough is formed. Scrape into ball and wrap tightly in plastic wrap; refrigerate at least two hours or overnight.

Remove dough from refrigerator and let sit about 30 minutes to slightly soften. Roll out dough on floured surface to ⅛-inch thickness and cut into rounds with 2½-inch cookie cutter. There should be about 30 rounds from this recipe. Carefully shape rounds over inverted gem muffin (miniature muffin) tin cups, taking great care not to puncture or tear dough. Press dough down and around cups to form cup-shape mold. Refrigerate tins 30 minutes.

Remove tins from refrigerator and prick top and sides of each dough cup. Bake at 350 degrees 12 to 15 minutes, until golden brown. Remove tins from oven, cool slightly and carefully lift dough cups from tins. Cool completely on wire rack.

In small bowl, combine remaining ½ cup softened butter with chopped eggs; mix thoroughly and set aside.

In another small bowl, combine sour cream, mayonnaise and scallions; mix thoroughly and set aside.

Spread about two teaspoons of egg mixture on bottom of each dough cup. Cover with about one heaping teaspoon sour cream mixture. Carefully spread about one heaping teaspoon caviar on top, pushing caviar to the edges of dough cup. Arrange cups on serving plate and refrigerate until serving time. Just before serving, sprinkle caviar lightly with fresh lemon juice. Makes about 30 Caviar Tarts.

**MAKES 40
TO 48 PIECES**

Crostini

8 T unsalted butter, softened, divided
1 large onion, chopped
2 cloves garlic, 1 minced and 1 cut in half
½ lb chicken livers, rinsed, membranes removed, and coarsely chopped
1 T sherry or white wine
½ c mayonnaise
¼ c freshly grated Parmesan cheese
2 to 3 T finely chopped black olives
1 T minced parsley
  Salt, pepper and nutmeg to taste
20 to 24 slices firm, thinly sliced white bread, crusts removed

In medium skillet, heat two tablespoons of the butter; add onion and minced garlic clove and cook until soft but not browned, about four minutes. Remove onion mixture with slotted spoon and set aside. To fat remaining in skillet add the remaining butter and heat. Add prepared chicken livers and cook until pink color disappears; remove with slotted spoon and drain on paper towel. Add sherry or white wine to liquid remaining in skillet and cook until reduced by half. Pour into blender or food processor with metal blade; add reserved livers and onion mixture. Puree mixture until smooth and scrape into bowl. Stir in mayonnaise, Parmesan cheese, olives and parsley; mix well and season to taste with salt, pepper and nutmeg. Cover and refrigerate until just before serving time.

Meanwhile lightly toast one side of the bread slices. Cut remaining garlic clove in half and rub the toasted sides of bread. Cut slices in half diagonally and spread untoasted side with prepared liver mixture, bringing spread to the edges of bread. Toast triangles about six inches from broiler unit, until bubbling and lightly browned. Serve hot. Makes about 40 to 48 Crostini.

MAKES 3 CUPS

Egg Mousse with Caviar

1 T unflavored gelatin
2 T lemon juice
2 T dry vermouth
6 hard cooked eggs, chopped
1 c mayonnaise
½ c grated onion
2 T anchovy paste
1 T Escoffier's au Diable
  Sour cream
1 jar (3½ oz) red lumpfish or salmon caviar
  Cherry tomatoes
  Pimiento strips
  Chopped parsley
  Assorted crackers or melba toast

In small bowl or cup, soften gelatin in lemon juice and vermouth for five minutes. Place container in pan of hot water and heat, stirring gelatin mixture, until completely dissolved; set aside.

In blender or food processor container, combine eggs, mayonnaise, onion, anchovy paste and Sauce Diable (or A-1 sauce); blend until smooth. With machine running, pour in prepared hot gelatin mixture and blend until thoroughly mixed. Pour mixture into oiled, oblong 3-cup mold and chill until firm. Before serving, unmold onto serving platter and "frost" with sour cream. Spread caviar on top and garnish with cherry tomatoes, pimiento strips and chopped parsley. Serve with assorted crackers or melba toast. Makes about three cups spread.

**MAKES 40
TO 46 ROUNDS**

French Parmesan Rounds

1 long, thin French bread (baguette) about 20 inches
2 large bunches scallions, trimmed with 4 inches of the green tops left on
1 c mayonnaise
¾ c freshly grated Parmesan cheese
1 to 2 cloves garlic, crushed

Slice bread into ¼-inch rounds and set aside.

In food processor or chopping bowl, chop scallions finely; add mayonnaise, cheese and garlic. Mix thoroughly. Spread about two teaspoons of mixture on each bread round and place on cookie sheet. Run under hot broiler until lightly browned and bubbling. Quickly transfer to serving tray and serve very hot. Makes about 40 to 46 rounds. Pre-baked hard rolls may be used for this appetizer instead of the French bread.

**MAKES 50
SANDWICHES**

Holiday Sandwich Wreath

Egg-Olive Spread:
6 hard cooked eggs, finely chopped
⅓ c finely chopped ripe pitted olives
⅓ c finely chopped pimiento-stuffed green olives
⅓ c finely chopped green onions, including green tops
½ c mayonnaise
¼ t tarragon
Dash hot red pepper sauce
Salt and freshly ground black pepper to taste

Corned Beef Spread:
1 can (12 oz) corned beef, finely chopped
½ c finely chopped dill pickle
⅓ c finely chopped celery
⅓ c finely chopped onion
½ c mayonnaise
1 T Worcestershire sauce
⅛ t cayenne pepper
Salt and pepper to taste

Chicken Curry Spread:
1 small whole chicken breast
1 bay leaf
¼ t tarragon
⅓ c minced celery
½ large tart apple, skinned, cored and minced
¼ c finely chopped pecans
½ c mayonnaise
1 to 2 t curry powder
Salt and white pepper to taste
2 loaves party rye bread (8 oz each)
1 loaf party pumpernickel (8 oz)

In a medium bowl, combine the ingredients for one spread and mix throughly. Repeat for each spread in separate bowl. Refrigerate, covered, until time to assemble the wreath.

Spread Egg and Olive on one loaf of the rye bread. Spread Corn Beef on pumpernickel loaf. Spread Chicken Curry on remaining loaf of rye. Alternate sandwiches on large platter in shape of wreath. Decorate with large fabric bow and sprigs of greenery or Christmas balls. Makes about 50 sandwiches.

MAKES 1 QUART DIP

Jane Reik's Seven Layer Dip

1 can (10½ oz) jalapeno bean dip
2 ripe avocados
1 T lemon juice
½ pkg taco seasoning (1¼ or 1¾ oz)
3 T mayonnaise
2 T sour cream
2 oz grated or shredded cheddar cheese
2 oz grated or shredded Monterey Jack cheese
2 ripe tomatoes, chopped and seeded
1 bunch green onions (about eight), chopped, including green tops
1 c ripe olives, chopped
Flavored corn chips

In shallow serving dish or pie plate, preferably glass or Pyrex, spread layer of jalapeno bean dip. In small bowl, mash avocados with lemon juice; spread on top of bean dip. Combine taco seasoning, mayonnaise and sour cream; blend well and spread on top of avocado mixture. Sprinkle cheddar and Monterey cheeses evenly on top of taco mixture. Arrange tomato on top of cheese and sprinkle evenly with green onions. Sprinkle olives on top of all. Chill until serving time. Serve with flavored corn chips. Makes about 1 quart dip.

MAKES 2 CUPS

Joe Lapointe's Guacamole

3 large, ripe chilled avocados
3 t lemon juice
1 large hard-boiled egg, chopped
1 large tomato, chopped
   Shredded scraps of chicken or turkey (optional)
2 T onion, finely chopped
   Chili powder to taste
   Garlic powder to taste
   Salt and pepper to taste
1 t prepared, mustard
   Dash of Worcestershire sauce

It is very important that the avocados be ripe. If they aren't, the dip won't be worth a hoot. The avocados should be soft to the touch and the skin should be dark green verging on black. (Avocados can get very soft and dark before they spoil.) Sometimes it is best to buy them a few days early and let them soften in room temperature in a brown paper bag.

Scoop out the avocado pulp, throwing out the pits and the skins. Put the pulp in a large mixing bowl. Pour the lemon juice directly on the avocado pulp. Add the chopped egg and the chopped tomato to the mixture. Mix in a few small scraps of shredded chicken or turkey, if desired. Add onion to mixture.

Season to taste with two or three shakes of chili powder, two or three shakes of garlic powder, two or three shakes of salt and pepper. Add mustard and Worcestershire sauce.

Using a potato masher, blend to an even consistency. Taste it. Because avocado is bland, the spices may be muted, so add extra spice to give it a sharper edge. Serve immediately with large corn chips or crackers in front of a televised football game.

MAKES 3/4 CUP

Dipping Sauce (Nuoc Cham)

1 fresh red chili or 2 small dried chilies
2 large garlic cloves, peeled
5 t sugar
  Juice and pulp of ¼ unpeeled lime
¼ c fish sauce (available at Oriental markets)
⅓ c water
1 T shredded carrot
1 T minced scallion

If using fresh chili, remove seeds and membrane. In food processor or blender, combine chili, garlic, sugar, lime, fish sauce and water. Process or blend until well minced. Pour into serving dish and sprinkle with carrot and scallion. Makes about ¾ cup.

SERVES 6 TO 8

Peppered Cheese

2 c grated Monterey Jack cheese (8 oz)
1 (8 oz) pkg cream cheese, room temperature
1 t fines herbes
1 t Worcestershire sauce
1 garlic clove, crushed
2 to 3 T seasoned pepper
  Plain or bacon-flavored crackers

In a medium bowl, combine Monterey Jack cheese, cream cheese, fines herbes, chives, Worcestershire sauce and garlic. Shape cheese mixture into a 5-inch ball; slightly flatten one side. Cut a 12-inch square of waxed paper. On a flat surface, spread seasoned pepper in an even thick layer on waxed paper. Roll cheese ball in pepper until completely covered. Refrigerate 6 hours or overnight. Cheese ball can be stored in refrigerator several days before serving. Cut into thin slices; serve on crackers. Makes one 5-inch cheese ball.

APPETIZERS

SERVES 12

Seafood Appetizer Cheesecake

1 c crushed buttery crackers (Ritz, Town Club, etc.)
3 T butter or margarine, melted
2 pkgs (8 oz) cream cheese, softened
3 eggs
¾ c sour cream, divided
1 can (7¾ oz) salmon, drained and flaked
1 t fresh lemon juice
½ t onion powder or 2 T grated onion
⅛ t freshly ground black pepper
    Crackers or melba toast

Combine cracker crumbs and melted butter or margarine and mix thoroughly; press onto bottom of nine-inch springform pan. Bake at 350 degrees 10 minutes. Remove from oven and set aside.

In medium bowl of electric mixer, combine softened cream cheese, eggs and ¼ cup of the sour cream; beat until well blended. Add prepared salmon, lemon juice, onion powder or grated onion and pepper. Mix well and pour mixture over prepared crust. Bake at 325 degrees 45 to 50 minutes, until middle is set. Remove from oven and run sharp knife around side of pan. Spread top evenly with remaining half-cup of sour cream. Serve with crackers or melba toast. Makes ample amount for 12 people.

MAKES 36 DUMPLINGS

Shao-Mai (Open-Faced Steamed Dumplings)

½ lb lean pork, ground
½ lb raw shrimp, shelled, deveined, diced into ¼-inch pieces
6 water chestnuts, minced
3 scallions, minced
1½ T fresh ginger, minced
1½ T light soy sauce
2 t Chinese sesame oil
1 t dry sherry
1 t sugar
½ t salt
⅛ t white pepper
3 large Chinese black mushrooms, soaked in hot water until spongy
36 thin won ton skins (available at Oriental markets)
Soy Vinegar Sesame Dipping Sauce

In medium bowl, combine pork, shrimp, water chestnuts, scallions, ginger, soy sauce, sesame oil, sherry, sugar, salt and white pepper. Remove stems from mushrooms and discard; mince mushrooms and add to bowl. Mix all ingredients well with hands but do not overmix until gluey.

Cut won ton skins into 3-inch circles. Place about one tablespoon pork/shrimp mixture in center of each circle. Gather the edges of the skin around filling to form pleat. Lightly squeeze center of dumpling and smooth surface of filling with knife. Tap bottom of dumpling on table surface to flatten bottom. Repeat procedure until all skins and filling are used.

Oil bottom of heat proof platter or steamer; place dumplings on it, leaving ½-inch space between the dumplings. Cover and steam over medium high heat 20 minutes. Serve hot with Soy Vinegar Sesame Dipping Sauce . Makes 36 dumplings.

MAKES 1/3 CUP

Soy Vinegar Sesame Dipping Sauce

¼ c light soy sauce
1 T Chinese red vinegar or red wine vinegar
½ T Chinese sesame oil

In small bowl, combine soy sauce, vinegar and oil; whip with fork to mix. Pour small amounts into individual dishes for dipping. Makes about ⅓ cup sauce.

APPETIZERS

MAKES 3 CUPS

Shrimp-Artichoke Party Spread

- ½ lb raw, peeled and deveined frozen shrimp or rock shrimp
- 1 can (14 oz) artichoke hearts, drained
- ½ c mayonnaise
- ½ c Parmesan cheese
- ¼ t lemon pepper
- ⅛ t salt
  Dash cayenne pepper
- ½ t paprika
  Melba toast or assorted crackers

In medium saucepan, bring water to the depth of one inch to a boil. Add shrimp and cook not more than 25 seconds (it is not necessary for the water to come to a second boil — *do not overcook*.) Drain shrimp and combine in medium bowl with artichoke hearts; chop finely. Add mayonnaise, Parmesan cheese, lemon pepper, salt and cayenne pepper; mix well. Place mixture in nine-inch pie plate or ovenproof serving dish. Sprinkle with paprika and bake at 400 degrees 10 minutes or until hot and bubbly. Serve hot with melba toast or crackers. Makes about three cups of party spread.

MAKES 30 BALLS

Shrimp Balls (Tom Vien)

- 1 lb raw shrimp, shelled and deveined
- 1 t salt
- 1 oz pork fat, minced
- 5 cloves garlic, minced
- 3 shallots, minced
- 1 egg white, lightly beaten
- 1 T cornstarch
- 1 T fish sauce
- 2 t sugar
- ⅛ t freshly ground black pepper
  Oil for frying
  Nuoc Cham (see recipe on Page 10)
  Fish sauce or soy sauce

Sprinkle shrimp with salt, mix well and let stand 30 minutes. Rinse in cold water and drain thoroughly. Chop shrimp very fine and mix with pork fat, garlic and shallots. Either pound in a mortar or whirl in blender or food processor until paste is formed. Add egg white, cornstarch, fish sauce, sugar and pepper and process again. With wet hands, form mixture into one-inch balls and set aside.

Pour oil to a depth of 1½ inches into wok or skillet and heat to about 375 degrees. Deep fry the shrimp balls, about six at a time, until golden, for two to three minutes. Drain on paper towels. Serve with Nuoc Cham, fish sauce or soy sauce. Makes about 30 Shrimp Balls.

13

APPETIZERS

MAKES 80 BALLS

Spinach Balls

2 pkgs (10 oz each) frozen chopped spinach
1 pkg (6 oz) chicken-flavored Stove Top Stuffing
1 c grated Parmesan cheese
6 eggs, lightly beaten
¾ c melted butter
Salt and pepper to taste

Cook spinach according to package directions and drain in sieve, pressing out as much moisture as possible with back of spoon.

In medium bowl, combine spinach, both packets of stuffing mix (do not add water), Parmesan cheese, eggs, butter and salt and pepper to taste. Mix thoroughly and roll into balls the size of large marbles, about 1½ inches in diameter. Place on cookie sheet and freeze. After balls are completely frozen, remove and store in plastic bag in freezer.

To serve: Replace frozen balls on cookie sheet and bake at 350 degrees 10 to 15 minutes (or seven to 10 minutes at 350 degrees for unfrozen balls) until lightly browned. Serve hot. Makes about 80 Spinach Balls.

MAKES 40 PIECES

Teriyaki Chicken Wings

⅓ c fresh or reconstituted lemon juice
¼ c soy sauce
¼ c vegetable oil
3 T chili sauce
2 cloves garlic, finely chopped
¼ t pepper
¼ celery seed
Dash dry mustard
3 lbs chicken wings

To make marinade, in medium bowl, combine lemon juice, soy sauce, oil, chili sauce, garlic, pepper, celery seed and mustard. Stir well and set aside. Cut chicken wings at joint and remove wing tips (reserve for use in soup or stock.) Place wing pieces in shallow baking dish. Pour marinade over chicken; cover and refrigerate at least four hours or overnight, turning occasionally. Drain and place on broiler tray; broil about 10 minutes on each side with broiler tray about seven inches from heating element. Brush occasionally with marinade. Makes about 40 pieces.

14

MAKES 50 SMALL, 30 LARGE

Vietnamese Egg Rolls (Cha Gio)

½ lb raw shrimp, minced
½ lb lean pork, minced
½ lb bean sprouts
2 medium carrots, grated
2 to 3 shallots, minced, if desired
1 oz cellophane noodles (bean threads)
1 pkg round rice paper (available at Oriental markets)
2 eggs, beaten
Oil for deep frying
Shredded scallions for garnish, if desired
Lettuce leaves
Dipping Sauce (recipe on Page 10)

In large bowl, combine shrimp, pork, bean sprouts, carrots and shallots; set aside.

Soak cellophane noodles in warm water about 15 minutes, until flexible; drain, cut into one-inch pieces and add to meat mixture. Toss until combined.

Run one sheet of rice paper quickly under tepid water, handling carefully because paper is very brittle. Place sheet on work surface and brush quickly with egg. Let stand a few seconds, until flexible. With very sharp knife, cut into quarters (or halves, if larger rolls are desired). Place one tablespoon filling on round edge of quarter piece; roll over once, then tuck in sides to enclose filling and continue rolling. If using halves, place about ⅓ cup filling on one end, roll once, tuck in sides and roll up. Continue filling and rolling until all filling is used. The egg will hold the rolls together.

In wok or 10-inch frying pan, heat oil until a drop of water jumps on the surface. Fry about eight rolls at a time until golden brown, about 15 minutes. Drain on paper towels, garnish with scallions and serve with lettuce leaves and Nuoc Cham (recipe on Page 10). Makes about 50 small or 30 large egg rolls.

APPETIZERS

Filo Triangles with Shrimp

    4 large green onions
    1 large clove garlic
    2 T butter
    ½ c dry vermouth
    ¼ c minced parsley
    1 pkg (8 oz) cream cheese, softened
    2 egg yolks
    4 anchovy fillets
   10 oz cooked shrimp
      Salt to taste
   10 to 11 sheets filo dough
      Melted butter

Finely mince onions and garlic or put through feeding tube of food processor. In small saucepan, melt butter; add onions and garlic and cook until golden, about five minutes. Add vermouth and bring to a boil; boil four minutes. Remove from heat and set aside to cool.

In blender, set on chop or food processor, combine parsley, cream cheese, egg yolks, anchovies and shrimp. Add prepared onion-vermouth mixture. With quick on and off motion, combine mixture thoroughly, stopping when shrimp are coarsely chopped. Season to taste with salt and set mixture aside.

Lay out filo dough, one sheet at a time on flat surface, keeping reserved dough covered at all times with a damp dish towel. With sharp knife, cut dough lengthwise into three equal strips. Brush strips with melted butter. Put one tablespoon prepared shrimp filling at the lower right hand corner of each strip; "furl" the strip into a triangle as you would fold a flag and place on cookie sheet. Continue process until all filling is used. Brush tops of triangles with melted butter. Bake at 350 degrees 15 to 18 minutes, until golden brown. Remove to serving platter and serve warm. Makes 30 to 33 triangles.

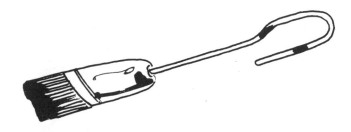

APPETIZERS

Filo Triangles with Curried Chicken

- 1 lb phyllo (filo) dough
- 2 whole chicken breasts, skinned and boned
- 2 T butter
- 1 T minced onion
- 2½ T flour
- 1 t curry powder, or to taste
- 1 c light cream
- ½ t salt
- ½ c chopped walnuts
- ¾ lb melted butter

If phyllo dough is frozen, defrost overnight in refrigerator.

Bake chicken breasts in buttered aluminum foil at 375 degrees 45 minutes. Remove from oven, unwrap and cool. Cut meat into small dice; set aside.

In medium saucepan, melt two tablespoons butter. Add onion and cook one minute. Add flour and curry powder and cook over low heat two minutes, stirring constantly. Add cream all at once and cook, whisking constantly, until mixture is thick and smooth. Season with salt. Stir in chicken and walnuts. Remove from heat and let cool completely.

To assemble: Place one sheet of phyllo dough on flat work surface. Brush with melted butter; top with two more sheets dough, buttering each. Cut sheet in half lengthwise; then cut each half crosswise into six equal parts. Spoon a heaping teaspoon chicken filling onto the end of each of the strips and form a triangle by folding right-hand corner to opposite side, as you would a flag. Continue folding until strip is used. Repeat whole process until all filling is used. Place triangles on greased baking sheet and brush liberally with melted butter. Triangles may be wrapped and refrigerated up to two days or frozen at this point. Bake at 400 degrees until golden brown and puffed, about 10 minutes. Makes about 50 appetizers.

Tyropitta Greek Cheese Triangles

    1 lb feta cheese
    2 eggs, beaten
    ⅓ c chopped chives, parsley, dill or a combination of herbs
      Salt and white pepper, to taste
    ½ c butter, melted
    1 pkg (16 oz) phyllo sheets

Mash feta cheese finely with fork or press through sieve. In medium bowl, combine cheese with beaten eggs, herbs, salt and pepper; set aside (you may use a food processor for this step.) Melt butter and keep it warm.

Lay out phyllo sheets on working surface and cover with damp towel. Remove one sheet and place on working surface. Brush lightly with melted butter. Lay another sheet on top and brush with butter, taking care not to tear dough. With a very sharp knife, cut phyllo lengthwise in four equal strips. Place about one teaspoon cheese mixture on bottom left-hand corner of dough. Fold into a triangle, toward righthand side of strip; continue folding and turning in triangles (as you would fold a flag) until the strip has been used up. Seal last fold by tucking under and brushing butter on the edge. Repeat process with remaining three strips. Continue procedure with the rest of the phyllo dough until cheese filling is used up. Place finished triangles on baking sheet and bake at 375 degrees 20 to 25 minutes, until golden brown and puffed. Serve warm. Makes about 48 triangles.

MAKES 2½ LBS.

April Murphy's Pate

- 2 T vegetable oil
- 1 onion, chopped
- ½ lb chicken livers
- ¾ c Madeira wine, divided
- ¾ lb fatty pork, ground
- ½ lb veal, ground
- ¼ lb boiled ham
- ¼ lb kosher-style salami
- 2 eggs
- 1 t salt
- ½ t pepper
- ½ t basil
- ½ t thyme
- ½ t sage
- ½ t allspice
- ¼ t mace
- 3 cloves garlic, peeled
- 6 to 8 slices bacon, blanched
- ¼ lb unsalted butter, softened and cut into bits
  Watercress, pimiento and parsley for decoration

In medium saucepan or skillet, heat oil and add onion. Cook until slightly soft, two or three minutes. Add chicken livers; cook five to 10 minutes, until still slightly raw inside. Add one-quarter cup of the Madiera, cook two minutes longer and set aside to cool. In food processor, using metal blade, grind and puree pork, veal, ham and salami individually until smooth; set aside in bowl.

Combine cooled chicken livers and eggs in processor bowl and puree finely, using metal blade. Add the pureed meats and process until well blended. Remove three-quarters of mixture to large bowl and set aside. To the quarter of the mixture remaining in the processor, add salt, pepper, basil, thyme, sage, allspice, mace, garlic and one-fourth cup of the remaining Madiera. Process until well blended. Add spiced mixture to reserved pureed meats and mix thoroughly with hands.

Line a 9x5x3-inch loaf pan with foil and pour mixture into pan. Cover the top with overlapping slices of blanched bacon. (To blanch the bacon, arrange slices in skillet, cover with boiling water and boil two to three minutes. Drain on paper towels.) Cover top of pan with foil, place pan on cookie sheet and bake at 350 degrees 1½ hours. Remove from oven; remove and discard bacon and let loaf cool 10 minutes. Break into chunks and return to food processor bowl with metal blade. Add butter and remaining Madeira, to taste, and process until smooth and creamy.

Put into loaf pan or decorative mold lined with plastic wrap or into tureen and chill until firm. If using loaf pan or mold, unmold onto serving plate and decorate with watercress, pimiento and parsley. Serve with crackers. Makes about 2½ pounds of pate.

MAKES 5 CUPS

Joanne Bacon's Chicken Liver Pate Maison

   1 lb butter, divided
   1 pkg (3 oz) cream cheese
   1 large onion, miced
   3 T minced shallots
   ½ c peeled, cored and finely chopped apple
1½ lb chicken livers, rinsed, dried and halved
   3 oz cognac or brandy
2½ t fresh lemon juice
   2 t salt
   ½ t freshly ground black pepper
       Crackers and/or melba toast

Place 2¼ sticks (18 T) of the butter and cream cheese in large bowl of mixer; set aside to soften.

In large skillet, melt 4 tablespoons of the remaining butter; add onion and cook until soft and golden, about five minutes. Stir in shallots and apple; cook about three minutes longer, stirring often. Scrape mixture into food processor or blender container and set aside.

Melt 4 more tablespoons of the butter in same skillet; add chicken livers and cook, stirring often, four minutes. Stir in cognac or brandy and simmer three minutes, stirring frequently. Add livers and liquid to mixture in processor or blender and let cool five minutes. Process or blend until mixture is smooth; cool thoroughly.

Meanwhile, beat the reserved softened butter and cream cheese until smooth and fluffy. Add cooled liver mixture and beat until thoroughly combined. Add lemon juice, salt and pepper and beat until well mixed. Spoon into small crocks or jars and smooth the top with back of a spoon; set aside.

In small saucepan, melt the remaining ¾ stick butter over low heat. Remove from heat and let rest 10 minutes. Carefully pour off the clarified butter from the top; reserve sediment for other uses. Pour clarified butter in thin layer over the tops of the crocks or jars. As butter hardens, it will form an edible seal. Cover tops of crocks or jars and store in refrigerator for five to seven days. Serve with crackers and melba toast. Makes five cups.

MAKES 2 CUPS

Salmon Camembert Pate

- 9 oz Camembert cheese
- 1 can (7¾ oz) salmon
- ⅓ c unsalted butter
- ¼ c chopped shallots or green onions
- 2 T coarsely chopped parsley
- ¼ t garlic powder
- ¼ t dried thyme, crushed
- ⅛ T dried basil, crushed
  Crackers

Remove rind if any, from Camembert and cut into chunks. Drain salmon thoroughly and flake. Place salmon, cheese, butter, shallots or onions, parsley, garlic powder, thyme and basil in food processor or blender. Process until smooth. Place in serving dish, cover and refrigerate until serving time. Serve with crackers. Makes about two cups paté.

Olive Pate

1½ c drained, pitted ripe olives
1 c grated Monterey Jack cheese
2 hard-cooked eggs
1½ t dried basil
1 t dried tarragon
1 t brandy
¼ t freshly ground black pepper
1 clove garlic, sliced
Salt to taste
2 T minced parsley
Raw vegetables or French bread and crackers

In medium bowl, or in food processor or blender, combine olives, cheese, eggs, basil, tarragon, brandy, pepper, garlic and salt to taste. Chop or puree until nearly smooth. Spoon into crock or serving dish; cover and chill until serving time. Sprinkle with chopped parsley and serve with raw vegetables or French bread and crackers. Makes about 2½ cups pate.

SOUPS

SOUPS

Barszcz

1 T butter
1 medium potato, peeled and sliced
1 small onion, chopped
3 large mushroom caps, sliced
4 c rich beef or veal stock or broth
4 large beets, cooked, peeled and sliced
⅓ small head cabbage, shredded
1 medium tomato, peeled and chopped
1 t fresh dill weed or ½ t dried dill weed
1 t chopped fresh parsley
1 t salt
1 bay leaf
4 whole peppercorns
1 c sour cream
Salt and pepper to taste

In large heatproof casserole or Dutch oven, melt butter; add potato, onion and mushrooms. Cook until soft, about four to five minutes. Add stock or broth, beets, cabbage, tomato, dill, parsley, salt, bay leaf and peppercorns. Simmer over medium heat, partially covered, about one hour, until vegetables are soft and flavors are well combined.

In medium bowl, beat sour cream until fluffy. Slowly add one cup of the hot broth and mix well. Return the sour cream mixture to soup and stir until well combined. Heat but do not boil. Serve hot. Makes about two quarts.

MAKES 2½ QUARTS

Canadian Cheese Soup

5 T butter or margarine
2 medium carrots, finely chopped
2 ribs celery, finely chopped
1 medium onion, finely chopped
½ green pepper, seeded and finely chopped
4 to 5 mushrooms, cleaned and finely chopped
½ c cooked ham, finely chopped, if desired
½ c flour
2 T cornstarch
1 qt chicken broth
1 qt milk
½ t paprika
¼ to ½ t cayenne
½ t dry mustard, if desired
1 lb process sharp cheddar cheese, grated
  Salt and freshly ground black pepper, if desired

In large heavy soup pot, melt butter or margarine; add carrots, celery, onion, green pepper, mushrooms and ham, if desired. Cook over medium heat until vegetables are crisp tender, about 10 minutes, stirring occasionally. Do not brown. Add flour and cornstarch and cook, stirring constantly, about three minutes. Add broth and cook, stirring constantly, until slightly thickened. Add milk, paprika, cayenne and mustard, if desired. Add cheese gradually, stirring constantly, until cheese is melted. *Do not allow soup to boil after cheese is added because it will curdle.* Season to taste with salt and black pepper, if desired. Serve very hot. Makes about 2½ quarts soup.

SERVES 6 TO 8

Charley's Chowder Soup

- ¼ c olive oil
- 3 medium-sized cloves garlic, smashed
- ⅓ c onions, finely chopped
- ⅛ t oregano
- ⅛ t basil
- ⅛ t thyme
- ½ c celery, finely chopped
- 6 oz finely chopped stewed tomatoes
- 3 qt water plus 2 oz clam base OR 3 qt clam juice (see note)
- 1 lb boneless pollack or turbot
- Salt to taste
- ½ c finely chopped fresh parsley

In large, heavy pot, heat olive oil until very hot. Add garlic cloves and cook just until golden; remove garlic and discard. *Do not burn the garlic or you will ruin taste of soup.* Add onions and cook, stirring, two minutes. Add oregano, basil and thyme and cook another minute, stirring. Add celery and cook until translucent, about three minutes. Add tomatoes and cook 20 to 25 minutes, stirring frequently to prevent sticking. Add water, clam base and fish. *Note:* If clam base is unavailable, substitute clam juice for the water and add no water at all. You may substitute fish stock for part of the clam juice but at least ⅓ of the liquid should be clam juice. Cook 15 minutes, uncovered, over high heat. Add salt to taste, cover pot, and continue cooking over low heat 20 minutes longer. Stir often by whipping to break up fish and blend flavor. Just before serving, add parsley. Makes six to eight servings.

SERVES 10 TO 12

Christ Church Cranbrook Choir Vegetable-Beef Soup

1 T olive oil
2 lbs round or flank steak, trimmed and cut into small cubes
2 large yellow onions, peeled and diced, divided
2 large cans (28 oz each) whole tomatoes, undrained
1 large can (24 oz) tomato juice
2 cloves garlic, mashed
2 cans (10½ oz each) condensed beef bouillon or 4 c beef stock
3 to 5 c red wine
4 to 8 c water, divided
2 to 3 T Italian herbs
Pinch oregano
Salt and pepper to taste
2 c green beans, cut into 1-inch lengths
2 large stalks celery, diced
2 medium yellow summer squash or zucchini, diced
1 large stalk or small bunch broccoli, trimmed and cut into flowerets and stalk diced
12 to 15 medium mushrooms, halved or quartered
3 large carrots, scraped and diced
3 to 5 ears corn, cut from cob
2 large baking potatoes, pared and diced
Sour cream, if desired

In very large soup pot or kettle, heat olive oil; add beef and one of the diced onions and brown thoroughly. Briefly whirl each can of tomatoes (about one to two seconds) in blender or food processor, just to coarsely break up tomatoes, and add to pot. Add tomato juice and garlic; bring to a boil: Add bouillon or stock, three cups of the wine and four cups of the water. Season with Italian herbs, oregano and salt and pepper to taste. Simmer for at least one hour, adding more wine and water as needed to keep the level of the broth.

About 30 minutes before serving, start adding the vegetables by order of length of time necessary to cook them. Start with green beans, then celery, squash or zucchini, broccoli, mushrooms, carrots, corn and potatoes. As soon as vegetables are tender, the soup is ready to serve. A dollop of sour cream on top of each serving adds a zesty taste. Makes about 10 to 12 servings.

SOUPS

Cream of Anything Soup

4 T butter
1 lb of any vegetable — carrots, beans, spinach, peas, whatever — trimmed, washed and chopped
6 scallions, sliced
3 c chicken broth or stock
½ c white wine
2 T chopped parsley
1 T lemon juice
1 t tarragon
1 t sugar
1 c heavy cream
Salt and freshly ground pepper to taste
Dill weed or chives for garnish

In large pot or soup kettle, melt butter; add vegetable and scallions and cook, stirring often, until vegetables are soft but not browned, about 20 minutes. Add chicken stock, wine, parsley, lemon juice, tarragon and sugar; simmer, covered, about 30 minutes, until vegetables are very soft. Puree soup in blender or food processor and transfer to large bowl. Add heavy cream and stir thoroughly. Season to taste with salt and pepper and garnish with dill weed or chives. Makes about six servings.

SERVES 12

Cream of Broccoli Soup

    1 lb fresh broccoli
    ½ c water
    5 T butter, divided
    ½ medium onion, chopped
    3 medium stalks celery, chopped
    4 T flour
    2 cans (14 oz each) chicken broth or 28 oz homemade broth
    ¼ lb mushrooms, chopped
    3 to 4 c light cream
    1 t salt
    ¼ t white pepper
    ¼ t crushed dried tarragon
    1 c chopped ham
      Grated cheddar cheese, if desired

Cut broccoli into one-half-inch slices, paring main stems and removing leaves. In medium saucepan, combine broccoli pieces and water; steam, covered, until tender, about 15 minutes. Set pan aside — do not drain.

In large soup pot or kettle, melt four tablespoons of the butter; add onion and celery and cook, stirring frequently, until soft, about six minutes. Add flour and stir until thoroughly mixed; cook, stirring constantly, about three minutes. Slowly add chicken broth, stirring constantly, until mixture is simmering and slightly thickened. Add prepared broccoli and cooking water. Bring to a boil and simmer five minutes, stirring occasionally. In small batches, puree soup in blender until smooth. Return to large soup pot.

Meanwhile, melt remaining tablespoon butter in small skillet. Add chopped mushrooms and cook over high heat until moisture disappears. Add to soup pot with light cream, salt, white pepper and tarragon. Heat slowly until hot, but do not boil. Stir in ham and serve with a sprinkling of grated cheese on top, if desired. Makes about 12 servings.

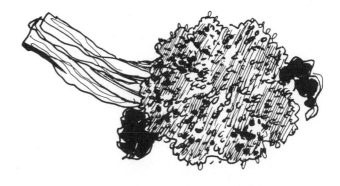

SOUPS

MAKES 3 DOZEN

Knaidlich (Matzo Balls)

    4 eggs, beaten
    2 T oil
    ½ t salt
      Freshly ground black pepper to taste
    1 c matzo meal
      Chicken soup made with parsley root, also known as
      Hamburg parsley

In medium bowl, combine eggs, oil, salt and pepper; mix well. Add matzo meal and stir until thoroughly mixed. Cover bowl and rest in refrigerator until mixture hardens enough to mold.

With wet hands, shape mixture into small balls, about the size of small walnuts. Drop into boiling, salted water and boil 30 minutes. Remove with slotted spoon and serve in hot homemade chicken soup which has been prepared with parsley root. Makes about three dozen matzo balls.

SERVES 6

Lentil-Sausage Soup

    1½ c dried lentils, washed and drained
      2 cloves garlic, peeled and chopped
      1 small onion, peeled and halved
      1 stalk celery, chopped
      1 medium carrot, chopped
      1 lb Polish kielbasa or other smoked sausage
      4 c beef broth
      3 c water
      2 T tomato paste
    1½ T red wine vinegar
      1 t paprika
      ½ t freshly ground black pepper
      1 small bay leaf
        Pinch thyme
        Salt to taste

In large, heavy soup pot or kettle, combine lentils, garlic, onion, celery, carrot and sausage. Stir in beef broth, water, tomato paste, vinegar, paprika, pepper, bay leaf and thyme. Simmer, covered, about one hour, until lentils are soft. Remove sausage and set aside. Puree soup in blender or food processor until smooth. Return soup to pot; slice sausage in ¼-inch diagonal slices and add to soup. Season to taste with salt and serve very hot. Makes six servings.

SOUPS

SERVES 6 TO 8

Minnesota Wild Rice Soup

3 T butter
1 medium onion, sliced
4 oz fresh mushrooms, sliced or chopped
¼ c flour
4 c chicken stock
1½ c cooked wild rice
1 c light cream
¼ c dry sherry
Chopped parsley for garnish
Salt and pepper to taste, if desired

In large, heavy saucepan, heat butter. Cut sliced onion into quarters and add to saucepan with mushrooms. Cook over low heat until onion is transparent, about five minutes. Stir in flour and cook, stirring frequently, over low heat about 15 minutes. Add chicken stock and cook, stirring constantly, until smooth and slightly thickened, about 10 minutes. Add wild rice, cream and sherry, stirring until heated through. Do not boil. Garnish with chopped parsley and season, to taste, with salt and pepper, if desired. Makes six to eight servings.

SERVES 6

Mrs. Iggers' Eintopf

3 qts water
2 c beef broth
1 ham bone or smoked ham hock
1 medium onion, coarsely chopped
1 clove garlic, minced
2 carrots, chopped
¼ small head cabbage, coarsely chopped
3 T barley
¾ lb knockwurst or garlic sausage, sliced in large pieces
1 oz imported dried European mushrooms, soaked in 1 c water for two hours and chopped, or 1 c fresh mushrooms, quartered
1 T fresh marjoram leaves or 1 t dried
1 t caraway seeds
4 large potatoes, peeled and cubed

In large soup pot or kettle, combine water, broth, ham bone or hock, onion, garlic, carrots, cabbage and barley. Bring to a boil, reduce heat and simmer one hour. Add sausage, mushrooms and soaking water, marjoram, caraway and potatoes. Return to boil, reduce heat and simmer at least two hours, until soup has thickened almost to the consistency of stew. This is even better reheated the next day. Makes about six servings.

32

SOUPS

SERVES 6

Patsy's Greek Buttermilk Soup

½ c walnuts
2 cloves garlic, crushed
¼ c olive oil
2 T white wine vinegar
1 qt buttermilk
1 cucumber, peeled and seeded
  Salt and white pepper to taste
10 small radishes, thinly sliced

In blender container, combine walnuts, garlic, olive oil and vinegar. Blend until smooth. Add buttermilk and cucumber and blend again until smooth. Season to taste with salt and pepper. Chill thoroughly and serve with sliced radishes floating on top. Makes about six servings.

SERVES 16 to 20

Picnique Clam Chowder

- 1 lb bacon, divided
- ⅓ c flour
- ½ medium onion, chopped
- ½ t white pepper
- 6 cans (7½ oz each) minced clams, drained, reserving liquid
- 2 bottles (8 oz each) clam juice
- 1 c water
- 2 medium potatoes, cut into ¼-inch cubes
- 2 c whipping cream

Set aside three strips bacon. In skillet fry remaining bacon until crisp. Drain bacon, saving drippings in skillet. Over low heat slowly whisk flour into bacon drippings to thicken. Set aside cooked bacon and flour-dripping mixture.

In large saucepan or kettle, cook together remaining three strips bacon and onion until onion browns. Stir in white pepper and drained clams. Cook for two minutes. Stir in liquid reserved from minced clams and bring mixture to boil. Stir in clam juice and water and return to boil. Reduce heat and let soup simmer, uncovered, 30 minutes.

Meanwhile, cook potatoes until tender in boiling, lightly salted water; drain and set aside. Mix ½ cup of hot soup with all of whipping cream and return that mixture to kettle. Let soup continue to simmer, uncovered, 20 minutes. Whisk in two tablespoons of bacon dripping-flour mixture to thicken soup. (Add more roux if desired but be careful not to make overly thick; reserve unused roux for other uses.) Continue to cook soup for 10 minutes. Remove from heat; stir in potatoes. Garnish soup with crumbled reserved cooked bacon. Makes 16-20 servings.

SERVES 12 TO 14

Pork and Rice Noodle Soup (Hu Tiu)

- 10 qts water
- 4 lbs pork neck bones
- 5 medium onions, coarsely chopped
- 1 c dried shrimp (available at Oriental markets)
- 3 T salt
- 2 T monosodium glutamate, if desired
- ⅓ c sugar
- 8 oz pork shoulder or butt
- 8 oz fresh medium shrimp, shelled and deveined
- 1 lb flat rice noodles (available at Oriental markets), broken
- 1 bunch scallions, chopped, including green tops
  Freshly ground black pepper to taste

In very large soup pot, combine water, pork bones, onions and dried shrimp; bring to a boil and skim off all residue that forms on surface. Add salt and monosodium glutamate, if desired. Simmer, uncovered, about four hours. Remove from heat and add sugar, stirring until dissolved. Let stand until partially cooled and skim off as much fat as possible from top of soup. Remove pork bones and pick off any meat clinging to bones. Add this meat to pot and discard bones.

Bring soup to boil again and add pork shoulder or butt. Cook about 20 minutes, until pork is tender. Remove pork with slotted spoon, slice into thin strips and set aside. Add fresh shrimp to boiling soup and cook about three minutes. Remove shrimp with slotted spoon and halve lengthwise. Set shrimp aside.

Bring large pot of lightly salted water to a boil and add broken rice noodles; cook about 10 minutes or until tender. Rinse with cold water in colander and return to cooking pot. Add a little of soup liquid and heat noodles. Return pork and shrimp to hot soup.

To serve, place about ⅔ cup of noodles in serving bowl; ladle soup with pork and shrimp on top of noodles and sprinkle with scallions and pepper to taste. Makes about 12 to 14 servings.

SERVES 6

Sandi Cooper's Senegalese Carrot Soup

4 to 6 T unsalted butter, divided
1 small onion, finely chopped
3 c peeled and coarsely chopped medium size carrots
3 c heated rich chicken or vegetable stock
1½ c rick milk or light cream
2 t curry powder
Salt and pepper to taste
Whipped cream flavored with ground coriander for garnish
Fresh parsley for garnish, if desired

In large skillet or heavy saucepan, melt four tablespoons of the butter. Add onions and cook until soft, about five minutes. Add carrots and cook until tender, stirring frequently, and adding more butter, if needed. When carrots are tender, add heated stock and bring mixture to a boil. Transfer soup to blender and puree until smooth. (If an extra-smooth velvety texture is desired, put mixture through a fine sieve). Return soup to saucepan and whisk in milk or cream. Add curry and salt and pepper to taste. Heat soup but do not boil. To serve, pour into individual soup bowls and garnish with dollop of whipped cream flavored with ground coriander. Place single parsley leaf on whipped cream if desired. Makes about six servings.

SERVES 8

Sopa de Aguacate con Ajo (Avocado Soup with Garlic)

3 medium, ripe avocados, peeled and pits removed
2 c chicken broth
2 t fresh lime juice
½ t salt
¼ t onion powder
⅛ t white pepper
2 large cloves garlic, crushed
1½ c heavy cream
Light cream or milk, if desired
Lemon slices

In blender container or food processor, puree avocados with a little of the chicken broth and lime juice. Add remaining broth, salt, onion powder, white pepper and garlic; puree until smooth and velvety. Pour mixture into large bowl and add heavy cream. If soup is too thick, thin with light cream or milk to desired consistency. Chill thoroughly. Serve in individual cream soup cups, garnished with slice of lemon. Makes about eight servings.

SERVES 4 TO 6

Soup of the Sea

- 2 T butter or margarine
- ¾ c sliced onion
- 1 can (15½ oz) whole peeled tomatoes, undrained
- 2 c clam broth (two 8-oz bottles)
- 1 T fresh lemon juice
- ¼ to ½ t hot red pepper sauce
- ¼ t dried thyme, crumbled
- 1 can (6½ to 7 oz) crabmeat, drained and flaked
- ½ c heavy cream
  Chopped parsley
  Herbed croutons, if desired

In a medium saucepan, melt butter or margarine. Add onion and cook until soft, about five to seven minutes. Do not brown. Add tomatoes and juice from can, clam broth, lemon juice, red pepper sauce and thyme; simmer over medium heat 10 minutes. Cool slightly and puree in blender or food processor. Return mixture to saucepan; add crab meat and cream. Mix well and heat just to boiling. Garnish with parsley and herbed croutons, if desired. Makes four to six servings.

MAKES 1 GALLON

Soup Kitchen's Corn Chowder

¾ lb salt pork, minced or ground
½ lb butter
1 large onion, peeled and diced
3 stalks celery, diced
1 large carrot, scraped and diced
1 to 1½ c flour
2 qts chicken stock
2 large potatoes, pared and diced
2 cans (16 oz each) whole kernel corn, undrained
¾ lb ham, diced
1 qt light cream
Salt and pepper to taste

In large, heavy soup kettle, cook salt pork until all fat has been rendered and pork bits are light brown and crispy. Add butter, onion, celery and carrot; cook over medium heat 10 minutes. Stir in flour; cook 10 minutes, stirring frequently to prevent flour from browning.

Meanwhile, in large pot, combine chicken stock, potatoes, corn and corn liquid and ham. Bring to a boil, reduce heat and simmer until potatoes are tender, about 10 minutes. Slowly add potato-corn mixture to thick butter-flour roux, stirring constantly until well mixed and roux is completely incorporated. Cook over low heat 15 minutes, stirring frequently. The chowder will be very thick. Add light cream (half and half) and salt and pepper to taste. Heat thoroughly but do not boil. Thin with additional light cream or milk, if desired. Makes about one gallon chowder.

SOUPS

Spring Garden Soup

- 7 c rich chicken broth
- ½ lb asparagus, tips reserved, stems snapped, peeled and sliced
- ⅓ small head iceberg lettuce, shredded
- 1 large onion, peeled and sliced
- 1 large leek, sliced (white part only)
- 2 ribs celery, leaves and strings removed, sliced
- 2 cloves garlic, peeled
- 1 c frozen small peas, thawed and divided
- 1 t dill weed
- ½ t basil, crumbled
- 1 t salt
  Freshly ground pepper, to taste
  Pinch of nutmeg
- 1 c fresh green beans, trimmed and sliced diagonally
- 1 large carrot, peeled and thinly sliced
- 1 small zucchini, trimmed but not peeled, thinly sliced
- 1 small turnip, peeled and sliced in matchstick strips
- 4 to 6 large fresh mushrooms, thinly sliced
  Minced parsley for garnish

In large heavy soup pot or kettle, combine chicken broth, asparagus stems, lettuce, onion, leek, celery and garlic. Cover and bring to a boil; reduce heat and simmer 40 minutes. Strain vegetables, reserving broth. Puree vegetables in food processor or blender 20 to 30 seconds. Add ¾ cup of the peas and process until peas are pureed. Return vegetables and broth to soup pot. Add dill, basil, salt, pepper and nutmeg. Return pot to boil and add beans, carrot, zucchini, turnip and reserved asparagus tips. Simmer 10 minutes, uncovered. Add mushrooms and reserved one-fourth cup of peas and simmer an additional five minutes. Pour into tureen or individual soup dishes and garnish with parsley. Makes about 10 servings.

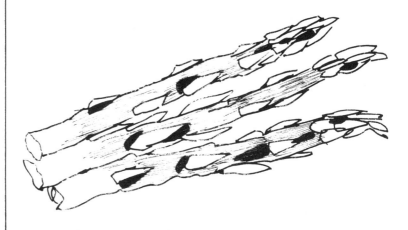

SOUPS

The Round Bar's Dill Pickle Soup

8 c chicken stock or broth
2 chicken bouillon cubes
2 medium carrots, coarsely grated
2 c peeled and cubed potatoes
1 c thinly sliced celery
5 coarsely grated Polish dill pickles
½ c milk
2 T flour
1 egg
5 T sour cream
Salt and pepper to taste
Finely chopped parsley, if desired
Finely chopped fresh dill, if desired

In large saucepan or soup pot with cover, combine chicken stock or broth, bouillon cubes, carrots, potatoes and celery. Cook, covered, over low heat until potatoes are soft, about 10 minutes. Do not overcook. Add pickles and continue cooking about 15 minutes.

In small bowl, beat milk and flour until completely smooth; stir a small amount of hot soup into flour mixture. Mix until smooth and return to soup pot, stirring until well combined. Bring soup to boil, stirring frequently until soup is slightly thickened. Remove from heat.

In small bowl, beat egg with sour cream until smooth. Pour a small amount of hot soup into sour cream mixture and mix thoroughly. Return sour cream mixture to soup pot and stir until smooth. Keep soup warm but do not boil after this point or egg-sour cream mixture will curdle. Add salt and pepper to taste. Garnish with parsley and dill, if desired. Makes about 10 servings.

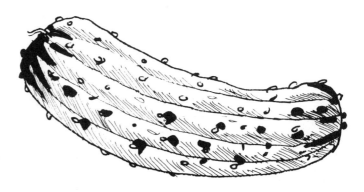

SOUPS

Turkey, Mushroom and Barley Soup

- 5 T butter, divided
- ⅓ c chopped onion
- ⅓ c chopped celery
- ½ lb fresh mushrooms, cleaned and diced
- 2 qts turkey broth, warmed
- ½ c pearl barley
- 1 chicken bouillon cube
- ½ t tarragon, crumbled
- ½ t basil, crumbled
  Salt and pepper to taste
- 3 T flour
- 2 T chopped parsley

In large saucepan, melt two tablespoons of the butter; add onion, celery and mushrooms. Cover and cook gently about 10 minutes, stirring occasionally. Pour in warm turkey broth; add barley, bouillon cube, tarragon and basil. Salt and pepper to taste. Simmer soup, uncovered 45 minutes. Set aside to cool slightly.

In another large saucepan, melt remaining three tablespoons butter; add flour and cook, stirring constantly, about three minutes. Gradually whisk in cooled broth and vegetables. Bring mixture to a boil, reduce heat and simmer 10 minutes. Serve hot, garnished with chopped parsley. Makes six to eight servings.

SOUPS

Vichyssoise

3 T butter
3 large onions, thickly sliced
3 to 4 leeks, carefully cleaned and sliced
1½ qts chicken stock
1 c chopped celery
4 medium potatoes, peeled and sliced
  Salt and white pepper, to taste
1 c sour cream
1 c medium cream
  Dash liquid hot pepper sauce
  Minced chives

In large soup pot or kettle, melt butter; add onions and leeks and cook until soft but not browned, about five to seven minutes. Add chicken stock, celery, potatoes and salt and white pepper, to taste. Cook over medium heat until potatoes are very soft, about 40 minutes. Puree cooked mixture in blender on fast speed; transfer soup to large bowl and cool to room temperature. Pour into jars or freezer containers, leaving about three inches of head room; cover tightly and freeze.

To serve: Thaw soup mixture and transfer to large bowl. Add sour cream, cream and hot pepper sauce. Puree in blender again; transfer to individual cream soup cups or a large tureen. Sprinkle with chives. Serve ice cold. Makes about 10 servings.

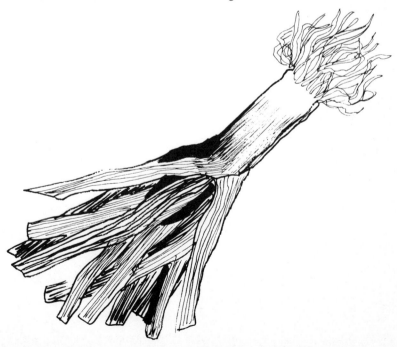

EGGS

SERVES 4 TO 6

Artichoke Frittata

1 can (14 oz) artichoke hearts, drained
3 cloves garlic, minced
3 T olive oil
Salt and freshly ground black pepper to taste
6 extra-large eggs
5 T freshly grated Parmesan cheese, divided
4 T butter
Chopped parsley

Slice artichoke hearts lengthwise and drain thoroughly on paper towels. In medium skillet, cook garlic in olive oil until soft, about three minutes. Add artichoke slices and cook four minutes, stirring gently. Season with salt and pepper to taste and remove from heat.

In medium bowl, beat eggs lightly; add artichoke mixture and four tablespoons of the cheese. In large, heavy skillet, melt butter. When butter is foaming, add egg/artichoke mixture and sprinkle with parsley. Cook, without stirring, over low heat until eggs have almost set, about 15 minutes. Sprinkle with remaining tablespoon cheese and run skillet under hot broiler just until top starts to brown, about one minute.

Run sharp knife around edge of skillet to loosen frittata and gently slide onto serving plate. Cut into wedges and serve warm or at room temperature. Makes four to six servings.

SERVES 4 TO 6

Cheese and Vegetable Quiche

1 10-inch pie shell, unbaked
8 strips lean bacon
1 c shredded Jarlsberg cheese
2 to 3 medium, firm tomatoes, skinned, seeded and chopped
4 T butter
1 medium onion, chopped
½ lb fresh mushrooms, sliced
2 c fresh broccoli flowerets, tightly packed, uncooked
3 eggs, beaten
1⅔ c light cream
Salt and pepper, to taste

With fork, prick bottom and sides of pie shell; bake at 350 degrees five minutes. Remove from oven and set aside. In large skillet, fry bacon until crisp; drain on paper towel, crumble and set aside. Sprinkle cheese evenly on bottom of prepared pie crust. Cover cheese with crumbled bacon. Sprinkle chopped tomatoes over bacon. Set aside pie.

In large skillet, melt butter; add onion and cook until soft, not browned, about four minutes. Add mushrooms and cook another three minutes. Add broccoli, cover and cook over medium heat 10 minutes.

Meanwhile, in medium bowl, beat eggs with cream, salt and pepper. Pour about one-third of the egg mixture over vegetables in skillet and stir well to incorporate pan juices; pour mixture into partially filled pie shell. Add remaining egg-cream mixture. Bake at 350 degrees 60 to 70 minutes, until tart is puffed and lightly browned on top. Remove from oven and let rest 10 minutes before cutting into wedges. Makes four to six luncheon servings, or eight to 12 appetizer servings.

SERVES 6

Farmer's Omelet

- 3 T butter or margarine
- 2 c cubed cold boiled potatoes
- ⅓ c finely chopped onion
- ½ c finely chopped green pepper
- 1 clove garlic, minced
- 1 c cubed ham
- ¼ c chopped fresh parsley
- 6 eggs
- 1 t salt
- ⅛ t freshly ground pepper
- 2 T low-fat milk
- 1 c shredded Monterey Jack cheese

In 9-inch skillet, melt butter or margarine. Add potatoes, onion, green pepper and garlic. Cook over medium heat, stirring occasionally, until lightly browned, about five minutes. Add ham and cook until heated throughout; sprinkle with parsley and reduce heat. In medium bowl, beat eggs, salt, pepper and milk until well blended. Pour egg mixture over potato mixture; cover and cook until eggs are almost set, about 10 minutes, slipping spatula around edges of pan occasionally to allow eggs to run down. Sprinkle with cheese, cover and cook until cheese melts. Cut into wedges to serve. Makes four to six servings.

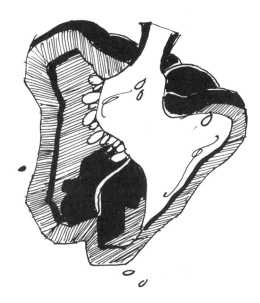

EGGS

French-Toasted Fruit Sandwiches

> 1 c plus 2 t sugar, divided
> 1 rounded T Fruit-Fresh (available at most supermarkets)
> 2 inch piece vanilla bean
> 6 thin slices large French bread
> ⅓ c soft butter
> 2 c sliced fresh strawberries (bananas, pears, nectarines or peaches may also be used)
> 2 eggs
> ½ c milk
> Dash salt
> Butter or margarine
> Confectioners' sugar

In small bowl, combine one cup of the sugar with Fruit-Fresh and vanilla bean; stir to mix and set aside. (Any leftover mixture may be kept in tightly sealed jar for other uses.)

Spread both sides of bread with softened butter. Top three slices with equally divided fruit slices, crushing slightly with fork. Sprinkle each with about one tablespoon prepared Fruit-Fresh mixture and top with remaining three slices buttered bread, pressing together firmly.

In small bowl, combine eggs, milk, salt and remaining two teaspoons sugar; beat until well mixed. Dip sandwiches in egg mixture until thoroughly coated and brown slowly in butter or margarine in large skillet. Sprinkle with confectioners' sugar and serve warm. Makes three sandwiches.

EGGS

SERVES 6 TO 8

French Women's Benevolent Club Quiche

Crust for 9-inch deep dish pie or 10-inch regular pie
6 slices boiled ham or Canadian bacon, shredded
½ to 1 c grated Swiss cheese
1 T flour
3 green onions, chopped, including green tops
3 eggs plus 1 egg yolk
2 c light cream
½ t salt
¼ t freshly grated black pepper
Generous pinch nutmeg

Line a 9-inch deep dish or 10-inch regular pie pan with butter crust of choice. Sprinkle ham over bottom of crust. Combine cheese and flour and sprinkle over ham. Distribute onions evenly over cheese.

In small bowl, combine eggs, egg yolk, cream, salt, pepper and nutmeg; beat until frothy and pour gently over ingredients in pie crust. Bake on rack in middle of pre-heated 400-degree oven 15 minutes. Reduce heat to 325 and bake 30 minutes longer or until set and lightly browned on top. Remove from oven and cool on wire rack five to 10 minutes before cutting into wedges. Makes six to eight servings.

SERVES 6 TO 8

Green Chili Souffle

12 slices white bread, crusts removed
Soft butter
1 can (12 oz) whole kernel corn, well drained
2 cans (3 oz each) or 1 7-ounce can whole green chilies, seeded and sliced
2 c shredded Monterey Jack cheese
4 large eggs, lightly beaten
3 c milk
1 t salt

Spread bread slices with butter and cut each slice in half. Arrange half the slices in the bottom of greased, shallow three-quart casserole. Cover with half the corn, half the chili slices and half the cheese. Repeat layers.

In medium bowl, combine eggs, milk and salt; beat well and pour over bread mixture. Cover with plastic wrap and refrigerate at least four hours or overnight in refrigerator. Bake, uncovered, at 350 degrees 45 to 50 minutes, until top is puffed and golden brown. Serve immediately. Makes six to eight servings.

SERVES 10 TO 12

Joe Moceri's German Pancakes

- 2 c water
- 1 c heavy cream
- ⅓ c powdered skimmed milk
- 10 eggs
- 1 c confectioners' sugar
- 3¼ c flour
- 1 T salt
- ¼ t baking powder
- Pinch nutmeg
- 20 T clarified butter (about ¾ lb), melted, divided
- Powdered sugar and lemon juice, or topping of your choice

In large bowl, combine water, cream and powdered skimmed milk; stir until well combined. Add eggs, confectioners' sugar, flour, salt, baking powder and nutmeg. Beat batter until smooth.

Pour two tablespoons of the clarified butter into a 12-inch ovenproof skillet; add six ounces of the pancake batter (about ¾ of a cup). Bake at 425 degrees 10 minutes, until golden brown. Sprinkle with powdered sugar and lemon juice, or topping of your choice. Repeat process for each serving. Makes 10 to 12 servings.

SERVES 6

Italian Fontina and Red Pepper Blossom Quiche

1⅓ c flour
6½ T chilled unsalted butter, cut into 10 pieces
¼ t salt
Pinch sugar
3 T ice water
3 eggs
1½ c heavy cream
6 oz Italian Fontina cheese (available at Italian markets), diced
¼ c Parmesan cheese, freshly grated
½ t salt
¼ t black pepper, freshly ground
⅛ t nutmeg, freshly ground
6 large red bell peppers, peeled and sliced into ½-inch wide strips
1 T butter, melted
Salt and pepper, to taste

To make pastry: In bowl of food processor, combine flour, butter, salt and sugar; process until mixture resembles coarse meal. With machine running, pour ice water through feed tube and process just until water is incorporated, before dough forms ball. Remove dough and scrape into ball; wrap in plastic wrap and refrigerate several hours or overnight. Roll out dough into a ⅛-inch-thick circle and place in 9-inch buttered quiche or tart pan with removable bottom. Remove excess dough from fluted edge and prick bottom surface in several places. Chill pastry crust at least 30 minutes. Cover bottom with buttered parchment or wax paper and fill with beans or pie weights. Bake at 425 degrees 15 to 20 minutes, until crust is firm. Remove beans or weights and parchment or wax paper. Return pastry shell to oven and bake another five minutes, until crust is light brown. Set aside to cook until ready to fill.

In large mixing bowl, stir together eggs, cream, Fontina and Parmesan cheeses, salt, pepper and nutmeg. Pour mixture into prepared pastry shell and bake at 375 degrees 30 to 40 minutes, until quiche is lightly browned and a knife inserted in center comes out clean. Starting at the outside pastry rim of the quiche, overlap pepper strips in petal shape — like apple slices in a French apple tart — and continue until entire top of quiche looks like a blossom. Coil up one pepper strip for a center bud. Brush pepper slices with melted butter and sprinkle with salt and pepper, to taste. Return quiche to oven and bake at 425 degrees five minutes or until peppers are heated through. Let stand at room temperature 15 minutes before cutting into wedges. Makes six servings.

EGGS

SERVES 3 TO 4

Mexican Omelet

    1 medium avocado, chopped
    ½ c sour cream
    3 green onions, chopped
    2 T canned green chilies, chopped
    1 t fresh lemon juice
    ½ t salt
      Dash liquid hot pepper sauce
    1 T butter
    1 corn tortilla, torn into small pieces
    4 slices cooked bacon, crumbled
    6 eggs, beaten
    1 c grated Monterey Jack cheese

In small bowl, lightly mix avocado, sour cream, green onions, chilies, lemon juice, salt and liquid hot pepper sauce; set aside. In oven-proof skillet, melt butter and fry tortilla pieces until soft. Add bacon pieces and pour in eggs. Cook, stirring occasionally until eggs start to set. Remove from heat, sprinkle with grated cheese and place in 325-degree oven three to four minutes, until cheese melts. Remove from oven and spread avocado mixture on half of the omelet. Return to oven until avocado mixture bubbles, about three minutes. Remove to hot serving plate and fold in half. Serves three to four.

SERVES 8

Scotch Eggs

    1 lb sausage
    2 T finely chopped parsley
    ½ t sage
    ½ t thyme, crumbled
    8 hard-cooked eggs, peeled and chilled
    ½ c flour
    ½ t salt
      Freshly ground pepper
    2 eggs, lightly beaten
    1 c fine bread or cracker crumbs
      Oil or shortening for deep frying

In medium bowl, combine sausage, parsley, sage and thyme. Mix well and divide into equal portions. Surround each hard-cooked egg with one portion of the sausage mixture, so that no part of the egg is showing. In small bowl, mix flour with salt and pepper. Roll sausage-coated egg in flour mixture, then dip into beaten eggs, then roll in bread or cracker crumbs. Fry in hot oil or shortening five to 10 minutes, or until sausage is cooked and browned. Serve hot or cold. Makes eight servings.

EGGS

SERVES 4

Scotch Woodcock

8 eggs
½ c milk
¼ c parsley, chopped
½ t salt
½ t hot red pepper sauce
¼ c butter or margarine
8 slices buttered toast
1 can (2 oz) anchovy fillets, drained
1 T capers, drained

In large bowl, combine eggs, milk, parsley, salt and hot red pepper sauce; beat with fork until well mixed.

In large skillet, melt butter or margarine over medium heat; pour in egg mixture and cook slowly, drawing spoon over bottom of pan occasionally to make large curds. Continue cooking until eggs are set but not dry. Arrange two slices of toast on each of four plates. Spoon egg mixture equally on all pieces of toast. Garnish with anchovies and capers. Makes four servings.

SERVES 2

Scrambled French Toast

4 slices stale bread
2 eggs, well beaten
½ c milk
Salt and pepper to taste
4 slices bacon
2 T butter or bacon grease
Syrup, if desired

Cut bread in small cubes but do not remove crusts. In medium bowl, combine eggs, milk, salt and pepper. Beat until well mixed. Toss bread cubes in egg mixture and let soak until all liquid is absorbed.

Meanwhile, in medium skillet, cook bacon until crisp; drain on paper towels. Pour out all but two tablespoons bacon grease or discard bacon grease and melt two tablespoons butter in skillet; when hot, pour in soaked bread cubes and cook, turning occasionally, until browned. Serve with bacon crumbled over top and choice of syrup, if desired. Makes two servings.

Torte Milanese

1½ lb puff pastry, divided
4 eggs
1 T water
1 t chopped parsley
1 t minced chives or green onion tops
½ t tarragon
4 T butter, divided
1 lb fresh spinach
2 shallots, minced
1 clove garlic, minced
    Salt and pepper to taste
    Pinch nutmeg
1 8 oz Jarlesberg or Swiss cheese, sliced 1/16-inch thick
8 oz thin-sliced smoked ham
1 jar (4 oz) pimiento, sliced

Roll out one pound of the puff pastry to line a greased 8-inch springform pan, allowing for about two inches overhang. In medium bowl, combine eggs, water, parsley, chives or green onion tops and tarragon; beat until well mixed. In small skillet, heat two tablespoons of the butter; pour one half of the egg mixture into skillet and cook over medium heat until eggs are set, about seven minutes. Slip omelet out of pan and set aside. Repeat procedure with remaining egg mixture and set aside.

Wash and drain spinach. In large pot, pour boiling water over spinach just to cover; boil until wilted, about two minutes. Drain thoroughly. In large skillet, heat remaining two tablespoons butter. Add shallots and garlic; stir until soft, about five minutes. Add wilted spinach and nutmeg; season to taste with salt and pepper. Cook until tender about 10 minutes. Place one of the prepared omelets on bottom of pastry lined pan. Cover with one half of the prepared spinach, one half of the cheese and one half of the ham. Spread pimiento on top and cover with remaining half of the ham, cheese and spinach. Place remaining omelet on top of mixture and fold pastry overhang towards center of pan. Roll out remaining ½ lb. puff pastry to an 8-inch circle and place on top of mixture, pinching edges to seal. Decorate top of pie with leftover pastry cut-outs. Bake at 375 degrees 15 to 20 minutes. Reduce heat and bake at 325 degrees about 40 minutes, until golden brown. Makes eight to 10 servings.

SALADS

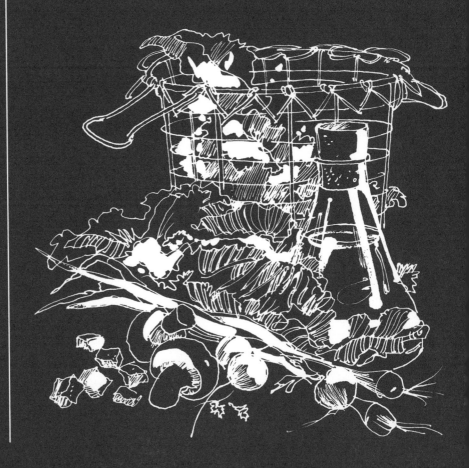

SERVES 6

Chicken Salad with Grapes

- 1 chicken, 2½ to 3 lbs
- 2 ribs celery, cut into pieces
- 1 medium onion, sliced
- 1 medium carrot, cut into pieces
- 1 t salt
- ⅛ t pepper
  Pinch tarragon
  Pinch summer savory
- 1 c green or purple grapes, cut in half lengthwise and seeded, if necessary (do not use the blue Concord grapes)
- 6 c scallions, thinly sliced using green ends
- ¾ c thinly sliced celery
- ¼ t tarragon, crushed
- ¼ t sour cream
- ½ c mayonnaise
  Salt and pepper to taste
  Lettuce leaves
- 2 hard-cooked eggs, cut lengthwise into thin wedges

In large kettle or soup pot, place chicken, cut up if desired, two ribs of the celery, onion, carrot, salt, pepper, pinch of the tarragon and savory. Barely cover with water and bring to a boil. Simmer, uncovered, for 30 minutes. Remove chicken and cool; set aside broth and vegetables. When chicken has cooled, remove skin and bone. Return bones to pot and make broth for other uses. Cut or tear chicken meat into large bite-size chunks and put into large bowl. Add grapes, scallions, ¾ cup sliced celery, and ¼ teaspoon tarragon. Toss together to mix. In small bowl, combine sour cream and mayonnaise and mix well. Add to chicken mixture and toss until mixture is well coated. Salt and pepper to taste. Line a serving bowl with lettuce leaves and place chicken salad in center. Garnish with thin wedges of hard-cooked eggs. Makes six servings.

SERVES 10

Chinese Chicken Salad

2 T cornstarch

7 T dark soy sauce, divided

1½ to 2 lbs skinless, boned chicken breasts, cut into ¾-inch pieces

6 to 8 oz very thin egg noodles
Oil for deep frying

10 wonton skins, cut into thin strips

2 eggs plus 1 egg yolk, beaten

2 T dry sherry

1½ t plus 1 T sugar, divided

2 t white vinegar

¼ c plus 3 T peanut oil, divided

2 t crushed red pepper

1 large clove plus 2 t garlic, minced, divided

1 pkg (8 oz) frozen snow peas

1 can (4 oz) water chestnuts, drained and sliced

1 bunch scallions, including some of the green tops, thinly sliced

2 c shredded Chinese cabbage or napa

1 T sesame oil

1 T minced ginger root

¼ t black pepper
Dash cayenne pepper

¼ c light soy sauce

3 T red wine vinegar

1 T peanut butter

½ c unroasted cashews, coarsely chopped

In large bowl, dissolve cornstarch in 5 tablespoons of dark soy sauce; add chicken pieces and toss until well coated. Let stand 20 to 30 minutes.

Meanwhile, cook noodles according to package instructions, until just tender (al dente). Drain and spread on extra-large serving platter; set aside. (It is not necessary to refrigerate noodles.)

In large skillet, heat ½ inch of cooking oil until hot but not smoking. Fry wonton strips until golden brown; remove with slotted spoon and drain on paper towel. Set aside.

Remove all but two tablespoons oil from skillet and pour in egg mixture to form large thin pancake. Cook until firm, turn carefully and cook other side one minute. Remove with wide spatula and drain on paper towel. Set aside.

In small bowl or cup, combine sherry, 1½ teaspoon of sugar and white vinegar; set aside. In wok or large skillet, heat ¼ cup of the peanut oil; add crushed red pepper and fry until darkened. Add large clove of minced garlic and chicken pieces; stir fry just until chicken turns opaque, about two to three minutes. Stir in prepared sherry mixture; stir fry just until chicken is cooked, about three minutes. Remove from heat and set aside to cool to room temperature.

Cook snow peas according to package instructions no longer than one minute. Drain and add to cooled chicken. Add water chestnuts and scallions and toss to mix.

Spread shredded cabbage on top of noodles on platter. Heap chicken mixture on top and set aside.

In small saucepan, slowly heat remaining three tablespoons peanut oil and sesame oil. Add ginger root, black pepper and cayenne pepper and cook over low heat five minutes. Meanwhile in blender, combine light soy sauce, red wine vinegar, remaining tablespoon sugar and peanut butter; process until smooth. Pour into sesame oil mixture and cook, stirring until sauce starts to foam. Remove from heat and set aside.

Just before serving, arrange prepared wonton strips around chicken mixture on platter. With very sharp knife, cut egg pancake into thin strips and sprinkle over chicken. Pour prepared sauce over all and sprinkle with cashews. Serve at room temperature. Makes about 10 servings.

SERVES 8 TO 10

Christmas Eve Salad

    2 medium oranges, peeled and sectioned
    2 bananas, peeled and sliced
    1 can (8¼ oz) sliced beets
    1 can (8 oz) chunk pineapple
    1 can (8 oz) water chestnuts, drained and sliced
    2 T lemon juice
    3 T sugar, divided
    ½ t salt
    3 c shredded lettuce
    1 lime, cut in wedges
    ¼ c chopped peanuts
    ⅓ c pomegranate seeds or sliced radishes
    1 T anise seed

In large bowl, combine oranges, bananas, beets, pineapple and water chestnuts; set aside. In small bowl, combine reserved beet liquid and pineapple juice, lemon juice, two tablespoons of the sugar and salt. Mix thoroughly and pour over fruit. Let stand 10 minutes; drain, discarding liquid.

Arrange fruit on lettuce. Garnish with lime wedges, peanuts and pomegranate seeds or radishes. Mix anise seed and remaining tablespoon sugar; sprinkle over salad. Makes eight to 10 servings.

SERVES 4

Curried Rice Salad

2½ c water
2½ t chicken bouillon granules
 ½ t salt
  1 c uncooked rice
 ½ green pepper, chopped
  3 to 4 green onions, sliced, using green tops
 ¾ c sliced pimiento-stuffed or pitted black olives
  2 jars (6 oz each) marinated artichoke hearts, drained, reserving oil from one jar
 ¾ c mayonnaise
  1 t curry powder (more if desired)
 ¼ t cayenne pepper
    Lettuce leaves
 ½ c chopped cashews, if desired

In medium saucepan, combine water, chicken bouillon granules and salt; bring to a boil and add rice. Cook, covered, about 20 minutes over medium heat, until rice is tender and liquid has been absorbed. Drain, if necessary, and set aside to cool. In large bowl, combine cooled rice, green pepper, onions, olives and drained artichoke hearts. In small bowl, combine oil from one jar of artichoke hearts, mayonnaise, curry powder to desired strength and cayenne pepper; mix thoroughly and toss with rice mixture. Chill thoroughly. Turn into lettuce-lined bowl and sprinkle with cashews, if desired.

SERVES 8

Hearty Beef Salad

10 small new potatoes
1 flank steak, about 1½ lbs
2 T sherry
1 T soy sauce
1 T lemon juice
1 T dried onion flakes
1 clove garlic, minced
2 c coarsely chopped celery
1 c finely sliced green onions, green tops included
1 medium dill pickle, finely chopped
3 fresh tomatoes, peeled, seeded and cut into eighths
1 medium cucumber, peeled, seeded and sliced
1 green pepper, roasted, skinned and cut into strips
¼ c capers, drained
6 hard-cooked eggs, separated
1 T Dijon-type mustard
1 c olive oil
1 t garlic salt
1 t freshly ground black pepper
⅓ c wine vinegar
Dash hot red pepper sauce
Lettuce leaves
Tarragon, crushed

In medium saucepan, cover potatoes with salted water and bring to a boil. Cook until just tender, about 12 to 15 minutes. Drain and set aside to cool. Unpeeled potatoes may be stored in the refrigerator overnight.

In low dish, marinate flank steak in mixture of sherry, soy sauce, lemon juice, onion flakes and garlic for at least three hours or overnight, covered, in refrigerator. Turn meat several times. Broil steak, about three inches from heat, until rare, about four minutes on each side. Do not overcook meat — it should be pink to red on the inside. Cool meat to room temperature; wrap meat and place in freezer until it feels solid but not frozen to the touch, about 1½ hours. Remove and slice as thin as possible; set aside.

When ready to assemble salad, peel potatoes and slice. In large bowl, combine prepared meat and potatoes, celery, onions, pickle, tomatoes, cucumber, green pepper and capers. Toss gently. Refrigerate while making dressing.

In medium bowl, place hard-cooked egg yolks and mash with fork. Work in mustard; stir in olive oil, garlic salt, pepper, vinegar and hot pepper sauce. Beat thoroughly with wire whisk or shake thoroughly in large jar.

Toss salad with desired amount of dressing and arrange in serving bowl lined with lettuce leaves. Garnish with chopped hard-cooked egg whites and sprinkle with tarragon. Makes about eight servings.

SALADS

SERVES 6 TO 8

Holiday Cran-Pineapple Mold

- 2 envelopes (¼ oz each) unflavored gelatin
- 3¼ c cranberry cocktail juice, divided
- 1 T sugar
- ⅛ t nutmeg
- ⅛ t allspice
- 1 can (8 oz) crushed pineapple, in juice
- 1 c non-dairy whipped topping

In small saucepan, combine gelatin, one-half cup of the cranberry juice, sugar, nutmeg and allspice. Cook and stir over low heat until gelatin dissolves, about five minutes. Drain pineapple, reserving juice. Add remaining cranberry juice to pineapple juice to make 3¼ cups; mix into dissolved gelatin mixture. Remove 1½ cups to a small bowl; chill until mixture mounds when stirred with a spoon. Fold in whipped topping. Coat the inside of a six-cup mold with vegetable oil and pour in whipped mixture. Chill until almost set, about 45 minutes. Meanwhile, chill remaining juice mixture until slightly thickened; fold in crushed pineapple. Carefully spoon over mixture in mold. Chill at least six hours or overnight. To unmold, run the tip of a sharp knife around edge of mold; unmold onto serving plate. Makes six to eight servings.

**MAKES 2 CUPS
OR 4 TO 6
LARGE SERVINGS**

Maurice Salad Dressing

- 2 T tarragon wine vinegar
- 1 T grated onion
- 1 c mayonnaise
- 1 c Miracle Whip
- 3 T parsley flakes
- 2 T chopped hard cooked egg
- 1 T minced chives
- 1 t sugar
  Salad greens
- 2 c each ham, Swiss cheese and chicken, cut into matchstick strips

In cup or small bowl, combine vinegar and grated onion and set aside to marinate.

Meanwhile, in medium bowl, combine mayonnaise, Miracle Whip, parsley flakes, eggs, chives and sugar; stir until well mixed. Add vinegar-onion mixture and mix thoroughly. Chill until use.

Line salad bowl with fresh salad greens. Combine strips of ham, Swiss cheese and chicken and turn into middle of bowl. Cover with prepared dressing, according to taste. Makes two cups dressing; four to six large servings Maurice Salad.

SERVES 8 TO 10

Molded Gazpacho Salad

- 3 T unflavored gelatin (3 envelopes)
- 2 c water
- 1 can (14½ oz) stewed tomatoes and liquid
- 2 cans (8 oz each) tomato sauce
- ½ c wine vinegar
- 1 T Worcestershire sauce
- 10 to 12 drops hot red pepper sauce
- 1½ t salt
- ½ t ground cumin
- 1 clove garlic, crushed
- ½ c onion, finely chopped
- ⅔ c celery, finely chopped
- ¾ c cucumber, seeded and finely chopped
- 1 c green pepper, finely chopped
  Lettuce leaves and lemon wedges for garnish, if desired

In small saucepan, soften gelatin in water; heat, stirring constantly, until gelatin is dissolved. Remove from heat and set aside. Drain stewed tomatoes, reserving liquid; chop tomatoes. In medium bowl, combine gelatin mixture, chopped tomatoes and reserved liquid, tomato sauce, wine vinegar, Worcestershire sauce, hot red pepper sauce, salt and cumin; stir to combine thoroughly. Add garlic, onion, celery, cucumber and green pepper; refrigerate until mixture mounds on a spoon when stirred. Turn into an oiled six-cup mold and refrigerate until firm, about four hours. Invert mold onto serving platter lined with lettuce leaves; garnish with lemon wedges, if desired. Makes eight to 10 servings.

SERVES 12

Paella Salad

4 c chicken broth
2½ t curry powder, divided
½ t salt
¼ t hot red pepper sauce
¼ t saffron threads or powdered saffron
2 cloves garlic, minced
6 T corn oil
1 c chopped onions
1½ c uncooked long grain rice
2 lbs skinned and boned chicken breasts, cut into 1-inch pieces
1 lb medium or large cooked shrimp, divided
2 jars (6 oz each) marinated artichoke hearts, drained and diced, juice reserved
1 can (4 oz) chopped green chilies, drained
1 can (6½ or 7 oz) crabmeat, drained and flaked
¾ c thinly sliced scallions, including green tops
¾ c sliced green pimiento-stuffed olives
1 c diced celery
1 c plus 1 T mayonnaise, divided
Salt and freshly ground pepper to taste
Lettuce leaves
Steamed clams, if desired
Sliced pimiento
Watercress
Lemon wedges

In large saucepan or pot, combine chicken broth, one teaspoon of the curry powder, salt, red pepper sauce, saffron and garlic; bring to a boil over medium heat.

Meanwhile in large skillet or paella dish, heat oil; add chopped onion and cook until translucent, about three minutes. Add rice and cook, stirring constantly, until rice is lightly browned. Carefully pour in hot seasoned broth, reduce heat, cover and simmer gently until broth is half absorbed, about 10 to 12 minutes. Add chicken and stir; cover and continue simmering until chicken is cooked and all liquid has been absorbed, about 12 to 15 minutes. Remove from heat and cool.

Turn chicken/rice mixture into very large bowl; add half of the shrimp, cut into bite size pieces if large. Reserve remaining shrimp for garnish and refrigerate in covered dish. Add artichoke, green chilies, crabmeat, scallions, olives and celery; set aside.

In medium bowl, combine 1 cup of the mayonnaise with reserved liquid from artichokes. Add remaining 1½ teaspoons curry powder and stir until smooth. Season to taste with salt and pepper. Toss dressing with salad until well coated. Grease a 10- to 12-cup mold with remaining tablespoon mayonnaise and press salad firmly into mold. Cover and refrigerate overnight.

Unmold salad on platter lined with lettuce leaves. Arrange reserved shrimp and clams, if desired, around edge. Garnish with sliced pimiento and watercress and serve with lemon wedges.

SERVES 8

Pasta Salad with Pesto

- **1 lb linguine, penne or thin macaroni**
- **12 oz cooked ham cut into strips 2x⅓x⅓ inches**
- **12 oz Jarlsberg, Emmenthaler or Gruyere cheese, cut into strips**
- **½ c scallions, thinly sliced**
  Pesto Dressing (recipe follows)

Cook linguine, penne or macaroni according to package instructions until just tender (al dente). Drain and rinse with cold water to stop cooking process; drain again and combine in large bowl with ham, cheese and scallions. Combine with Pesto Dressing (recipe follows) and toss to coat thoroughly. Cover and refrigerate several hours or overnight to blend flavors. Bring salad to room temperature before serving. Makes eight servings.

MAKES 2 CUPS

Pesto Dressing

- **2 c fresh basil leaves, loosely packed**
- **½ c pine nuts or walnuts**
- **½ c grated Parmesan cheese**
- **3 garlic cloves, peeled**
- **¾ c olive oil**
- **½ c wine vinegar**
  Salt, to taste

In blender or food processor with metal blade, combine basil, pine nuts or walnuts, cheese, garlic, olive oil and wine vinegar. Blend or process until smooth, scraping sides of container. Add salt, to taste. Makes about two cups of dressing.

SALADS

SERVES 6

Pesto Potatoes

5 or 6 medium potatoes, peeled, cooked and sliced
½ lb green beans, trimmed, cut in 2-inch pieces and cooked crisp-tender
1 c cherry tomatoes, halved and drained
½ c hot water
½ c lightly packed parsley sprigs
⅓ c grated Parmesan cheese
¼ c vegetable oil
2 T white wine vinegar
2 T dries basil, or ¼ c minced fresh basil leaves
1 or 2 cloves garlic, peeled and sliced
½ t salt
¼ t pepper
Lettuce leaves

In large bowl, combine potatoes, beans and tomatoes; set aside. In container of electric blender or food processor, combine water, parsley, cheese, oil, vinegar, basil, garlic, salt and pepper. Blend or process until smooth. Pour mixture over reserved vegetables and toss gently to coat. Line serving bowl with lettuce leaves; spoon in potato mixture and chill one or two hours. Makes six servings.

SERVES 16 TO 20

Ribbon Salad

2 pkgs (¼ oz each) unflavored gelatin
2½ c cold water, divided
2 c milk
½ c sugar
2 c (1 pint) sour cream
2 t vanilla
1 pkg (3 oz) lime-flavored gelatin
1 pkg (3 oz) orange-flavored gelatin
1 pkg (3 oz) lemon-flavored gelatin
1 pkg (3 oz) cherry- or raspberry-flavored gelatin
4 c boiling water, divided

In small bowl, soften unflavored gelatin in ½ cup of the cold water; set aside. In small saucepan, bring milk to a boil; remove from heat, add sugar immediately and stir to dissolve. Add sour cream, vanilla and softened gelatin mixture to the hot milk and beat until smooth and creamy. Set mixture aside but *do not refrigerate*.

In small bowl, dissolve lime gelatin in one cup of the boiling water. Stir in ½ cup of the cold water and stir until gelatin is completely dissolved. Pour into bottom of 9x13-inch Pyrex dish. Refrigerate until set, about one hour. It is important that each layer be entirely set before pouring on the next layer. Be sure that your dish is level on refrigerator shelf so that the end result will not be lopsided.

When lime layer is set, spoon over it one-third of the reserved milk/sour cream mixture, about 1½ cups. Tilt dish so that white layer is evenly distributed. Refrigerate until white layer is set, about 45 minutes.

Dissolve orange gelatin in another cup of the boiling water; add ½ cup of the cold water and stir until entirely dissolved. Pour orange layer carefully over white layer and refrigerate again about one hour, until set. Add another white layer. Repeat process with lemon gelatin, another white layer and end with cherry or raspberry layer, using 1 cup boiling water and ½ cup cold water for each of the flavored gelatins and about 1½ cups of milk mixture for each of the white layers.

When all layers have been added, let chill in refrigerator, covered with plastic wrap, at least four hours before cutting into squares to serve. Makes about 16 to 20 servings.

SERVES 6

Sameer Eid's Fattoush (Vegetable Pita Salad)

        4 small stale pita breads
        3 small tomatoes, seeded and diced
        1 large onion, diced
        1 medium unpeeled cucumber, seeded and diced
        1 bunch parsley, minced
       ¾ c minced fresh mint leaves
       ⅓ c olive oil
        1 T lemon juice
        1 t sumac
           Salt and pepper to taste
        1 T sesame seeds

With sharp knife, separate pita breads into flat disks, cutting through pockets. Place on cookie sheet and toast under broiler until golden. Remove, cool and break into crisp, bite-size pieces. Set aside.

In large bowl, combine tomatoes, onion, cucumber, parsley and mint. In small bowl, whisk together olive oil, lemon juice, sumac and salt and pepper to taste. Toss salad with dressing and chill until ready to serve. Just before serving, add pita pieces and toss salad again. Sprinkle with sesame seeds. Makes about six servings.

SALADS

SERVES 6 TO 8

Slightly Oriental Salad

½ c salad oil
4 T catsup
3 T red wine vinegar
¼ c minus 1 T sugar
1 t salt
1 small onion, minced
1 lb fresh spinach, thoroughly rinsed, veins removed
1 can (16 oz) bean sprouts, drained
¼ lb fresh mushrooms, thinly sliced
1 can (6 oz) water chestnuts, drained and thinly sliced
1 or 2 hard-cooked eggs, chopped
½ c bacon bits, real or imitation

In medium jar with top, combine salad oil, catsup, vinegar, sugar, salt and onion. Cover jar and shake well; store in refrigerator until ready to use.

In large serving bowl, combine spinach, bean sprouts, mushrooms and water chestnuts. Just before serving, pour enough reserved dressing over greens to just coat them (do not over-dress). Sprinkle with chopped egg and bacon bits. Makes six to eight servings.

SERVES 6 TO 8

Sweet Potato Salad

1 lb sweet potatoes or yams (dry-packed canned potatoes may be used, well-drained)
3 to 4 stalks celery, chopped
4 hard-cooked eggs, chopped
2 or more small green onions, minced
Dash salt
Hellman's mayonnaise to taste
Durkee's Dressing to taste

Cook potatoes with skins on until tender. Drain, cool slightly and peel. Mash potatoes in large bowl and add celery, eggs, onions and salt. Moisten to desired consistency with mayonnaise and season to taste with Durkee's Dressing. Spoon into serving bowl and serve chilled. Makes six to eight servings or more, if used as appetizer.

SERVES 8

Vermicelli Salad with Shrimp

1 lb vermicelli or other thin spaghetti, broken into 2-inch
  pieces and cooked al dente
1 lb cooked shrimp, cut into bite-size pieces
1 c chopped celery
1 c chopped onion
2 c mayonnaise
½ c chopped sour pickles, well drained
2 T capers, finely chopped
1 T Dijon-style mustard
1 T fines herbes
  Lettuce leaves

In large bowl, combine vermicelli, shrimp, celery and onion; toss well and set aside. In medium bowl, combine mayonnaise, pickles, capers, mustard and fines herbes. Stir to mix well, and combine with vermicelli mixture. Toss salad until vermicelli and shrimp are coated. Serve very cold, on lettuce leaves. Makes eight servings.

SERVES 6 TO 8

Wild Rice Salad with Orzo and Spinach

- ¾ c wild rice
- 2 c water
- ½ c orzo (tiny rice-shape pasta)
- ½ c thinly sliced scallions, including green tops
- ½ c thinly sliced radishes
- ½ c chopped red onion
- 1 large stalk celery, halved lengthwise and thinly sliced on the diagonal
- 1 c (4 oz) chopped green chilies, drained
- 4 oz thinly sliced hard salami, cut into fine julienne, if desired
- 3 T tarragon wine vinegar
- 1 clove garlic, pressed
- 1 t salt
- ½ t freshly ground black pepper
  Pinch tarragon
- ½ c olive oil
- 2 c shredded fresh spinach
  Spinach leaves
  Greek olives

In medium saucepan, combine wild rice and water (a clove of garlic may be added, if desired.) Bring to a boil, reduce heat and simmer over low heat until water is almost absorbed and rice is tender, 45 to 60 minutes. Drain rice and turn into large bowl; set aside to cool.

Meanwhile cook orzo in lightly salted boiling water until just tender (al dente), about 10 to 12 minutes. Drain and add to rice. Add scallions, radishes, red onion, celery, green chilies and salami, if desired. Toss to combine and set aside.

In small bowl, combine vinegar, pressed garlic, salt, black pepper and tarragon. Whisking constantly, add the olive oil in a thin stream. Continue whisking until emulsion is set. Pour dressing over rice mixture and toss to coat. Chill until 30 minutes before serving time. Just before serving, toss with shredded spinach and turn into salad bowl lined with crisp spinach leaves. Garnish with small Greek olives. Serve at room temperature. Makes six to eight servings.

PASTA

SERVES 6 TO 8

Bob Phillips' Spaghetti with Clam Sauce

- 6 oz imported olive oil
- 4 cloves garlic, minced
- 4 T butter
- 2 c broccoli flowerets
- 1 c minced parsley leaves
- 2 cans (6½ oz each) chopped or minced clams and juice
- 1 c light cream
- 1 lb vermicelli
- ¼ c freshly grated Romano or Parmesan cheese

In large skillet, heat olive oil; add garlic and sauté one minute. Add butter, broccoli and parsley and cook just until broccoli is crisp tender, about three minutes. Add clams and clam juice; cook 10 minutes, stirring frequently. Add light cream and cook, stirring frequently, an additional 10 minutes.

Meanwhile, cook vermicelli according to package instructions just until tender, about four to five minutes. Drain thoroughly and return to cooking pot. Pour prepared clam sauce over vermicelli and mix thoroughly. Let stand over low heat, mixing occasionally, about five minutes, until pasta has absorbed most of sauce. Sprinkle with grated cheese and serve immediately. Makes six to eight servings.

SERVES 6 TO 8

City Delights' Pasta Primavera

- 1 t vinegar
- 1½ c tiny broccoli flowerets
- 1 c tiny cauliflower flowerets
- 1 c sliced small zucchini (slices about ¼-inch thick)
- 1 c fresh asparagus, trimmed and sliced diagonally into 1½-inch pieces
- 1 c fresh peas
- 12 cherry tomatoes, halved if large
- ½ c thinly sliced scallions
- ½ c chopped parsley
- ½ c shredded carrots
- ½ c olive oil
- ¼ c wine vinegar or fresh lemon juice
- 4 cloves garlic, finely minced
- ½ t dry mustard
- ½ t basil
- ½ t oregano
- ¼ t thyme
- ¼ t savory
- 1 lb fresh pasta or ¾ lb dried pasta

In large pot of boiling water acidulated with one teaspoon vinegar, blanch broccoli, cauliflower, zucchini, asparagus and peas until crisp-tender, about two minutes. Do not overcook. Set aside to drain thoroughly in colander.

In medium bowl, combine tomatoes, scallions, parsley and carrots; set aside.

In small bowl or medium jar with top, combine olive oil, vinegar or lemon juice, garlic, mustard, basil, oregano, thyme and savory. Whisk or shake until well blended; set aside.

In large kettle or pot, cook pasta in large amount of boiling salted water until just tender (al dente), six to eight minutes depending on what type of pasta is used. Drain in colander; rinse with cold water to stop cooking action and drain thoroughly.

In large serving bowl, combine cooled pasta, prepared blanched vegetables and fresh vegetables. Pour prepared dressing over all and toss until well combined and coated. Serve at room temperature. Makes six to eight servings.

SERVES 4

Dolly Sinelli's Prizewinning Pesto

- 4 c basil, loosely packed
- ½ c curly parsley
- 2 to 3 cloves garlic
- ¾ c olive oil
- 5 T butter, divided
  Salt and pepper to taste
- 1 lb linguine
- ½ c freshly grated Parmesan cheese

In food processor container with steel blade, combine basil, parsley, garlic, olive oil and four tablespoons of the butter. Process just until finely chopped. Do not process to a paste. Add salt and pepper to taste and set aside.

In large pot, bring about four quarts of lightly salted water to boil; add linguine and cook until just tender (al dente). Drain and toss with the remaining tablespoon butter. Add one half of the prepared basil mixture and one half of the Parmesan cheese and toss. Add remaining basil mixture and remaining Parmesan and toss again. Serve immediately. Makes four servings.

SERVES 4

Falafel with Tahini Sauce

        2 c dry chick peas (garbanzo)
        1 c small dry fava beans
    1¼ t baking soda, divided
        ½ bunch parsley
        ½ head garlic, about 6 cloves, peeled
        1 medium onion
        ½ t dried mint
        ½ t ground cumin
        ½ t marjoram
        ¼ t cinnamon
            Salt and pepper to taste
        ½ t coriander, if desired
        1 small Hungarian pepper, peeled and seeded, if desired
            Cooking oil
            Tahini Sauce (recipe follows)
            Pita Bread
            Chopped tomato, onion, cucumber, alfalfa sprouts and yogurt for garnish

In large bowl, combine chick peas, fava beans and one teaspoon of the baking soda. Cover with water by one inch and let stand overnight or at least 12 hours.

The next day, drain beans and rinse well. In large bowl, combine beans, remaining baking soda, parsley, garlic, onion, mint, cumin, marjoram, cinnamon, salt and pepper to taste and coriander and Hungarian pepper, if desired. Mix thoroughly and put mixture through meat grinder or food processor until mealy but smooth. Form into small patties and deep- or pan-fry in cooking oil until golden brown. Drain on paper towels and serve with Tahini Sauce in halved pita bread. Garnish with chopped tomato, onion, chopped cucumber, alfalfa sprouts and yogurt.

Tahini Sauce

        4 T Tahini (soybean paste)
        4 T lemon juice
        3 T minced parsley
        ½ t garlic powder
            Salt and freshly ground pepper to taste

In small bowl or blender, combine all ingredients and stir or blend until smooth. Makes about ½ cup sauce.

SERVES 4

Fettucine with Avocados and Cream

¼ c pecans

3 T finely chopped fresh basil or ¼ c finely chopped fresh parsley

1½ T finely minced lemon peel (white pulp removed)

2 t finely chopped garlic

1 c heavy cream, at room temperature

2 large, ripe avocados

2 T lemon juice

1 T plus 1 t salt

¾ lb fettuccine

2 T unsalted butter

¼ t white pepper

¾ c freshly grated Parmesan cheese, divided

1 c alfalfa sprouts, if desired

In small skillet, toast pecans over low heat about five minutes, until lightly browned; chop finely and set aside.

Combine basil or parsley, lemon peel and garlic; chop together until well mixed but not soft; set aside.

In small saucepan, bring cream to a simmer over medium-low heat, stirring occasionally, until reduced to two-thirds cup. Keep warm.

Halve avocados; peel and remove pits. Cut each half into eight lengthwise slices; cut each slice in half. Toss avocado with lemon juice. Toss again with prepared basil-lemon-garlic mixture and set aside.

In large pot, bring about four quarts water to rapid boil; add one tablespoon of the salt and fettucine. Cook until just tender (al dente), drain and toss with remaining salt, butter and pepper. Add warm cream and one-half cup of the Parmesan cheese and toss to coat fettuccine; add avocado mixture and gently toss to combine. Sprinkle with remaining cheese and alfalfa sprouts, if desired, and serve immediately. Makes four servings.

Joanne's Lasagna

     6 slices bacon, chopped
     2 T margarine
     2 medium onions, chopped
     1 stalk celery, chopped
     1 medium carrot, diced
    ¼ lb chicken livers, cut into quarters
     1 lb ground beef
   1½ c beef bouillon
   1½ c tomato sauce, fresh or canned
     1 t salt
        Freshly ground black pepper, to taste
    ¼ t nutmeg
    ½ lb fresh mushrooms, sliced
    ½ c dry white wine
        Pinch of sugar, basil and rosemary
     3 T butter
     3 T flour
     1 c milk
     1 c light cream
     1 lb ricotta cheese
    ½ t salt
    ¼ t pepper
     4 qt salted boiling water
    ½ lb lasagna noodles (12 strips)
     1 c grated Parmesan cheese
     1 c grated mozzarella cheese

In large, heavy skillet, cook bacon until browned; remove with slotted spoon and set aside. Add margarine to the fat in the pan and stir until melted. Add onions, celery and carrot; cook vegetables until onion is soft but not browned. Push vegetables to one side of the pan and add chicken livers; cook until livers are firm and lightly browned. Remove pan from heat and set aside.

In separate pan, cook ground beef until browned. Pour off excess fat and add beef to vegetable-liver mixture to heat and add bouillon, tomato sauce, salt, pepper and nutmeg. Cover and simmer over low heat 30 minutes. Add mushrooms, wine, sugar, basil and rosemary; simmer, covered, another 30 minutes. Add reserved bacon pieces, stir and set aside.

In large saucepan, melt butter; add flour and stir until mixture is bubbly. Add milk and cream all at once and cook, stirring until mixture starts to thicken. Add ricotta and break it up with fork; cook, stirring until mixture is smooth but grainy and thickened. Season with salt and pepper, remove from heat and set aside.

PASTA

To large kettle of boiling salted water, add lasagna noodles, one at a time. Cook, at high boil, until noodles are just tender, five to seven minutes. Drain, rinse in cool water and lay out on tabletop or damp cloth to cool.

To assemble: In two 9x13-inch well greased baking dishes, spread a layer of the meat sauce. Top with a layer of three noodles, then with a layer of the ricotta sauce. Sprinkle with Parmesan cheese. Repeat layers, ending with the Parmesan cheese. Sprinkle half the mozzarella over the top of each dish. Wrap tightly in plastic wrap, foil or freezer paper and freeze.

To serve: Remove freezer paper or plastic wrap, cover with foil and bake at 375 degrees about 45 minutes or until sauce starts to bubble. Remove foil and continue baking 15 or more minutes, until lightly browned on top. Makes eight servings per casserole.

SERVES 3 TO 4

Linguine with Clam Artichoke Sauce

¼	c olive oil
4	T butter
1	t flour
1	c chicken broth
2 to 3	cloves garlic, crushed
1	T minced fresh parsley
2	t lemon juice
	Salt and pepper to taste
1	can (14 oz) drained artichokes, quartered
1	can (10 oz) whole baby clams, drained
2 to 3	T freshly grated Parmesan cheese
2	t drained capers, chopped
½	lb linguine

In heavy skillet or 2-quart saucepan, heat olive oil and butter; stir in flour and cook three minutes over medium heat, stirring often. Stir in broth, reduce heat and cook one minute. Add garlic, parsley, lemon juice and salt and pepper to taste; cook over low heat about five minutes. Stir in artichokes, clams, Parmesan cheese and capers; continue cooking, stirring frequently, 10 minutes.

Meanwhile, cook linguine in rapidly boiling, lightly salted water until al dente (just tender), about six minutes. Drain thoroughly and combine with prepared artichoke/clam sauce; toss to distribute and serve at once. Makes three to four servings.

SERVES 4 TO 6

Colette Wismer's Linguine with Pesto Sauce

- 12 almonds
- 12 walnut halves
- 2 c fresh basil
- 1 c Italian parsley
- 1 T pine nuts
- 3 T butter
- ½ c olive oil
- 2 garlic cloves
- ½ c grated Asiago cheese
- ½ c grated Romano
- 1 lb linguine

Blanch almonds and walnuts in boiling water to remove skins, if desired. Combine almonds and walnuts with basil, parsley, pine nuts, butter, olive oil, and garlic cloves in blender jar. Blend until smooth. Transfer to large serving bowl, and stir in grated Asiago and Romano cheeses. Cook linguine al dente (just tender) and drain, reserving 4 tablespoons hot water. Toss pasta in serving bowl with sauce, add reserved hot water, and toss again. Makes four to six servings.

PASTA

Microwave Creamy Stuffed Pasta Shells

  6 oz bulk sausage, mild or hot
  ¼ c finely chopped green onions, including green tops
  1 c finely diced cooked chicken or turkey
  1 can (3 oz) mushrooms, chopped or ¼ lb fresh mushrooms, chopped and lightly browned in butter
  ½ c coarsely crushed saltine cracker crumbs
  2 T snipped parsley
  2 T dry white wine or sherry
  ½ t celery salt
  16 jumbo macaroni shells (conchiglioni), about 5 oz, cooked according to package directions, rinsed and well drained
    Mornay Sauce (recipe follows)
    Snipped parsley, Parmesan cheese and paprika for garnish, if desired

In 1-qt. microwave-safe casserole dish, crumble sausage and add green onion; microwave on high three to four minutes, until lightly browned, stirring twice. Pour off fat. Add chicken or turkey, mushrooms, crumbs, parsley, wine or sherry and celery salt; mix with spoon until well combined. Stuff about two heaping tablespoons into each prepared pasta shell. Place four stuffed shells, filling side up, into each of four individual casserole dishes. Pour Mornay Sauce (recipe follows) over each of the dishes, covering pasta completely. Cover each dish with vented plastic wrap. Microwave on high seven to eight minutes, until very hot and bubbly, giving dishes a half turn once. Remove wrap and spoon sauce over pasta again. Garnish, if desired, with snipped parsley, Parmesan cheese and paprika. Makes four servings.

Microwave Mornay Sauce

  6 T butter or margarine
  6 T flour
  ¼ t salt
  1½ c chicken broth
  1½ c milk or light cream
  ¼ c grated Parmesan cheese

In microwave-safe 1½-qt casserole or dish, melt butter or margarine on high one to 1¼ minutes. Remove dish and stir in flour until thoroughly mixed. Microwave on high 30 seconds. Remove dish and stir in salt, chicken broth, milk or cream and Parmesan cheese; mix well. Microwave on high about eight minutes, or until thick and bubbly, stirring four times. Mixture should be thick and smooth. Makes about 3½ cups Mornay Sauce.

SERVES 8 TO 10

Pastitsio

8 T butter
3 medium onions, chopped
2 large cloves garlic, minced
1 lb lean ground beef
1 can (1 lb 13 oz) Italian tomatoes with basil, juice reserved
¾ c dry red wine
2 t salt, divided
½ t freshly ground black pepper
½ t cinnamon
½ t oregano
½ t nutmeg
12 oz elbow macaroni
1 T vegetable oil
6 T flour
4 c milk
¼ t white pepper
4 eggs, beaten
1¼ c freshly grated Parmesan cheese, divided
¾ c unseasoned fine dry bread crumbs, divided
Butter for topping

In large deep skillet or Dutch oven, melt two tablespoons of the butter; add onions and garlic and cook until soft but not brown, about five minutes. Crumble meat into skillet and cook until lightly browned. Add drained tomatoes (reserve juice) and chop up with fork or knife. Add wine, one teaspoon of the salt, black pepper, cinnamon, oregano and nutmeg. Bring mixture to a boil, reduce heat and simmer about 20 minutes, until most of the liquid has evaporated. Remove from heat and cool; spoon off excess fat.

Meanwhile, in large pot, bring four to five quarts of lightly salted water to boil; add macaroni and vegetable oil. Boil briskly until macaroni is just tender (al dente), about eight minutes; drain well and set aside.

In large saucepan, melt remaining six tablespoons butter; add flour and cook, stirring, until mixture is bubbly. Gradually add milk, stirring with wire whisk; cook, whisking constantly, until sauce is thickened and smooth. Stir in remaining teaspoon salt and white pepper. Remove from heat and cool, stirring occasionally to prevent skin from forming on top. When white sauce is lukewarm, beat in eggs and ¼ cup of the Parmesan cheese; set aside.

PASTA

In lightly greased 13x9x2-inch baking dish, sprinkle ¼ cup of the bread crumbs evenly on bottom. Cover with one-half the macaroni; sprinkle with ¼ cup of the Parmesan cheese. Stir ¼ cup of bread crumbs and ¼ cup Parmesan into the prepared meat sauce; if mixture is too dry, stir in some of the reserved tomato liquid from can. Spread meat sauce evenly over macaroni and cover with one-half of the white sauce. Cover with remaining half of macaroni; spread remaining half of white sauce over macaroni and sprinkle with remaining crumbs and Parmesan mixed together. Dot top evenly with butter. Bake at 350 degrees 40 to 50 minutes, until top is golden brown and puffed. Remove from oven and let stand 15 minutes before cutting into squares to serve. Makes eight to 10 servings.

SERVES 16

Oak Park Drive In's Macaroni and Cheese

    1½ lbs elbow macaroni
    1½ qts milk
    2½ lbs sharp American cheese
     18 eggs, beaten
     ¼ lb grated Romano cheese

Cook macaroni according to package instructions. Drain into colander and rinse with cold water; set aside.

In large saucepan, combine milk and American cheese; heat, stirring, until cheese melts. In very large bowl, combine milk mixture, drained reserved macaroni and beaten eggs. Turn into two four-quart-casseroles, and sprinkle with Romano cheese. Bake at 350 degrees about 45 minutes, until edges are lightly browned. Do not overbake. Makes about 16 servings.

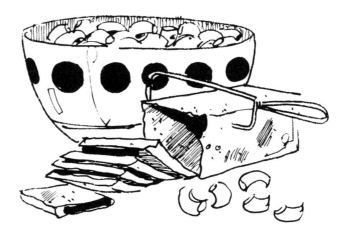

SERVES 10

Spinach Lasagna

- 3 T olive oil
- 1 c chopped onion
- 1 c chopped green pepper
- 1 T minced garlic
- 1 t dried basil
- 2 t dried oregano
- 1 bay leaf
- 2 t sea salt
- 1 c chopped fresh tomatoes
- 1 can (29 oz) tomato puree
- 1 can (6 oz) tomato paste
- 1 c dry red wine
- Juice and grated peel of 1 lemon
- 2 t nutmeg, divided
- 1 t cinnamon
- ¾ t black pepper, divided
- Dash Worcestershire sauce
- ½ c chopped fresh parsley
- 1 lb coarsely chopped fresh mushrooms
- 1½ c ricotta cheese
- ½ c cottage cheese
- 2 beaten eggs
- 1 lb fresh spinach, steamed three minutes, drained and chopped
- ½ t salt
- 12 lasagna noodles, plain, whole wheat or spinach, cooked, drained and rinsed in cold water
- 1 lb grated mozzarella cheese
- ½ c grated Parmesan or Romano cheese

In large skillet or Dutch oven, heat olive oil; add onion, green pepper, garlic, basil, oregano, bay leaf and sea salt. Cook, stirring frequently, until onions are translucent, about five minutes. Add tomatoes, tomato puree, tomato paste, red wine, lemon juice and peel, one teaspoon of the nutmeg, cinnamon, ¼ teaspoon of the black pepper and Worcestershire sauce; mix thoroughly and simmer at least 45 minutes. Add parsley and mushrooms and correct seasoning; remove from heat and set aside.

In large bowl, combine ricotta cheese, cottage cheese, eggs, spinach, salt, remaining nutmeg and black pepper; mix thoroughly and set aside.

To assemble: Place about one cup of the prepared tomato sauce in bottom of large lasagna pan, 11x15 inches. Arrange four cooked noodles on top. Cover with ½ of the ricotta/spinach mixture. Spread with ⅓ of the remaining tomato sauce and ½ of the mozzarella cheese. Arrange four more noodles over cheese; spread with remaining ½ ricotta/spinach mixture, ⅓ remaining tomato sauce and remaining mozzarella cheese. Place final four noodles on top and spread with remaining tomato sauce. Sprinkle with Parmesan or Romano cheese. Cover tightly with foil and bake at 375 degrees about 40 minutes. Remove foil and return to oven 10 minutes longer to brown lightly on top. Let stand 10 minutes before cutting into squares. Makes about 10 servings.

SERVES 4

Knedlik (Bread Dumpling)

   2 eggs
   ⅔ c milk
   2 T melted butter
   1 t salt
   4½ c slightly stale dense white bread, cubed
      Lard, butter or margarine

In small bowl, beat eggs, milk, melted butter and salt together until well mixed. Place bread cubes in medium bowl and pour egg mixture over; mix lightly with spoon until liquid is absorbed. Set aside.

Grease a large napkin or tea towel with lard, butter or margarine; place bread mixture in center and mold into large oval sausage shape, about 9 inches long and about 3½ inches in diameter. Roll up lightly and tie ends of roll securely with twine, letting two "tails" hang loose. Immerse in boiling water and boil 30 minutes. Remove to cutting board; remove twine and unroll dumpling carefully. Slice into ½-inch rounds to serve. Makes about four servings.

**MAKES FILLING
FOR 36 KREPLACH**

Chicken Filling for Kreplach

   3 T chicken fat
   2 large onions, grated
   1 clove garlic, minced
   ¼ c grated green pepper
   2¼ c ground, cooked chicken
   2 large eggs yolks
   2 T minced parsley
      Salt and pepper, to taste

In medium pan or skillet, melt chicken fat. Add onions and garlic and cook until partially browned. Add green pepper and cook until mixture is browned. Combine with chicken, egg yolks, parsley, salt and pepper, to taste; mix thoroughly. Cover and chill in refrigerator until ready to use. Makes filling for about 36 kreplach.

Yellow Egg Pasta Dough

2 c unbleached or regular flour
4 large eggs, at room temperature
2 T milk

In large bowl or on work surface, pour out flour. Make a hollow in the center of the flour and break the eggs into the hollow. Pour milk on top of eggs and beat mixture lightly with a fork, incorporating flour from the sides, little by little. When eggs are no longer runny, draw in the sides of the flour mound, working the dough with your fingertips until the egg is fully incorporated into the flour and a pasty dough is formed. Let dough rest 10 minutes.

Turn out dough onto lightly floured surface and knead with the heel of your palm 10 minutes or until dough is elastic and smooth. (Kneading time is important — don't skimp.) Wrap the dough in plastic and let it rest at least 15 minutes before proceeding. Then knead the dough one minute more before rolling it or feeding it into a pasta machine. Either put dough through pasta machine (at proper setting for type of noodle desired), or roll with rolling pin.

If you roll the dough by hand, turn the dough continuously as you roll it, to ensure that the dough is stretched in all directions. Continue rolling and stretching until dough is paper-thin.

To make wonton or kreplach wrappers, cut the sheet of dough into three-inch squares.

For wonton: Place one-half teaspoon of filling in the center of each square. Fold the square in half to form a rectangle, and press the edges to seal, moistening with a few drops of water if necessary. Fold wrapper in half again (so it is one-quarter as wide as it is long); then fold the rectangle in half lengthwise and pinch together the shorter inside edges.

For kreplach: Place one teaspoon of filling in a corner of each square. Pull the opposite corner of the dough over the filling to form a triangle, and seal the edges of the kreplach by pressing the two layers of dough together with the tines of a fork.

For noodles: Allow the dough to dry until it becomes somewhat leathery but not brittle. Then roll the dough like a jelly roll and, with a sharp knife, slice it into circles of desired width. Unroll the circles of dough. They can be used immediately, or hung to dry and stored for later use.

SERVES 6

Marvelous Molded Olive Rice Ring

```
 1  T butter
¼  c slivered almonds
 1  medium onion, chopped
 1  c uncooked brown rice
3½  c broth or stock
 1  c shredded Swiss, fontina or gruyere cheese
¼  c chopped ripe olives
¼  c chopped stuffed green olives
 2  T chopped parsley
```

In large skillet, melt butter; add almonds and cook until lightly browned. Remove almonds with slotted spoon and drain on paper towel. Add onion and rice to skillet; cook, stirring frequently, five minutes. Add broth, cover and simmer about 35 to 45 minutes, until liquid is absorbed. Stir in cheese, black and green olives, parsley and reserved browned almonds. Press mixture into lightly buttered small ring mold. Cover mold with metal foil and bake at 350 degrees 25 minutes. Uncover and let stand a few minutes. Carefully invert onto serving plate. Makes about six servings.

MEATS

SERVES 6 TO 8

Annette Liberson's Roast Beef Brisket with Mushrooms

3½ **to 4 lb brisket of beef**
½ **lb fresh mushrooms sliced**
1 **small onion, chopped**
1 **t salt**
¼ **t pepper**
¼ **t garlic powder, if desired**
2 **flowers fresh dill, if desired**
⅓ **c dry red wine**

Line a large roasting pan or jelly roll pan with heavy-duty aluminum foil, leaving about four inches of foil around the edges of the meat. Place brisket on foil and broil about five minutes on each side, until browned. Remove from broiler and sprinkle with mushrooms, onion, salt and pepper. Add garlic powder and dill, if desired. Sprinkle wine over all. Place another sheet of heavy-duty aluminum foil, the same size as the one used to line the pan, over the meat. Seal the package with double folds so that no cooking liquid or steam can escape. Roast meat at 325 degrees for 2½ hours. Remove to serving platter and serve the pan gravy in a separate bowl. Makes six to eight servings.

SERVES 4

Beef Burgundy in Gougere Shells

- 3 slices bacon, diced
- 1 lb tenderloin, sirloin or stewing beef, cut into 1-inch cubes
- 1 large clove garlic, minced
- 1 c water
- ½ c canned beef bouillon, undiluted
- ¼ c dry red wine
- 1 T tomato paste
- 1 bay leaf
- ½ t thyme
- ¼ t salt
- ⅛ t pepper
- 1½ c whole pitted ripe olives, drained and cut into wedges
- 1½ c small whole frozen or canned onions or fresh pearl onions, peeled and cooked
- ¼ lb fresh mushrooms, sliced
- 2½ T flour mixed with ⅓ c dry red wine
  Gougere Shells (recipe follows)

In large skillet or Dutch oven, cook bacon bits until browned and crispy; remove with slotted spoon and drain on paper towel. Add beef cubes and garlic to fat in skillet and cook, stirring frequently until just browned. If you are using beef tenderloin or sirloin, remove with slotted spoon and set aside on plate. If you are using stewing beef, leave in skillet. (The better the cut of beef, the better the taste; if you are using tenderloin or sirloin, the cooking time should be very short. If you use stew beef, it will take the full hour to cook until tender.) Stir in water, bouillon, red wine, tomato paste, bay leaf, thyme, salt and pepper. Bring mixture to a boil, reduce heat, cover and cook over low heat 45 minutes, or until beef is tender. Add olives, onions and mushrooms; cover and cook another 15 to 20 minutes. Stir flour/wine mixture into skillet and cook briefly until sauce is thickened. Return tenderloin or sirloin to skillet, if applicable, and cook until heated throughout. Spoon mixture into prepared Gougere Shells (recipe follows) and serve at once. Makes four servings.

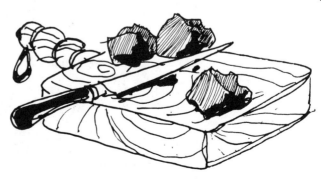

MAKES 4 SHELLS

Gougere Shells

⅓ c butter, in small pieces
⅔ c water
⅔ c flour
3 eggs
¼ c grated Parmesan cheese
2 T diced ripe olives

In medium saucepan, bring butter and water to a boil over medium heat. When butter is melted, remove pan from heat and stir in flour all at once. Stir vigorously with wooden spoon until mixture comes away from sides of pan and forms ball. Stir in eggs, one at a time, beating thoroughly after each addition. Stir in cheese and olives. Spoon mixture around sides, not bottom of four buttered 1¾-cup individual oval baking dishes or ramekins. Bake at 400 degrees 20 minutes, or until puffed and golden brown. Makes four Gougere Shells.

SERVES 4

Beef with Broccoli and Mushrooms

¾ lb to 1 lb beef flank steak, thinly sliced across the grain
3 T soy sauce
3 T vegetable oil, divided
1 T sherry
½ t finely minced ginger root
½ t brown sugar
½ t onion powder
⅛ t pepper
1 T cornstarch
2 stalks broccoli, cut into 1-inch pieces
¼ lb fresh mushrooms, thinly sliced
2 green onions, shredded
⅓ t salt
⅛ t monosodium glutamate, if desired

In large bowl, mix steak slices, soy sauce, two tablespoons of the oil, sherry, ginger root, brown sugar, onion powder and pepper. Add cornstarch and mix well; set aside (this part of the recipe may be done in advance and stored in the refrigerator to marinate).

In 2-qt. casserole or container suitable for microwave cooking, toss together broccoli, mushrooms, onions, salt, monosodium glutamate, if desired, and remaining tablespoon of oil. Cover with plastic wrap and cook in microwave oven on full power two minutes, stirring once. Remove from oven and spread reserved meat over vegetables. Cover with plastic wrap and cook on full power four minutes. If meat has not lost its pink color, return to microwave oven for an additional two minutes, but do not overcook. Transfer to platter before serving. Makes four servings.

SERVES 8

Beef Tongue in Sweet and Sour Sauce

    3 lbs fresh beef tongue
    2 medium onions, peeled and quartered
    1 large carrot, coarsely sliced
    3 ribs celery with leaves, coarsely sliced
    4 sprigs parsley
   10 peppercorns
    ½ c raisins
    ½ c chopped pitted prunes
    2 c water
    ½ c unsweetened prune juice
    ¼ c chicken fat or margarine
    1 medium green pepper, diced
    1 large onion, diced
    ¼ c dark brown sugar
    2 T cornstarch
    ½ c vinegar
      Salt and pepper to taste

In large heavy pot or Dutch oven, combine fresh tongue, quartered onions, carrot, celery, parsley and peppercorns. Add water just to cover tongue; bring to a boil, reduce heat and simmer three hours, adding more water to keep the level just covering ingredients. Remove tongue and discard water and vegetables. Let tongue stand until just cool enough to handle. Remove roots, small bones and gristle. Pull off skin and slice tongue in ¼-inch to ½-inch slices; set aside.

Meanwhile, in medium saucepan, combine raisins, prunes, water and prune juice. Bring to a boil, reduce heat, cover and simmer 30 minutes.

In medium skillet, melt chicken fat or margarine; add green pepper and onion. Cook until soft, stirring occasionally, about five minutes. Mix brown sugar, cornstarch, vinegar and salt and pepper to taste and add to green pepper mixture alternately with prepared prune mixture. Cook over medium heat, stirring constantly, until sauce thickens and boils.

Arrange sliced tongue in skillet and spoon sauce over; heat gently for 20 to 30 minutes. Makes about eight servings.

SERVES 10

Beery Beef

⅓ c vegetable oil, divided
2 lbs onions, peeled and thickly sliced
3½ to 4 lbs lean beef, trimmed and cut into 1-inch cubes
½ c flour
6 cloves garlic
2 c beef broth or consomme
1 bottle or can (12 oz) beer
½ c chopped fresh parsley
¼ c red wine vinegar
3 T brown sugar
2 bay leaves
2 t thyme
1 t salt
Freshly ground black pepper, to taste
Hot buttered noodles, if desired

In large Dutch oven or fireproof casserole with lid, heat half the vegetable oil. Add onions and cook over low heat, stirring occasionally, until onions are soft but not brown, about 10 minutes. Remove onions with slotted spoon and set aside. Add remaining oil to the Dutch oven or casserole and heat. In paper bag, shake beef in the flour until well coated. Cook half the beef at a time in the oil, adding more oil if necessary, until beef is well browned on all sides. Spoon off excess oil and return onions to pot. Add garlic, broth or consomme, beer, parsley, vinegar, brown sugar, bay leaves, thyme, salt and pepper, to taste. Bring mixture to a boil, cover and simmer over low heat 90 minutes. Remove from heat and cool completely, skimming off excess fat on top. When cool, seal with foil or plastic wrap, cover and freeze.

To serve: Remove foil or plastic wrap. With cover on again, heat in 350-degree oven one hour or until mixture is thick and bubbly. Serve with hot buttered noodles, if desired. Makes about 10 servings.

Chopped Beef with Peas

- ½ lb flank steak
- 2 T vegetable or peanut oil
- 1 t minced fresh garlic
- 2 T light dry sherry
- 1½ c chicken broth or stock
- 1 c frozen peas or snow peas, thawed
- 2 T oyster sauce (available at most supermarkets)
- 2 T dark soy sauce
- ½ t salt
- ½ t sesame oil
- ¼ t sugar
- 2 T cornstarch
- 4 T water
- Hot cooked rice

In food processor with metal blade or sharp cleaver, shred flank steak — do not chop too finely. Set aside.

Heat wok until very hot; add oil and heat. Add garlic and stir-fry 20 seconds. Add prepared steak and stir-fry just until pink color disappears. Add sherry and stir in. Add chicken broth or stock and peas or snow peas. Cover wok and boil five minutes. Add oyster sauce, soy sauce, salt, sesame oil and sugar; stir until well mixed. Dissolve cornstarch in water and add to mixture in wok; stir-fry until sauce thickens. Serve at once over hot cooked rice. Makes two to three servings.

Curry Beef (Ca-Ri Bo)

- 2 T cooking oil
- 6 to 8 oz lean beef, cut into small cubes
- 1 small onion, sectioned
- 1 t fresh garlic, minced
- 1 T curry powder
- ¾ c water
- 1 green pepper, seeds and membrane removed, cut into large pieces
- 1 T chili powder
- 1 t sugar
- 1 t cornstarch dissolved in 2 t water
- 2 c hot cooked rice

Warm wok or 12-inch skillet over high heat one to two minutes. Reduce heat to medium and add oil, beef, onion, garlic and curry powder. Stir-fry two minutes. Add water, green pepper, chili powder and sugar; cook until beef is tender, about five minutes. Add cornstarch mixture and cook, stirring constantly until sauce is thickened, about one minute. Serve at once over hot cooked rice. Makes two entree servings.

MAKES 10 LARGE

Finlandia's Pasties

8 c flour
  Dash salt
3 c solid vegetable shortening
2 c water
1 lb coarsely ground (chili grind) or chopped beef
½ lb coarsely ground or chopped pork
3 medium potatoes, peeled and finely diced
4 medium carrots, scraped and finely diced
1 small onion, chopped
½ medium rutabaga, peeled and finely diced
½ c beef suet, finely chopped
1 T parsley flakes or ¼ cup minced fresh parsley
1 t salt
  Dash pepper
2 T melted butter
  Gravy or catsup, if desired

In large bowl, combine flour and dash salt. With pastry blender or two knives, cut shortening into flour until mixture resembles gravel. Slowly add water until mixture forms ball. The pastry will be much stickier than regular pie crust. With floured hands, shape pastry into ball, cover with plastic wrap and let rest in refrigerator while preparing filling.

In large bowl, combine beef, pork, potatoes, carrots, onion, rutabaga and suet; sprinkle with parsley, salt, pepper and melted butter. Toss mixture thoroughly until all ingredients are well distributed. Set aside.

Divide prepared pastry dough into 10 equal parts. On well-floured surface, roll each part into an 8-inch circle. Mound about 1¼ cups filling on half of a dough circle; fold other half of the dough over filling, making a half-moon shape, and crimp edges together firmly. With spatula, transfer pasty to ungreased cookie sheet. Continue procedure until all dough and filling are used. Bake at 350 degrees about 1¼ hours, until lightly browned. Serve with gravy or catsup, if desired. Makes 10 large pasties.

SERVES 6

Ginger Pot Roast

1 round-bone or chuck pot roast, about 4 lbs, with most of the fat removed
  Cooking oil
4 medium carrots, pared and sliced
4 stalks celery, sliced
1 medium onion, sliced
1 medium potato, peeled and cut into eighths, if desired
2 cloves garlic, minced or pressed
1 t salt
¼ t freshly ground black pepper
2 cans (12 oz) or 3 c Vernors
  Flour or cornstarch for thickening

In large skillet, brown meat thoroughly on both sides in a little cooking oil. Remove meat to roasting pan; add carrots, celery, onion, potato, if desired, and garlic. Sprinkle with salt and pepper and cover with Vernors. Cover pan and bake at 325 degrees about three hours, until meat is fork-tender, Drain meat and vegetables and remove to hot platter. Skim off excess grease from cooking liquid and discard. Thicken cooking liquid with flour or cornstarch to make gravy and pour over meat and vegetables. Makes about six servings.

SERVES 8 TO 10

Howard Camden's Roast Style Brisket of Beef

- 1 6 to 8 lb flat cut brisket of beef
- 3 T cooking oil
- 2 c chopped onion
- 4 stalks celery, leaves included, chopped
- 1 diced carrot
- 1 diced parsnip
- 1 large green pepper, chopped
- 2 cloves garlic, minced, or 1 t garlic powder
- 2 t beef bouillon granules
- ½ t freshly ground pepper
- 2 c dry red wine
- 2 cans (16 oz each) small whole potatoes or 2 lbs tiny fresh new potatoes
- 10 small carrots, halved
- 10 small parsnips, peeled and halved
- ½ bunch parsley
- 2 medium size ripe tomatoes, cut into wedges or ornamental shapes

Trim off all excess fat from beef and discard. In large Dutch oven or roasting pan with cover, heat oil; add beef and brown thoroughly on all sides. Remove meat from pan and set aside. To fat remaining in pan, add onion, celery, diced carrot, diced parsnip and green pepper; cook, stirring frequently until well browned and lightly caramelized. With slotted spoon, remove half of the vegetable mixture and set aside on plate. Return beef to pan and place on top of remaining vegetable mixture. Rub meat with garlic, bouillon granules and pepper and cover with reserved half of vegetable mixture. Add wine, cover and roast at 325 degrees about three hours, until meat is almost done. Add potatoes, carrots and parsnips to the liquid surrounding meat. Continue roasting, covered, until meat is fork tender and vegetables are cooked, about 30 minutes. When roast is done, remove from pan and let stand about 20 minutes to distribute juices. Keep vegetables warm. Slice meat across grain and arrange in large platter surrounded by vegetables. Garnish with parsley and tomato wedges or shapes. Makes eight to 10 servings.

SERVES 10 TO 12

Jeremy Igger's Mom's Spiced Beef (Svickova)

    4 to 5 lbs beef tenderloin of rib-eye roast
    3 c water
 1½ c white vinegar
    1 medium onion, diced
    2 small carrots, diced
    2 small bay leaves
  10 peppercorns, bruised
    4 to 5 whole allspice
       Celery root, if desired
  ½ lb bacon
    1 T salt
    3 T goose or chicken fat
    1 c sour cream
    2 T flour

Wipe beef with damp cloth and pat dry. Trim off excess fat; set beef aside. In large saucepan, combine water, vinegar, onion, carrots, bay leaves, peppercorns, allspice and celery root, if desired. Bring to a boil and simmer 15 minutes; let cool to room temperature. Place beef in oval or rectangular dish and pour marinade over it. Refrigerate, uncovered, 12 to 24 hours, turning once.

Remove beef from marinade, reserving marinade. Using larding needle or sharp thin knife, thread strips of bacon through the beef lengthwise. Rub beef with salt. Melt goose or chicken fat in large roasting pan. Add beef and pour reserved marinade over it; roast at 325 degrees 30 minutes per pound, about 2½ hours for a five-pound roast. When beef is done, remove to serving platter and slice thinly; keep warm.

Meanwhile, in small bowl, mix sour cream and flour. Add one cup of the pan juices in roasting pan and mix well. Pour sour cream mixture into roasting pan and mix with remaining pan juices. Cook, stirring constantly, over medium heat until gravy thickens. Pour some of the gravy over the sliced beef and serve the rest in a gravy boat. Makes 10 to 12 servings.

SERVES 6 TO 8

Mary Ruggles' Cabbage Stroganoff

⅛ c bacon drippings or vegetable oil
1 c chopped green onions
1 lb ground sirloin or other lean ground beef
1 small head or ½ large head green cabbage, chopped coarsely
1 c water, divided
1 pkg (1.37 oz) Lipton's onion soup mix
1 can (10½ oz) cream of mushroom soup, undiluted
1 c sour cream
Mashed potatoes or noodles, if desired

In large heavy skillet, heat bacon drippings or oil; sauté onions until limp. Add beef, crumbling with fork, and cook until browned. Add cabbage and ¾ cup of the water. Cover and simmer over medium heat until cabbage is wilted. Sprinkle with onion soup mix and stir, mixing thoroughly. Add mushroom soup; rinse can with remaining ¼ cup water, and add that water to the skillet, stirring to combine. Stir in sour cream, cover and simmer over low heat 45 minutes, until cabbage is tender. Serve plain or over mashed potatoes or noodles, if desired. Makes six to eight servings.

MAKES 3 GALLONS

Bob Vargo's Prizewinning Chili

- ½ corn oil
- 2 lbs boneless pork, cut into small dice
- 3½ lbs round steak, cut into small dice
- 4 lbs ground round steak
- 3 large onions, diced
- 3 large green peppers, diced
- 2 large bulbs garlic, peeled and chopped
- 6 small hot green peppers, seeded and finely diced
- 2 bunches celery, chopped
- 1 can (4 oz) green chilies, chopped
- 6 bay leaves
- 6 oz chili powder
- 4 oz powdered cumin
- 4 oz beef base granules
- 2 T monosodium glutamate
- ½ oz dried minced onion
- ½ oz dried minced garlic
- 1 t celery salt
- 1 t sugar
- 1 t freshly ground black pepper
- ½ allspice
- ½ t Lawrey's Seasoned Salt
- ¼ t basil
- ¼ t oregano
- 4 cans (1 lb 12 oz each) whole tomatoes with juice cut up
- 3 cans (15 oz each) tomato puree
- 3 cans (6 oz each) tomato juice

In a very large soup kettle or pot, heat corn oil. Add pork, round steak and ground round steak and cook until pink color is gone. Add onions, green peppers, garlic, hot green peppers, celery and chilies and cook until onion is transparent. Add bay leaves, chili powder, cumin, beef base granules, monosodium glutamate, dried minced onion, dried minced garlic, celery salt, sugar, black pepper, allspice, Lawrey's Seasoned Salt, basil and oregano. Simmer mixture 30 minutes, uncovered. Add canned tomatoes and juice, tomato puree and tomato juice; simmer over low heat, uncovered, two hours. Makes three gallons.

MEATS

Jim Adamski's Original Sin Chili

3 lbs ground beef
3 lbs round steak, tendons and fat removed, cut into small cubes
2 large cans (28 oz each) stewed tomatoes
1 large can (46 oz) V8 juice
2 pkgs (1½ oz each) dried onion soup mix
1 large Spanish onion, chopped
3 celery stalks, chopped
2 green peppers, seeded and chopped
2 pickled mild banana peppers, seeded and chopped
½ c banana pepper juice
½ c white vinegar
2 cloves garlic, crushed
1 bay leaf
3 oz chili powder
¼ c barbecue sauce
¼ c catsup
¼ c liquid hot pepper sauce
2 t cumin powder
2 t instant beef bouillon granules
2 t salt
1 t oregano
1 t onion powder
½ t paprika
½ t black pepper
Dash crushed red pepper
Dash dried basil
Dash dried thyme
1 dried red pepper
1 to 2 c beer, to taste

In large vat or stock pot, brown ground beef; drain off excess fat and discard. Add cubed round steak, tomatoes, V8 juice, onion soup mix, onion, celery, green peppers, banana peppers, banana pepper juice, vinegar, garlic, bay leaf, chili powder, barbecue sauce, catsup, liquid hot pepper sauce, cumin powder, beef bouillon granules, salt, oregano, onion powder, paprika, black pepper, crushed red pepper, basil, thyme and dried red pepper. Bring mixture to a boil, reduce heat and simmer two hours, stirring occasionally. Correct seasonings and add beer to taste. Simmer one additional hour, stirring occasionally. Makes about six quarts chili.

SERVES 8 AS ENTREE OR MAKES 15 SANDWICHES

Meat Loaf for Sandwiches

- 4 slices white bread, cubed
- 3 T milk
- 2 lbs lean beef, or combination of beef, pork and veal twice ground (see below)
- 1 medium onion, minced
- ¼ c parsley leaves, minced
- 2 t seasoning salt
- 1 t salt
- ½ t nutmeg
- ½ t sage
  Freshly ground pepper, to taste
- ⅔ c vegetable-tomato juice
- 1 t Worcestershire sauce
  Dash liquid hot pepper sauce
- 1 large egg

Note: Ask butcher to put the meat through the commercial grinder twice, use your grinder with a fine blade, or put half the meat mixture in a food processor and process about three seconds, repeating for the second half.

In small dish, soak bread cubes in milk; set aside. In large bowl, combine meat, onion, parsley, seasoning salt, salt, nutmeg, sage and pepper. Add reserved bread cubes and milk; mix thoroughly with your hands.

In medium bowl, whisk together vegetable-tomato juice, Worcestershire sauce, liquid hot pepper sauce and egg. Add to meat mixture and mix thoroughly with hands. Shape mixture into loaf form and cook, or wrap securely with foil or freezer paper, label and freeze.

To glaze and cook: Let meat loaf thaw completely in refrigerator. When thawed, cover with Meat Loaf Glaze and Garnish (recipe follows). Bake at 350 degrees 60 minutes, pour off fat and serve immediately, or cool and refrigerate for sandwiches, or freeze for later use. Makes eight servings as entree or enough for about 15 sandwiches.

Meat Loaf Glaze and Garnish

- ¼ c catsup
- 1 t dry mustard
- ½ t nutmeg
- 1 T brown sugar
  Dash liquid hot pepper sauce
- 1 lemon, thinly sliced

In small bowl, mix catsup, mustard, nutmeg, brown sugar and hot pepper sauce. Spread over meat loaf. Arrange lemon slices in overlapping line on top of loaf.

MEATS

Mexican Chimichangas

      1 T vegetable oil
     ¾ lb lean ground beef
      1 large onion, chopped
      1 large green pepper, seeded and chopped
      1 clove garlic, minced
      2 T chili powder
     ½ t salt
     ½ t ground cumin
     ⅛ t cayenne pepper
     ½ c canned refried beans
      1 c shredded Monterey Jack cheese
     12 flour tortillas
        Vegetable oil for frying
    1½ c mashed ripe avocado
      1 can (10 oz) tomato and green chili relish (available at
        most supermarkets)
    1½ c sour cream

Heat wok over medium high heat. Add oil and heat. Add beef, onion, green pepper and garlic; stir-fry until meat is browned and onion is limp, about five to seven minutes. Pour off excess fat and discard. Add chili powder, salt, cumin, cayenne pepper and refried beans. Cook, stirring constantly, until heated through. Fold in cheese and set mixture aside.

In eight-inch skillet, heat a small amount of vegetable oil. Fry one tortilla at a time about five seconds on each side and remove to drain on paper towel. Continue until all tortillas are briefly fried and pliable, adding small amounts of oil as needed.

Place about ¼ cup of prepared meat mixture in the center of each tortilla; fold tortilla around mixture, tucking in sides. Fasten with wooden skewers or toothpicks.

Heat wok over high heat; add oil to the depth of about 1½ inches and heat until a drop of water bounces on the oil. Add three or four chimichangas at a time and deep fry until browned, turning often, about five minutes. Remove with tongs and drain on paper towels; keep warm while frying remaining chimichangas. Serve with bowls of mashed avocados, tomato and green chili relish and sour cream to spoon over the top. Makes 12 chimichangas or about six servings.

MEATS

Reuben Pie

½ c dry, non-dairy creamer
1 egg, lightly beaten
1 medium onion, chopped
1 t sharp mustard
¼ t salt
⅛ t pepper
1 can (12 oz) corned beef, flaked
1 c sauerkraut, drained and packed
½ lb uncooked lean ground beef
1 c soft pumpernickel bread crumbs (about 2 large slices)
1 prepared deep-dish pie crust
4 oz shredded Swiss cheese
Chopped parsley, if desired

In medium bowl, combine non-dairy creamer, egg, onion, mustard, salt and pepper; set aside.

In large bowl, mix corned beef, sauerkraut, ground beef and bread crumbs. Add reserved egg-onion mixture and mix with hands until thoroughly combined. Pat one-half of the mixture into prepared pie shell. Sprinkle cheese evenly over top. Cover with remaining mixture and sprinkle with chopped parsley, if desired. Bake at 375 degrees 35 to 40 minutes. Serve at once or bring to room temperature, cover with plastic wrap and freeze up to three months.

To serve: Partially thaw in refrigerator and bake at 350 degrees 40 to 50 minutes, until heated throughout and bubbly. Makes six to eight servings.

Steak and Kidney Pie

    2 beef kidneys
    2 T vegetable oil
1½ lbs round steak, trimmed and cut into bite-size pieces
    1 medium onion, coarsely chopped
    1 c fresh sliced mushrooms, if desired
    1 can (10½ oz) beef bouillon
 ½ c water
 ¼ c chopped parsley
 ¼ t Worcestershire sauce
 ¼ t pepper
    1 hard-cooked egg, chopped
 ¼ c dry sherry
    2 T flour and ¼ c water, stirred into paste
      Pastry Dough (recipe follows)

In large saucepan, place kidneys; cover with cold water and bring to a boil. Remove from heat, discard water. Refill pan with cold water to cover kidneys, and repeat process until fresh water has been discarded four times. Cook kidneys; trim, cut into bite-size pieces and set aside.

In large, heavy skillet, heat oil. Cook steak until brown on all sides. Remove from pan with slotted spoon and drain on paper towel. In fat remaining in pan, brown onion and mushrooms, if desired. Return steak to pan; add reserved kidneys, bouillon, water, parsley, Worcestershire sauce, pepper and chopped hard-cooked egg. Bring to a boil, cover and simmer about 40 minutes, until meat is tender. Add sherry. Stir in flour-and-water paste, stirring constantly, to thicken mixture. Remove from heat and cool.

Prepare Pastry Dough (recipe follows) for double-crust nine-inch pie. Fill with steak-kidney mixture, crimp edges and bake 15 minutes at 425 degrees. Lower oven heat to 350 and bake an additional 30 minutes, until crust is brown. Makes six servings.

**MAKES 1 8-
OR 9-INCH
DOUBLE PIE
CRUST**

Pastry Dough

2 c flour
1 t salt
½ c butter, frozen and cut into six pieces
⅓ c ice water

In medium bowl, or in food processor bowl, combine flour, salt and butter. If using processor, use knife blade and process 15 seconds, until mixture resembles gravel. If using knives or pastry blender, let butter soften 10 minutes, then cut into flour and salt until gravely.

Add ice water all at once and process or stir just until mixture forms a ball, 20 to 30 seconds. Wrap dough in plastic wrap and refrigerate one hour before rolling, for easier handling.

Roll out on lightly floured surface not more than one-quarter inch thick for pie crust. Use slightly more dough for the bottom crust than for the top. Makes one eight- or nine-inch double pie crust.

MEATS

Stir-Fried Beef Slices

- 1½ lbs eye of round or sirloin roast of beef
- 5½ T soy sauce, divided
- 3½ T rice wine, divided
- 2 t sesame oil, divided
- 1 T plus 2 t cornstarch, divided
- 6 T water, divided
- 10 dried wood ears (edible fungus, available at Oriental markets)
- 1 c water chestnuts
- 1 T sugar
- 2 t Chinese black vinegar or Worcestershire sauce
- ¼ t black pepper
- 1 c peanut oil
- 3 T minced scallions
- 2 T minced ginger root
- 2 T minced garlic
- 2 t (or less) Szechwan chili paste

Remove any fat or gristle from meat and cut into paper-thin slices. Cut the slices cross-wise into thirds so that they measure 2 inches by 1 inch. Place meat in medium bowl and add 1½ tablespoons of soy sauce, 1½ tablespoons of rice wine, one teaspoon of sesame oil, one tablespoon of cornstarch and two tablespoons of water. Toss mixture to coat meat and let stand 30 minutes at room temperature.

Meanwhile soften wood ears in warm water for 25 minutes; drain and cut off any hard edges. Shred wood ears and set aside.

Blanch water chestnuts in boiling water 10 seconds. Remove and refresh in cold water; slice finely.

In small bowl, combine remaining four tablespoons soy sauce, remaining two tablespoons rice wine, sugar, vinegar or Worcestershire sauce, remaining teaspoon sesame oil, black pepper, remaining four tablespoons water and remaining two teaspoons cornstarch; mix well and set sauce mix aside.

Heat wok or large skillet; add peanut oil and heat until almost smoking. Add prepared meat slices and stir-fry over high heat just until pink color is gone. Remove with slotted spoon and set aside.

Pour off all but two tablespoons of oil remaining in wok or skillet. Reheat wok until very hot. Add scallion, ginger root and garlic; stir fry until fragrant, about two minutes. Add chili paste and stir-fry another 10 seconds. Add wood ears and water chestnuts; stir-fry about one minute. Add prepared sauce mix and stir constantly until thickened. Add reserved meat slices and toss until coated and heated throughout. Turn onto serving platter and serve immediately. Makes about six servings.

MEATS

Tomato Beef with Green Peppers

1 lb bottom round
6 T vegetable oil, divided
3 T soy sauce, divided
1 t rice wine or sherry
1 t minced fresh ginger root
2 t cornstarch, divided
2 t sugar, divided
¼ t pepper
¼ c chicken broth
¼ c water
1 t sesame oil, if desired
10 scallions, cut in one-inch lengths
1 green pepper, chopped in one-inch squares
1 t salt
1 tomato, chopped in one-inch cubes
Hot cooked rice

With very sharp knife or cleaver, slice beef across grain into thin strips about two inches long. In medium bowl, combine two tablespoons of the vegetable oil, two tablespoons of the soy sauce, rice wine or sherry, ginger root, one teaspoon of the cornstarch, ½ teaspoon of the sugar and the pepper. Add beef strips and mix well; let stand at room temperature 20 minutes.

In wok or large skillet, heat remaining four tablespoons of oil for one minute. Add beef and stir-fry over high heat until lightly browned. Remove beef with slotted spoon and set aside. In small bowl, combine chicken broth, water, remaining teaspoon cornstarch, remaining tablespoon soy sauce, remaining 1½ teaspoons sugar and sesame oil, if desired; set aside.

Heat oil remaining in pan 30 seconds. Add scallions and stir-fry 30 seconds. Add green pepper and salt; stir-fry one minute. Add tomato and stir-fry one minute. Add reserved chicken broth mixture and stir-fry until mixture thickens slightly. Return cooked beef to pan and mix well. Serve at once over hot cooked rice. Makes four servings.

SERVES 4 TO 5

Rolladen

8 to 10 large, thin slices rump steak or end sirloin, about 1½ lbs
8 to 10 small scallions, trimmed
1 to 2 medium carrots, cut in 8 to 10 thin, long wedges
1 to 2 medium dill pickles, cut in 8 to 10 thin wedges
4 to 5 bacon strips, cut in half crosswise
3 T vegetable oil or margarine
1 can (10½ oz) consomme or bouillon
1 c water
½ c dry red wine
1 t thyme
1 bay leaf
½ t black pepper
¼ t rosemary
¼ t sugar
2 t cornstarch, mixed with ¼ c water
Buttered noodles

Lay beef slices flat on work surface; pound thinner if necessary — slices should be no more than ¼-inch thick. On lower half of each slice, arrange one scallion, one wedge of carrot, one wedge of pickle and half a bacon strip. Roll up and fasten with toothpicks. In large skillet, heat oil or margarine; brown meat roll-ups thoroughly on all sides. Pour consomme or bouillon, water and wine into skillet and bring to a boil. Add thyme, bay leaf, pepper, rosemary and sugar. Simmer over low heat, covered, 45 minutes. Remove from heat and cool. When cool, transfer meat to casserole or freezer container and pour sauce over it. Seal tightly and freeze.

To serve: If freezer container was used, thaw slightly and transfer meat and sauce to casserole. Heat covered casserole in 375-degree oven about 45 minutes, until sauce is bubbling and rolls are heated through. Remove from oven and thicken gravy with cornstarch mixture. Return to oven and cook, uncovered, 10 minutes. Serve with buttered noodles. Makes four to five servings.

MEATS

Grilled Butterflied Leg of Lamb

    6 lbs leg of lamb, boned and butterflied
    ½ c red wine
    ¼ c olive oil
    ¼ c vinegar
    1 clove garlic, minced
    ½ t thyme
    ½ t oregano
      Salt and pepper to taste

Trim lamb and remove most of the fat. In large bowl, combine wine, oil, vinegar, garlic, thyme, oregano, salt and pepper. Add butterflied leg of lamb and turn to coat with marinade. Marinate in refrigerator 3-4 hours. Place lamb on a moderately hot grill, about five inches from coals, fat side down. Grill approximately 15 minutes per side for rare lamb, 20-25 minutes for medium. Cooking time will vary depending on heat of coals, size and shape of leg of lamb. Covering the grill will concentrate the heat and speed up cooking time. Makes six to eight servings.

Gyros Meat

1½ lbs shoulder lamb, including some fat
1 lb beef chuck, including some fat
¼ c dehydrated minced onions
⅓ c water
1 T salt
1 t sugar
2 t oregano
2 t freshly and coarsely ground black pepper
1 t cumin
1 t hot paprika
½ t cinnamon
2 cloves garlic, pressed or minced
2 T vegetable oil
Butter
8 or more slices blanched bacon or fresh pork belly slices, if available
Pita Bread
Onion rings and chopped tomatoes
Tzatziki Sauce (recipe follows)

Grind lamb and beef together, using large hole plate on meat grinder. Regrind, using small hole plate.

In small bowl, reconstitute dehydrated onion in water. In another small bowl, combine salt, sugar, oregano, pepper, cumin, paprika and cinnamon; mix thoroughly.

In large bowl, combine ground meat, onions and water and mixed spices. Add garlic and vegetable oil; mix thoroughly with hands until spices are well distributed; refrigerate, covered, several hours.

In small skillet, fry a small amount of meat mixture in a little butter. Taste for seasoning and adjust, if desired.

Blanche bacon by simmering in hot water about three minutes. If pork belly is used, blanching is not necessary. Drain on paper towels. Line loaf pan, 8½x5x3 inches, with bacon or pork slices, covering sides and bottom; pack gyros meat into pan, filling to top of pan. Cover with remaining slices of bacon or pork. Place filled pan in hot water bath, reaching three-fourths of the way up the loaf pan. Bake at 375 degrees 20 to 30 minutes. Reduce heat and continue baking 30 minutes longer.

Remove pans from oven; remove loaf pan from hot water bath and place on wire rack to cool. Cover with metal foil and weigh with about two pounds weight to compress loaf. Cool to room temperature; refrigerate meat covered with weight 12 hours or overnight to ripen and increase flavor. Meat will keep up to four days refrigerated. Slice thin and serve in pita bread with sliced onions, tomatoes and Tzatziki Sauce (recipe follows). Makes two pounds Gyros Meat.

Tzatziki Sauce

> 2 cucumbers, pared, seeds removed, grated and well-drained
> 1 to 2 large cloves garlic, pressed or minced
> ½ t salt
> ¼ t white pepper
> 1 t white vinegar
> ¼ c vegetable or olive oil
> 1 lb plain thick yogurt

In medium bowl of electric mixer, mix all ingredients except yogurt. Add yogurt and beat on medium speed until mixture has a creamy appearance. Refrigerate, covered, overnight to blend flavors. Makes about three cups sauce.

SERVES 8 TO 10

Mary Dawud's Baked Kibbee (Lamb with Bulgur)

    3 c bulgur (cracked wheat), available at some markets and
       all Mideastern markets
    2 lbs extra-lean ground round steak
    1 large onion, finely grated
  2½ t salt, divided
  1½ t allspice, divided
    ¾ t pepper, divided
    ¼ t cumin
    ½ c water
    4 T butter
  1½ lbs ground lamb or ground beef
    1 medium onion, chopped
    ¼ c pine nuts
    ¼ c vegetable oil

In large bowl, wash bulgur in water to cover; drain well in fine sieve or colander. Dry bowl and return drained bulgur; add ground round, grated onion, two teaspoons of the salt, one teaspoon of the allspice, ½ teaspoon of the pepper and the cumin. Knead with hands, adding water gradually, until mixture is well combined and bulgur has swelled slightly. Mixture should be soft and smooth. Pat half of the mixture onto bottom of greased 9x13 baking pan, pressing evenly and firmly; set aside.

In large skillet, melt butter; add ground lamb or ground beef, chopped onion, remaining salt, allspice and pepper. Cook, stirring often and breaking up large meat pieces with fork, until pink color has disappeared from meat. Add pine nuts and spread mixture evenly on top of bulgur mixture in pan. Cover with reserved half of bulgur mixture and spread evenly over filling. Wet hands and rub over top of mixture until entirely even and uniformly smooth. With sharp knife, cut through layers, making squares or diamond shapes. Pour vegetable oil evenly over top and smooth with hands. Bake at 375 degrees 30 to 40 minutes until browned on top. Makes eight to 10 servings.

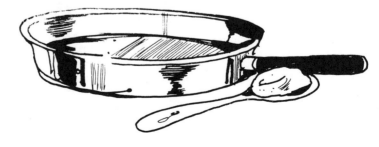

Kibbee Nyee

- 1 c cracked wheat (bulgur), measured after rinsing and draining
- ½ lb raw lamb (leg or shank meat)
- 1 large onion
- ½ c chopped parsley
- ½ t salt
- ½ t pepper
  - Dash allspice
  - Dash cayenne pepper
- 2 T olive oil
  - Lettuce leaves
  - Pita bread, crackers or small rye or pumpernickel bread

Rinse cracked wheat thoroughly in sieve; drain and set aside in large bowl. Using meat grinder or food processor, grind lamb to the consistency of fine hamburger; set aside.

In blender or food processor, combine onion, parsley, salt, pepper, allspice, cayenne and olive oil; blend or process until well mixed and almost smooth. Combine onion mixture and lamb with reserved cracked wheat, mixing thoroughly with hands. Chill until serving time. To serve, mound mixture on serving plate lined with lettuce leaves, and offer a choice of pita bread, crackers or small slices of rye or pumpernickel bread. Makes one main course serving.

Mike Bazzi's Ghallaba (Lamb with Vegetables)

- 3 T butter or olive oil
- 1 lb lean lamb, cut into bite-size pieces, fat removed
- ¼ large onion, cut into slivers
- ½ medium green pepper, seeded and cut into slivers
- 1 to 2 cloves garlic, minced or pressed or ½ t granulated garlic
  - Salt and pepper to taste
  - Pinch cayenne pepper
- 1 large tomato, seeded and coarsely chopped

In large skillet, heat butter or olive oil; add lamb and cook, stirring frequently, until browned, about 10 minutes. Add onion, green pepper and garlic and stir into meat. Season with salt, pepper and cayenne pepper. Cook until onions and peppers are limp, about five minutes. Add tomato, cover skillet and cook eight to 10 minutes, until tomatoes are cooked and partially liquefied. Makes two to three servings.

MEATS

Blanquette de Veau (White Veal Stew)

- 3 lbs stewing veal, trimmed and cut into 1½-inch cubes
- 6 c chicken broth
- 2 celery stalks, halved
- 1 large onion, studded with 1 clove
- 1 large carrot, pared and cut into four pieces
- 1 lemon slice
  Bouquet garni (8 parsley stems, 1 small bay leaf, ½ t thyme, all tied in cheesecloth bag)
  Salt, to taste
- 24 tiny pearl onions, peeled
- 6 T unsalted butter, divided
- ¼ t salt
- ¼ c flour
- ¼ c lemon juice
  Salt and freshly ground white pepper, to taste
- 24 small fresh mushroom caps
- 3 egg yolks
- ½ c heavy cream
  Freshly cooked hot rice

Place veal in large, heavy pot or Dutch oven; cover with cold water and bring to a boil. Boil exactly two minutes; drain and rinse veal with cold water. Return veal to same pot and add chicken broth. Simmer over low heat 20 minutes. Add celery, onion, carrot, lemon slice and bouquet garni. Simmer, covered, about 1¼ hours or until veal is tender, skimming off any surface scum from time to time. Season with salt, to taste.

Meanwhile, cut an X in the bottom of the larger pearl onions. Put onions, one tablespoon of the butter, ¼ teaspoon salt and ¼ cup of the broth from the simmering veal into small saucepan and simmer, covered, until tender, about 10 to 15 minutes. Remove from heat and set aside.

With slotted spoon, remove meat, vegetables and bouquet garni from cooking pot. Discard vegetables and bouquet garni and reserve meat. Boil broth, uncovered, until reduced to three cups. In small bowl, work flour and remaining five tablespoons butter into roux; stir into hot broth, whisking rapidly. Simmer, uncovered, over low heat 10 minutes. Stir in lemon juice. Season with salt and white pepper, to taste. Add reserved meat, reserved onions and mushroom caps. Cook, covered, over low heat five minutes.

In small bowl, whisk egg yolks with cream. Remove stew from heat and whisk in yolk mixture, blending thoroughly. Return to low heat and cook, stirring constantly, until slightly thickened, about five minutes. Spoon into six shallow ramekins or individual baking dishes. Lay a sheet of plastic wrap, cut to size, directly on top of the veal. Cool completely on wire rack. Freeze until solid, about 45 minutes. Remove from freezer and wrap dishes in plastic wrap or foil and again in freezer wrap. Seal. Freeze and store up to six months.

To serve: Remove all wrappings. Bake, uncovered, at 375 degrees 35-40 minutes, or until bubbling. Serve with freshly cooked rice. Makes six servings.

SERVES 4 TO 6

Oriental Pearl Balls

    1 c Oriental short-grain sweet rice
    1 lb ground lean pork
    1 can (8 oz) water chestnuts, finely minced
    2 green onions, minced, both white and green parts
    1 T minced fresh ginger
    1 egg, slightly beaten
    2 T dark soy sauce
    1 T sherry
       Vinegar-Soy Sauce (recipe follows)

Rinse rice thoroughly, in sieve, until water runs clear. Transfer rice to medium bowl and cover with warm water; let stand one hour. Meanwhile, in large bowl, combine pork, water chestnuts, onions, ginger, egg, soy sauce and sherry. Mix thoroughly with hands and form into walnut-size balls; set aside. Drain rice well and spread on cookie sheet. Roll each pork ball in rice until well coated. Arrange balls on steamer rack with ½-inch space between balls to allow for expansion of rice. Steam 45 minutes or until rice is glutinous and tender. Serve with Vinegar-Soy Sauce (recipe follows). Makes four to six servings.

Vinegar-Soy Sauce

    4 T cider vinegar
    2 T wine vinegar
    1 T sherry
    3 T soy sauce
    1 t sesame oil
    1 t crushed garlic
    1 t minced ginger root
    ¼ t liquid hot pepper sauce

In medium bowl or jar, mix vinegars, sherry, soy sauce, sesame oil, garlic, ginger and hot pepper sauce. Cover and refrigerate. This sauce should be made the day before serving with Oriental Pearl Balls, and will keep six months if refrigerated. Makes about ½ cup of dipping sauce.

MEATS

Microwave Hoison Sauce Pork with Nuts

- 1 lb lean pork, cut into ½-inch cubes
- 4 T Hoison sauce (available at Oriental markets and some supermarkets)
- 1 T soy sauce
- ¼ t pepper
- 1 t or more minced fresh ginger root
- ¼ t onion or garlic powder
- 1 T sherry
- ¼ lb fresh mushrooms, quartered
- 1 T sesame oil
- 3 T vegetable or peanut oil
- 1 T cornstarch
- ½ c or more nuts of your choice
- ½ c sliced water chestnuts, if desired
  Coriander or parsley for garnish
  Hot cooked rice, if desired

In 2-qt. container suitable for microwave cooking, combine pork, Hoison sauce, soy sauce, pepper, ginger root, onion or garlic powder, sherry, mushrooms, sesame oil, peanut or vegetable oil and cornstarch, mix thoroughly. Cover container with plastic wrap; microwave on high six minutes. Stir well; add nuts and water chestnuts, if desired, and stir again. Cover and microwave on high three minutes. Garnish with coriander or parsley. Serve hot with cooked rice, if desired. Makes four servings.

SERVES 6

Indonesian Pork Sate with Peanut Sauce

```
      Juice of one lemon
 ¼  c sherry
 3  T tempura sauce (available at supermarkets)
 3  large cloves garlic, minced
 3  shallots, minced
 1  T ground coriander
 1  t crushed, dried red pepper, with seeds
 ¼  t cumin
 ¼  t black pepper
2½  to 3 lbs lean pork, cut into 1-inch cubes
 3  T olive oil
    Peanut Sauce (recipe follows)
    Rice Pilaf or brown rice
```

In large glass or pottery baking dish, mix together lemon juice, sherry, tempura sauce, garlic, shallots, coriander, red pepper, cumin and black pepper. Add pork cubes and toss until completely covered with marinade. Marinate, unrefrigerated, three to four hours. Thread meat onto six skewers. Reserve four tablespoons of the marinade and set aside (for the Peanut Sauce). To the remaining marinade, add olive oil and mix thoroughly. Charcoal-broil the meat — about six inches from the coals — 10 to 15 minutes or until brown, basting frequently with marinade-oil mixture. Serve with Peanut Sauce (recipe follows) and rice pilaf or brown rice. Makes six servings.

MAKES ⅔ CUP

Peanut Sauce

```
 4  T reserved marinade
 3  T crunchy-style peanut butter
 2  T butter
 ⅓  c light cream
```

In small, heavy saucepan, mix together marinade, peanut butter and butter. Cook over low heat, stirring about five minutes. Just before serving, add cream and reheat. Serve as a dipping sauce for Indonesian Pork Sate. Makes about ⅔ cup sauce.

SERVES 6

Mole Verde de Cacahuate (Pork in Green Peanut Sauce)

2¼ lbs pork with some fat, cut into 1-inch cubes or 3½ lbs
country spareribs, in small pieces
¼ onion, roughly chopped
2 cloves garlic, roughly chopped
2 t salt, or to taste
4 T peanut or safflower oil, divided
5 oz raw (unroasted, unsalted) peanuts, shelled weight
1½ c fresh cooked or drained canned tomatillos
6 sprigs fresh coriander
4 peppercorns
3 to 4 chilies serranos or any fresh, hot green chili, roasted
and peeled
2 cloves garlic, whole and peeled
⅓ medium onion, sliced
Fresh hot tortillas

In large saucepan, combine pork, chopped onion, chopped garlic
and salt; cover with water, bring to a simmer and cook until almost
tender, about 40 minutes. Drain meat, reserving broth; discard onion
and garlic.

Meanwhile, in medium skillet, heat one tablespoon of the peanut or
safflower oil; add peanuts and cook, turning constantly, until golden
brown. Transfer to blender and add tomatillos, coriander,
peppercorns, chilies, whole garlic and ¾ cup of the reserved pork
broth; blend until smooth, adding more broth if necessary to make
smooth but not watery sauce. Set aside.

In large skillet, heat remaining three tablespoons oil; add reserved
pork and sliced onion and cook until golden, stirring constantly. Add
blended sauce and cook about three minutes, stirring and scraping
bottom of skillet constantly. Add about 2½ cups of the remaining
broth and simmer about 15 minutes. Sauce should be consistency of
thin cream; it will thicken as it cooks. Serve meat with sauce and
fresh, hot tortillas. Makes six servings.

Note: Roast chilies by placing on baking sheet under hot broiler,
turning frequently until skins are blackened and loose. Remove
immediately and place peppers in plastic bag. Let stand until
lukewarm before peeling.

SERVES 6

Root Beer Ribs

    5 lbs spareribs, cut into two-rib pieces
    2 t salt, divided
    1 can (16 oz) sliced cling peaches in light syrup
    2 cans (12 oz each) root beer
    ½ c brown sugar
    ¼ c cornstarch
    ¼ c vinegar
    3 t powdered ginger

Place ribs in the bottom of shallow baking pan. Sprinkle with 1½ teaspoons salt, cover tightly with aluminum foil and bake at 375 degrees one hour. Remove from oven and pour off accumulated fat.

Drain peaches, reserving syrup, and set aside. In medium saucepan, combine peach syrup, root beer, brown sugar, cornstarch, vinegar, ginger and remaining salt. Cook over low heat, stirring constantly, until smooth, thickened and clear, about five minutes. Pour two cups of the sauce over spareribs and return to oven. Reserve remaining sauce. Bake ribs at 375 for 30 to 45 minutes longer, turning and basting with sauce several times. Add sliced peaches to remaining sauce, heating throughout. Pour over ribs just before serving. Makes six servings.

SERVES 6

Teriyaki Pork Tenderloin

    4 T soy sauce
    1 to 2 cloves garlic, minced or crushed
    2 T olive oil
    2 t light brown sugar
    1 t ground ginger
    ½ t freshly ground black pepper
    2 pork tenderloins, about ¾ lb each

Combine soy sauce, garlic, olive oil, brown sugar, ginger and pepper; whisk until well mixed and pour over pork in shallow dish. Let stand three to four hours at room temperature, turning frequently.

Place pork on rack in broiling pan and broil 12 to 15 minutes, turning once. Baste frequently with reserved marinade. Slice thinly and serve. Makes about six servings.

MEATS

SERVES 2 TO 3

Black Bean Spareribs

- 2 T fermented black beans (available at Oriental markets), finely chopped
- 3 cloves garlic, minced
- 1 t grated or minced fresh ginger root
- 1 T cornstarch
- 1 T dry sherry
- 1 T soy sauce
- 1 t honey
- ½ t salt
- 1½ lbs baby spareribs, cut 1½ inches long, then cut into one-rib pieces
- 2 T vegetable oil
- 3 green onions, thinly sliced, including some green tops

In medium bowl, combine black beans, garlic, ginger, cornstarch, sherry, soy sauce, honey and salt; mix well. Add sparerib pieces and toss until each one is well coated; let stand 30 minutes.

Place wok on high heat; when wok is heated add oil and heat. Add meat and juices and cook two to three minutes on each side, until well browned. Scrape contents of wok into eight- or nine-inch round, shallow heatproof bowl. (A pie plate works well for this step). Rinse out wok and fill with 1½ to two inches boiling water. Place bowl or pie plate on rack *(see note below)* in the water. Cover wok and steam one hour or until meat is very tender. Just before serving, skim excess fat from dish and sprinkle meat with green onions. Makes two to three servings as main dish or four servings as part of Chinese meal.

Note: If you do not have a rack to fit the wok, a simple one can be made by poking many holes in a disposable pie tin and inverting it in the water.

SERVES 4

Rufus Sharp's Barbecued Ribs

- 3 to 3½ lb slab of ribs
- 2 T seasoning salt
- 1 T liquid smoke
- 20 oz vinegar
- 1 t Worcestershire sauce
- 10 oz water
- Wham Bam Sauce (recipe follows)

Wash and trim ribs, sprinkle with seasoning salt and liquid smoke. Place in 350-degree oven. Mix vinegar, Worcestershire sauce and water. After ribs begin to cook, baste with mixture and turn regularly. (If open pit, keep flame low.) Bake for about one hour and 45 minutes. When ribs are golden brown, add Wham Bam Sauce.

Wham Bam Sauce

1½ c vinegar
 2 c barbecue sauce
½ c hot sauce
 1 T liquid smoke
 2 T Worcestershire sauce
 2 T mustard (mild yellow)
¼ t ground red pepper (optional)
 1 small onion, chopped finely
 2 T sugar
   Dash of salt
 1 t lemon juice

Mix all ingredients in a three-quart pot. Bring to a boil, reduce heat and simmer for 30 minutes.

SERVES 6

Washington Pork with Cherries

 1 T vegetable shortening
1½ lbs lean pork, cut into 1-inch cubes
 1 t salt
½ c water
 2 T red wine vinegar
½ t dry mustard
¼ t ground cloves
 1 can (16 oz) tart, pitted red cherries, drained, liquid reserved
¼ c sugar
 2 T cornstarch
⅓ c slivered almonds
   Hot cooked rice

In large, heavy skillet, melt shortening and evenly brown the pork. Season with salt; add water, vinegar, mustard and cloves. Cover and cook slowly until meat is tender, about 30 to 40 minutes. Combine cherry liquid, sugar and cornstarch and add to the pork. Cook, stirring constantly, until sauce is thick and clear. Gently stir in cherries and heat through. Sprinkle with almonds and serve on platter with a rice border. Makes six servings.

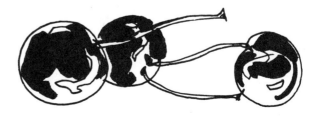

MEATS

Mitchell Lewandowski's Polish Bigos

- 1 lb lean pork, cut into large cubes
- 2 T margarine
- 1 lb sauerkraut
- ½ lb smoked slab bacon, in one piece
- 2 large dried mushrooms
- 1 lb fresh cabbage, cored and shredded
- ½ lb Polish smoked sausage
- 1 medium onion, chopped
- 1 bay leaf
- 1 t salt
- ½ t black pepper
  Dash marjoram
- 1 t mashed stewed prunes
- 1 c dry white wine

In large skillet, cook pork in margarine until well browned; drain on paper towels and set aside.

Meanwhile, in large heavy pot or Dutch oven, combine sauerkraut and bacon. Add almost enough water to cover mixture. Cook, uncovered, one hour.

In small saucepan, place mushrooms in water just to cover; cook until soft. Reserve cooking liquid; remove and chop mushrooms. Return to cooking liquid and set aside.

When sauerkraut and bacon have cooked one hour, remove bacon and cut into small dice. Return bacon to pot, add prepared mushrooms and liquid, fresh cabbage, sausage, onion, bay leaf, salt, pepper and marjoram. Cook slowly one hour, uncovered, stirring occasionally. Add mashed prunes and mix well. Cook 30 minutes. Add wine and bring to a boil. Serve with bread. Makes about eight servings.

MAKES 3 LBS.

Fresh Polish Kielbasa

1½ lbs boneless pork butt
1 lb pork back fat
12 oz boneless beef chuck
4 t coarse salt (sea salt or kosher salt)
3 T sweet Hungarian paprika
3 t finely minced fresh garlic
2 t black pepper
1 t sugar
1 t marjoram, crushed
½ t savory, crumbled
⅓ c ice water
Hog casings

Cut pork into one-inch chunks. Trim all gristle and sinew off pork. Cut pork back fat into ½-inch dice. Cut beef into ½-inch dice and trim. Refrigerate pork, fat and beef separately until well chilled. In medium bowl, combine salt, paprika, garlic, black pepper, sugar, marjoram and savory; mix well.

When meats and fat are chilled, combine the beef, half the fat, half the mixed seasonings and half the ice water. Grind through ¼-inch plate of meat grinder or process into fine grind in bowl of food processor. Scrape into large bowl and set aside. In another bowl, combine pork, remaining pork fat, remaining seasonings and remaining ice water. Grind through ½-inch plate of meat grinder, or process to coarse grind in food processor with a few on and off turns. Add pork mixture to beef mixture and combine thoroughly. Cover bowl with plastic wrap and refrigerate overnight.

The next day, stuff mixture into hog casings, tying off links every 10 to 30 inches, as desired. Refrigerate, uncovered, 12 hours to dry. Store up to three days in refrigerator until ready to use. Makes about three pounds of kielbasa.

SERVES 6 TO 8

Tarragon Rabbit

2 rabbits, cleaned and cut into serving pieces
¼ c flour
¼ c butter or margarine
4 T vegetable oil
1 large onion, diced
4 carrots, diced
3 c veal or beef stock or bouillon
1 c dry white wine
2 T tarragon, crushed
1 t thyme
1 bay leaf
1 t salt
¾ c sour cream
2 T flour
3 t Dijon-style mustard
Hot buttered noodles, if desired

Rinse rabbit pieces and pat dry; sprinkle lightly with flour. In large skillet, heat butter or margarine and vegetable oil. Add rabbit, a few pieces at a time, and brown thoroughly. Remove and drain on paper towels. To grease left in pan, add onion and carrots; cook until onion is translucent but not brown. Spoon off any excess grease and return rabbit pieces to skillet. Over the rabbit, pour veal or beef stock or bouillon, wine, tarragon, thyme, bay leaf and salt. Cover and simmer over medium heat 45 minutes, or until fork-tender.

In small bowl, combine sour cream, flour and mustard; mix thoroughly. Stir in a small amount of the pan gravy; return sour cream-gravy mixture to skillet and stir until combined. Serve with hot buttered noodles, if desired. Makes six to eight servings.

POULTRY

SERVES 8

Dorothy Morgan's Chicken and Dumplings

  1 **stewing hen, about 5 lbs**
    Water
  1 **carrot, cut in thick slices**
  1 **stalk celery, cut in thick slices**
  ½ **medium onion, sliced**
  1 **t salt**
  ½ **t pepper**
4½ **c flour, divided**
  ½ **c water**
  4 **T softened butter or chicken fat**
  3 **whole eggs**

Place hen in large stewing pot or kettle. Add 10 cups water, carrot, celery, onion, salt and pepper. Bring to a boil, skim off froth and simmer over medium heat 1½ to two hours. Remove hen and let cool. Strain broth and add more water to bring liquid quantity to 10 cups again. Set aside.

Bone hen and place large chunks of chicken in a heavy casserole. Discard skin and bones. In large saucepan bring five cups of the broth to a boil. Mix ½ cup flour and ½ cup water; shake or stir vigorously until there are no lumps. Pour flour mixture into boiling broth, stirring constantly with whisk, until gravy is thickened and smooth. Pour over chicken in casserole.

In large bowl, combine remaining four cups flour, butter or chicken fat, the eggs and about one cup water. Mix with hands, adding more water if necessary, to make stiff dough. Turn out on lightly floured surface; roll out to rectangle ¼- to ⅛-inch thick. Cut in 1x2-inch rectangles.

Meanwhile, in large saucepan, bring remaining five cups broth to a boil. Drop the dough rectangles, a dozen or so at a time, into simmering broth. When dough puffs up slightly and rises to surface (after about five minutes), remove dough with slotted spoon and add to chicken and gravy in casserole. Repeat process until a sufficient amount of dumplings has been made. Heat casserole until chicken and dumplings are heated through and gravy is bubbling. Makes about eight servings.

POULTRY

Mock Chicken Tetrazzini with Casserole Sauce Mix

    4 T butter or margarine
    ½ lb fresh mushrooms, cleaned and thinly sliced
    1 small onion, chopped
    ⅔ c Casserole Sauce Mix (recipe follows)
    2 t cornstarch
 2½ c water
 1¼ c chicken broth
    ½ c Parmesan cheese, divided
    2 T fresh chopped parsley
    ¼ t thyme
      Pinch marjoram
    3 c cooked chicken, torn into bite-size pieces
    ¼ c sherry
    6 oz thin spaghetti or fettuccine, broken in half
      Paprika

In medium saucepan, melt butter or margarine; add mushrooms and onion and cook until soft, about five minutes, stirring frequently.

In another medium saucepan, combine Casserole Sauce Mix (recipe follows), cornstarch and water. Cook until thick, stirring constantly with wire whisk. Combine mushroom mixture and sauce mixture; add broth, ¼ cup of the Parmesan, parsley, thyme and marjoram. Cook, stirring frequently, until well combined and heated. Add chicken and sherry; keep warm.

Cook spaghetti or fettuccine in large amount of lightly salted water until just barely tender, about seven minutes. Drain thoroughly and mix with the prepared chicken mixture. Turn into ovenproof 2-qt. casserole and sprinkle with the remaining ¼ cup Parmesan. Bake at 350 degrees for 30 to 40 minutes, until top is lightly browned. Sprinkle top with paprika.

POULTRY

Casserole Sauce Mix

- 2 c instant nonfat dry milk crystals
- ¾ c cornstarch
- ¼ c instant chicken bouillon granules
- 2 T dry onion flakes
- ½ t pepper
- 1 t dried basil, crushed, if desired
- 1 t dried thyme, crushed, if desired

In medium bowl, combine dry milk, cornstarch, bouillon, onion, pepper and basil and thyme, if desired; mix thoroughly and store in airtight container. Makes three cups, or the equivalent of nine 10½-oz. cans of condensed soup.

To substitute for one can of condensed soup, combine ⅓ cup dry mix with 1¼ cups water in saucepan. Cook over medium heat, stirring constantly, until thickened. If a thicker sauce is required for a recipe, add one teaspoon cornstarch to the ⅓ cup mix and cook as directed.

SERVES 4

Chicken Breasts and Zucchini in Tarragon Cream Sauce

- 2 whole boneless chicken breasts, (four halves)
- 6 T butter, divided
- 1½ lbs zucchini, cut into julienne strips
- 1 c heavy cream
- 1 t tarragon
  Salt and pepper to taste
  Hot cooked rice or noodles

Cut chicken breasts into matchstick strips. Heat three tablespoons of the butter in large skillet, add chicken strips and sauté until completely cooked. Remove chicken and set aside. Add remaining butter and saute zucchini strips until tender but still crisp — do not overcook. Remove zucchini with slotted spoon and add cream and tarragon to skillet. Bring to a boil and allow cream to reduce by almost half. Return chicken and zucchini to pan just long enough to heat through. Season with salt and pepper to taste. Serve immediately with rice or noodles.

SERVES 6 TO 8

Chicken-Groundnut Stew

5 lbs frying chicken, cut into serving pieces
3 T powdered ginger
1 T salt
½ c peanut oil
1 c finely chopped onions
5 medium tomatoes, peeled, seeded, chopped and pureed in blender
¼ c tomato paste
1 t finely minced garlic
½ t cayenne pepper
½ t white pepper
5 to 6 c boiling water
2 whole hot chili peppers, each about three inches long
1 c peanut butter
1 c cold water
12 okra, fresh or frozen, stemmed
Fufu
Chopped hard cooked eggs, unsalted roasted peanuts, chopped onions, sliced bananas, diced pineapple for garnish, if desired

Rinse chicken pieces and pat dry. Combine ginger and salt; rub evenly over each piece of chicken. In large skillet or Dutch oven, heat peanut oil. Add chicken pieces and brown evenly over medium heat; remove chicken to plate. (The browning will probably have to be done in two batches.) Discard all but ¼ cup of oil remaining in pan. Add onions and cook five minutes, stirring frequently. Add pureed tomatoes, tomato paste, garlic, cayenne and white pepper and any remaining salt and ginger left over from rubbing chicken. Bring mixture to a boil; reduce heat and simmer five minutes. Stirring constantly, add boiling water and chili peppers; return chicken to pan and cook over low heat about 15 minutes. Combine peanut butter and cold water and beat until smooth; add to chicken mixture. Add okra; continue cooking until chicken is tender, 45 minutes to an hour. Serve stew at once with Fufu and chopped hard-cooked eggs, unsalted roasted peanuts, chopped onions, sliced bananas and diced pineapple, if desired. Makes six to eight servings.

POULTRY

Fufu (Yam Paste Balls)

1½ lb yams
2 c water
2 t salt

Peel yams and cut into ½-inch slices. (Drop slices into bowl of cold water to prevent discoloration.) In large saucepan, combine yams, water and salt; bring to a boil. Reduce heat, cover pan and cook 30 to 45 minutes, until yams are tender enough to be mashed with fork. Drain yams well in colander; puree in food processor or blender or pound with heavy mallet or pestle until smooth.

Shape yams into smooth, firm, walnut-sized balls with moist hands and arrange in serving plate. While forming balls, dip hands periodically into bowl of water to prevent their sticking to yam paste. Let balls stand at room temperature until outside has hardened slightly, about 30 minutes. Cover with plastic wrap and set aside at room temperature up to two hours before serving time. Makes about 24 Fufu.

SERVES 4 TO 6

Indian Chicken Curry

2½ lbs skinned chicken legs, thighs and divided breasts
3 t salt, divided
½ c vegetable oil
1½ c finely chopped onion
1 T minced garlic
1½ t finely minced fresh ginger root
1 t ground cumin
1 t turmeric
1 t ground coriander
1 t ground cayenne pepper
¼ t ground fennel seed
½ c water, divided
1 c chopped fresh or canned tomatoes, drained
2 T finely chopped fresh coriander, or parsley
½ c unflavored yogurt
½ t cinnamon
¼ t ground cardamom
1 T fresh lemon juice

Rinse chicken pieces, pat dry with paper towel and sprinkle with two teaspoons of the salt. In large, heavy skillet, heat oil until a drop of water flicked into it sputters instantly. Add chicken and fry three to five minutes, turning pieces with a spoon until they are white and slightly firm. Transfer chicken to plate and set aside. To the remaining oil, add onion, garlic and ginger and fry until onion is soft, about five minutes. Reduce heat to low and add cumin, turmeric, coriander, cayenne pepper, fennel and one tablespoon of the water. Fry for one minute, stirring constantly. Stir in tomatoes, fresh coriander or parsley, yogurt and remaining teaspoon of salt. Increase heat to moderate and add chicken and any juices that have accumulated on the plate. Pour in remaining water and bring to a boil, turning chicken pieces to coat evenly. Sprinkle top with cinnamon and cardamom, cover tightly and simmer until chicken is tender, about 20 minutes. Arrange on platter and sprinkle with lemon juice. Makes four to six servings.

SERVES 6

Sesame Chicken Shred Noodles

8 to 10 oz extra-thin egg noodles
1 c Chinese celery cabbage, cut crosswise in thin strips
4 qts water
6 bay leaves
3 whole chicken breasts, each cut in half
¼ c red or green bell pepper, chopped in pea-size pieces
¼ c snipped parsley
¼ c sesame seeds
3 T peanut or vegetable oil
1 T sesame oil (available at Chinese market)
¼ c scallions, cut into pea-size pieces, including green part
2 dried chili peppers, torn into small pieces (use seeds also)
1 T minced fresh ginger root
2 t minced fresh garlic
¼ t black pepper
¼ t cayenne pepper
6 T soy sauce
4 T red wine vinegar
2 T sugar
2 T peanut butter

Cook noodles according to package instructions; drain well and spread on large serving platter. Sprinkle evenly with celery cabbage, cover with plastic wrap and set aside.

In large pot, bring water and bay leaves to a rapid boil. Add chicken breasts and return to a boil. Cover pot and turn off heat. Allow chicken to poach in water 20 to 25 minutes. Remove chicken, drain well and chill in refrigerator. (Save water for other cooking purposes.) When chicken has cooled, bone, skin and tear into ½-inch strips. Arrange chicken evenly on top of noodles and cabbage. Sprinkle with red or green bell pepper and parsley. Cover with plastic wrap and set aside. In small, heavy, ungreased saucepan, heat sesame seeds over low heat, stirring constantly, until golden brown, about 15 minutes. Sprinkle over chicken-noodle mixture. In small saucepan, combine peanut or vegetable oil and sesame oil and heat slowly. In small bowl, combine scallions, chili peppers, ginger root, garlic, black pepper and cayenne pepper. When oil is hot, drop in seasoning mixture and brown slightly, about five minutes over medium heat. In blender container, combine soy sauce, vinegar, sugar and peanut butter; blend until smooth. Add soy mixture to oil and seasonings and cook, stirring, until sauce starts to foam. Pour over chicken-noodle mixture, just before serving. (You may cook the seasoned sauce in advance and keep it in a covered jar until use.) Serve at room temperature. Makes six servings.

Suzanne Franklin's Moroccan Chicken

- 1 **frying chicken, about 3 lbs, cut into small serving pieces**
- 3 **cloves (or more) finely minced garlic**
- ¾ **to 1 c meaty black Greek olives**
- ¾ **c raisins**
- ½ **c olive oil**
- 1 **lemon, sliced thinly**
  Juice of ½ lemon
  Salt to taste
  Hot cooked rice or pilaf

Place chicken in roasting pan and sprinkle evenly with garlic. Arrange olives and raisins around and in between chicken pieces. Pour olive oil over chicken, spreading evenly. Cover chicken with lemon slices and sprinkle with lemon juice and salt to taste. Bake at 350 degrees 1¼ to 1½ hours, until golden brown. Baste frequently with pan juices. Serve with hot cooked rice or pilaf. Makes four to six servings.

POULTRY

Tipsy Chicken

½ c dark rum
½ c finely chopped chives or green onion tops
3 cloves garlic, minced
1 T Worcestershire sauce
2 t soy sauce
½ t monosodium glutamate
Salt and freshly ground black pepper to taste
1 chicken, about 4 lbs, cut into eight sections
6 T vegetable oil, divided
2 T brown sugar
1 c finely chopped onions
½ lb fresh mushrooms, sliced
2 t sugar
½ c water
2 t cornstarch dissolved in 2 T water
2 pimientos, sliced in strips
1 can (8 oz) crushed pineapple
Hot cooked rice

In large shallow dish, combine rum, chives or green onion tops, garlic, Worcestershire sauce, soy sauce, monosodium glutamate and salt and pepper to taste. Mix thoroughly, add chicken pieces, turning until well coated. Marinate at room temperature two to three hours, turning chicken. In large heavy skillet, heat four tablespoons of the oil; add brown sugar and stir until sugar is melted. Add chicken, reserving marinade, and cook until golden brown on all sides. Add remaining two tablespoons of the oil, the onions and reserved marinade; cook five minutes on high heat. Add mushrooms, sugar and water; simmer, covered, about 30 to 40 minutes over low heat, until chicken is tender. Thicken cooking liquid with cornstarch mixture; add pimientos and pineapple and cook until heated throughout. Serve at once over hot cooked rice. Makes four servings.

POULTRY

Duckling a La Vernors

- 1 duckling, about 3½ to 4 lbs
  Salt and freshly ground black pepper to taste
- 2 cans (12 oz each) Vernors
- 2 dime-size slices fresh ginger
- 1 c freshly squeezed orange juice
- ½ c brown sugar
- ⅓ c orange marmalade
- 2 t Dijon mustard
- 1 T minced shallot
- ¼ c brandy, divided
  Parsley sprigs or watercress for garnish
  Orange slices

Quarter duck and remove lumps of fat from cavity and save for other purposes. Cut off extra neck skin and discard. Wipe duck pieces with damp cloth and season with salt and pepper to taste. Place, skin side down on rack in roasting pan and bake for 60 minutes at 350 degrees.

Meanwhile, in medium saucepan, combine Vernors and ginger slices. Simmer until reduced to one cup. Add orange juice, brown sugar, marmalade, mustard, shallots and two tablespoons of the brandy. Bring to a boil, reduce heat and simmer until mixture is the consistency of thin syrup.

After an hour of roasting, turn duck pieces skin side up and baste thoroughly with prepared orange sauce. Return to oven and bake another 45 minutes, basting with sauce every 10 minutes. Add remaining two tablespoons brandy to sauce and simmer until thickened. Remove duck to heated platter and pour sauce over. Garnish platter with parsley or watercress and orange slices. Makes four servings.

SERVES 6

Apricot Glazed Cornish Hens and Wild Rice Bake

3 large Cornish hens (about 1 lb each)
Salt and pepper
3 T vegetable oil
Chopped giblets
2¼ c giblet stock
1 pkg (6 oz) long grain and wild rice mix
½ c chopped walnuts
½ c chopped onion
⅓ c apricot preserves, divided

With poultry shears or heavy knife, cut hens evenly in half; reserve necks and giblets for making stock. Rub hens inside and out with salt and pepper and set aside. In medium saucepan, cover reserved necks and giblets with two inches of water. Sprinkle with a little additional salt and pepper and bring to a boil. Reduce heat and simmer, uncovered for about 30 minutes.

Meanwhile, in large skillet, heat oil. Add hens, three halves at a time, and brown thoroughly on all sides. Drain, cut side down, on paper towels. Drain stock through colander into bowl, reserving giblets and discarding necks. Chop giblets and set aside. Measure giblet stock and add enough water to measure 2¼ cups liquid. Return stock to saucepan and bring to a boil. Combine contents of rice and seasoning packets with walnuts and reserved giblets in 13x9-inch baking pan. Stir in boiling stock and onions. Arrange hens on top, cut side down. Brush hens with half of the apricot preserves. Cover pan tightly with metal foil and bake at 350 degrees for 45 minutes. Remove foil and brush hens with remaining preserves. Continue baking, uncovered, until all liquid is absorbed by the rice, about 10 minutes. Makes six servings.

**SERVES 10 OR
MAKES 20 APPETIZERS**

Dilled Turkey Tarts

20 slices whole wheat bread (one loaf)
Melted unsalted butter, about 1½ sticks
 4 T butter
 1 medium onion, chopped
 ¼ lb fresh mushrooms, chopped
Salt and freshly ground black pepper to taste
 1 t dried dill weed
 1 T minced fresh parsley
 1 c sour cream
 2 t flour
 1 c finely chopped cooked turkey

Trim crusts from the bread and brush slices on both sides with melted unsalted butter; fit them gently into muffin tins, taking care not to tear the bread. Bake the bread cups at 350 degrees about 15 minutes, or until crisp and edges are golden brown. Remove from oven and set aside.

Meanwhile, in medium saucepan, melt the four tablespoons butter; add onion and sauté until golden. Add mushrooms, salt and pepper; cook 10 minutes, stirring frequently. Add dill weed and parsley. In small bowl combine sour cream and flour; mix thoroughly and add to mushroom mixture. Add turkey and cook, stirring often, over low heat about five minutes. Do not let mixture come to a boil. Fill prepared shells with mixture and place in 250-degree oven just until heated through, about 10 minutes. Makes 10 servings or 20 appetizer servings.

SERVES 6

Janice Bernheardt's Impossible Turkey Pie

   2 c cooked turkey, cut into small cubes
   1 jar (4 oz) sliced mushrooms, drained
   ½ c chopped onion
   ½ t salt
   1 c shredded Swiss cheese (about 4 oz)
 1½ c milk
   ¾ c Quick Baking Mix or Bisquick
   3 eggs
     Parsley for garnish

Lightly grease 10-inch pie plate and arrange turkey and mushroom pieces on bottom; sprinkle with onion, salt and Swiss cheese. Set aside.

In medium bowl, combine milk, baking mix and eggs; beat until smooth and pour over turkey mixture. Bake at 400 degrees 30 to 35 minutes, until golden brown and knife inserted in center comes out clean. Let stand five minutes before cutting into wedges. Makes about six servings.

SERVES 6

Turkey Enchiladas Puerto Vallarta

    4 c shredded cooked turkey
    1 medium onion, chopped
    8 oz Monterey Jack cheese (about 3 c) grated, divided
    4 T grated Parmesan cheese
    1 can (4 oz) chopped green chilies
 1¾ c drained canned tomatoes
    ¼ c cilantro or parsley leaves
    1 c heavy cream
    1 large egg
       Salt to taste
       Vegetable oil
  12 large corn tortillas
    1 can (14 oz) refried beans
    2 large ripe avocados
    1 medium tomato, seeded and chopped
    4 T minced onion
    1 t lemon juice
    ½ t garlic powder
    ½ t salt
    2 dashes hot red pepper sauce
       Shredded lettuce
       Sour cream
       Ripe olives for garnish

In medium bowl, combine turkey, chopped onion, one cup of the Monterey Jack cheese and Parmesan cheese; toss to mix well and set aside.

In blender or food processor, combine chilies, canned tomato, cilantro or parsley, cream and egg; blend or process until smooth. Add salt to taste and set chili-cream mixture aside.

Heat a small amount of vegetable oil in medium skillet; place one tortilla at a time in skillet and cook about four seconds. Flip tortilla carefully and cook on other side just long enough to soften. Drain on paper towel. Repeat process until all 12 are lightly cooked and drained.

Spread each tortilla with about one heaping tablespoon refried beans. Place about two heaping tablespoons turkey-cheese mixture on each tortilla and roll up compactly. Place, seam side down in lightly greased 9x13-inch baking dish. Pour prepared chili-cream mixture evenly over tortillas. Sprinkle evenly with remaining Monterey Jack cheese. Bake 20 minutes, or until heated through and sauce is bubbly.

Meanwhile, in medium bowl, mash avocados with fork. Add chopped tomato, minced onion, lemon juice, garlic powder, salt and hot red pepper sauce; mix thoroughly and set aside.

To serve, place two enchiladas per serving on small mound of shredded lettuce. Place about two tablespoons sour cream over the top and a small mound of avocado mixture (guacamole) on top of the sour cream. Garnish with ripe olives. Makes six servings.

SERVES 6 TO 8

Mexican Bean, Rice and Turkey Casserole

    3 c cooked brown or white rice
    2 c sour cream
 2½ c (10 oz) shredded Monterey Jack cheese, divided
    2 cans (4 oz each) chopped green chilies, drained
    2 to 2½ c leftover chopped turkey
    1 jar (24 oz) Randall pinto beans, drained

In large bowl, combine rice, sour cream, two cups of the cheese, chilies, turkey and beans; mix well. Turn into large 2½- or 3-qt. casserole and sprinkle with remaining ½ cup cheese. Bake at 350 degrees 35 to 45 minutes, until mixture bubbles and cheese melts. Makes six to eight servings.

SERVES 6 TO 8

Turkey in the Straw (Chinese Style)

8 to 10 oz extra thin straight egg noodles
4 T peanut oil, divided
2 T sesame oil, divided
1 c seeded, unpeeled cucumber, shredded and drained
1 c shredded carrot
2 to 3 c shredded cooked turkey
Vegetable oil
2 large eggs, beaten
¼ c sesame seeds
½ c scallions cut into thick slices
2 small dried red chili peppers, crumbled, seeds included
1 T minced fresh garlic
1 T minced fresh ginger root
¼ t black pepper
¼ t cayenne pepper
5 T soy sauce
¼ c turkey broth
1 T Worcestershire sauce
4 T red wine vinegar
4 T peanut butter
2 T sugar
2 c shredded lettuce

Cook noodles until just tender, according to package instructions, adding one tablespoon of the peanut oil to the cooking water. Drain thoroughly and toss with one tablespoon of the sesame oil. Arrange noodles on large flat platter or in large shallow serving bowl. Cover noodles with a layer of shredded, drained cucumber and top with layer of shredded carrots. Cover mixture with the shredded turkey.

Add a little vegetable oil to a medium skillet and heat. Pour in half of the beaten eggs and rotate skillet so egg covers bottom. Cook without stirring until eggs are set and form a thin pancake; flip pancake and cook a few seconds until lightly browned on other side. Repeat process with other half of eggs, making two thin pancakes. Cool slightly and cut into matchstick strips; sprinkle over turkey.

In small ungreased skillet, cook sesame seeds, stirring constantly, until toasted a golden brown, about seven to 10 minutes. Sprinkle over egg strips. Cover platter or bowl with plastic wrap and set aside or refrigerate until one hour before serving.

In small saucepan, combine remaining peanut oil and sesame oil and heat gently. In small bowl, combine scallions, chili peppers, garlic, ginger root, black pepper and cayenne pepper. Add mixture to hot oils and cook over medium heat about five minutes, or until lightly browned. In blender, combine soy sauce, turkey broth, Worcestershire sauce, wine vinegar, peanut butter and sugar; blend until smooth and add to oil-spice mixture in saucepan. Cook until sauce foams and comes to a boil; remove from heat and set aside. (The seasoned sauce may be made in advance and kept in covered jar until time for use.)

Surround edge of platter or bowl with shredded lettuce and pour prepared sauce over salad just before serving. Serve at room temperature. Makes six to eight servings.

MAKES 8 CUPS

Jambalaya Dressing

    1¼ c long grain rice
     ¼ lb sweet Italian Sausage
     1 t vegetable oil
     1 c chopped onion
     2 cloves garlic, minced
     2 T unsalted butter
     ¾ c diced green pepper
     2 c peeled, seeded, chopped tomatoes
     ½ t sugar
     ¼ c chicken broth
     1 T dried basil, crumbled
     ½ t grated lemon peel
     ¼ t chili powder
        Pinch thyme
     1 c diced cooked ham
     ½ lb tiny salad shrimp or larger shrimp cut into ½-inch dice
        Salt and freshly ground pepper, to taste

Cook rice according to package directions (you should wind up with about 3½ cups); set aside. In medium skillet, cook sausage in oil over medium heat until browned on all sides; cool, cut into ⅛-inch slices and set aside. In large skillet, cook onion and garlic in butter until golden, about five minutes. Add green pepper and cook three minutes. Add tomatoes; sprinkle with sugar. Add chicken broth, basil, lemon peel, chili powder and thyme; cook five minutes. Transfer mixture to large bowl; stir in ham, shrimp, reserved sausage and rice. Season with salt and pepper, to taste. Serve as a casserole or as a stuffing. (Cool completely before stuffing turkey.) Makes about eight cups stuffing.

MAKES 8 CUPS

Wild Rice Dressing

½ c wild rice
2 c water
½ c pecan rice (available at most markets)
4 pork sausages
1 medium onion, finely chopped
2 stalks celery, finely chopped
2 T butter
2 c packaged herbed bread dressing
1 medium apple, peeled, cored and chopped
1 t sage
1 t thyme
Salt and pepper to taste

In medium saucepan, combine wild rice and water; bring to a boil, reduce heat and simmer 10 minutes. Add pecan rice and continue cooking another 20 minutes or until rices are just barely tender. Add additional water as needed to prevent mixture from cooking dry. Meanwhile, in small skillet, cook sausages until light brown and have lost some of their fat, about 15 minutes. Drain on paper towels and cut into small dice. Set aside.

Rinse out skillet and add onion, celery and butter; cook just until vegetables are tender, about five minutes. In large bowl, combine cooked rice and any pan liquid left (up to ½ cup), sausages, onion and celery, herbed bread dressing, apple, sage and thyme; toss until thoroughly mixed. Season with salt and pepper, if desired, and toss again. Makes about eight cups dressing.

FISH and SEAFOOD

SERVES 4

Bacalao

- **1 lb salt cod**
- **3 T olive oil**
- **2 c frozen shoestring potatoes**
- **1 large onion, chopped**
- **6 eggs, lightly beaten**
- **½ c milk**
- **¾ t hot red pepper sauce**
- **2 T chopped parsley**
- **Black olives and parsley sprigs for garnish, if desired**

Soak cod overnight in cold water, changing and discarding the water several times. Drain and rinse in cold running water. In large saucepan or skillet, cover fish with fresh water and bring to a boil; simmer, uncovered, 20 minutes or until fish flakes easily with fork. Drain and flake fish; set aside.

In large skillet, heat olive oil; add potatoes and cook, turning often, until golden brown, about seven minutes. Stir in onion; cook until soft, stirring occasionally, about four minutes. Add prepared cod and mix well. In small bowl, combine eggs, milk, hot pepper sauce and parsley; mix well and add to mixture in skillet. Stir until eggs form soft curds. Cover skillet and cook over medium heat until eggs are set, about five minutes. Garnish with black olives and parsley sprigs, if desired, and serve at once. Makes four servings.

SERVES 6

Catfish, Oriental Style

3 lbs boneless catfish fillets, skinned and cut into 4-inch pieces
1 c stone-ground cornmeal
½ c sesame seeds, coarsely ground
1 small, fresh hot chili pepper, seeded
¾ c tamari soy sauce, available at Oriental or health food stores
2 t rice wine vinegar or white wine vinegar
1 t sesame seed oil
½ t sugar
2 scallions, including green tops, minced
1 c peanut oil

Wash catfish pieces and pat dry with paper towels. In plastic bag, combine cornmeal and sesame seeds; shake a few fillets at a time in mixture and place on cookie sheet. Chill for one hour.

Meanwhile, in blender or food processor, combine chili pepper, soy sauce, vinegar, sesame seed oil and sugar. Process until chili pepper is pureed. Pour into small individual bowls and sprinkle with scallions. Set aside.

In wok, or skillet, heat oil to 370 degrees; add fish pieces, a few at a time, and cook about three minutes on each side or until golden brown. Drain well on paper towels and serve hot with dipping sauce. Makes about six servings.

FISH and SEAFOOD

Ceviche

1 lb skinned filets of pollock
Fresh lime juice, about 4 to 6 limes
1 medium tomato, skinned, seeded and chopped
1 small avocado, peeled and chopped
1 small onion, thinly sliced
3 or 4 unseeded canned hot chilies serranos en escabeche
(available at most markets), chopped
¼ c olive oil
1 T minced coriander
½ t oregano
½ t salt
Freshly ground black pepper to taste
Minced fresh coriander, avocado slices and onion rings
for garnish

Drain pollock on paper towels, removing as much moisture as possible; chop into ½-inch cubes and place in non-metal dish. Cover fish with fresh lime juice and cover dish with plastic wrap. Refrigerate for at least five hours overnight, stirring occasionally so that each fish piece will get "cooked" in the lime juice.

In larger serving dish, combine tomato, avocado, onion, chilies and fish pieces with juice. Add olive oil, coriander, oregano, salt and black pepper to taste; mix well so flavors are well distributed. Just before serving, sprinkle mixture with fresh coriander and garnish with avocado slices and onion rings. Makes about eight to 10 servings. (Crackers may be served as an appetizer.)

SERVES 4

Chinese Skewered Shrimp

⅓ c olive oil
⅓ c dry sherry
⅓ c soy sauce
2 cloves garlic
2 T minced fresh ginger
24 large shrimp, shelled and deveined, uncooked
6 slices boiled ham, cut in quarters
½ lb large fresh mushrooms, cut in half
1 can (6½ oz) water chestnuts, cut in half lengthwise
2 T butter
Plain or fried rice
Chutney

In large, flat dish, mix together oil, sherry, soy sauce, garlic and ginger. Add shrimp and ham and marinate one hour, stirring occasionally. Meanwhile, in small saucepan, cook mushrooms and water chestnuts in butter two to three minutes, until softened (pre-cooking will prevent the mushrooms and water chestnuts from splitting on the skewers); set aside. When ready to assemble, thread shrimp, mushrooms, water chestnuts and ham squares, folded in half, onto metal skewers. Broil over hot coals, turning and basting often with marinade, until shrimp is pink and ham begins to brown at the edges, about five to seven minutes. Do not overcook. Serve with plain or fried rice and chutney. Makes four servings.

SERVES 6 TO 8

Creole Gumbo

½ c butter or margarine
2 c finely chopped celery
1 c finely chopped onion
½ c finely chopped green pepper
2 c sliced okra
6 c hot water
1 c tomatoes, mashed
1 T salt
1 T sugar
1 t garlic powder
1 t allspice
½ t bay leaf powder or 1 large bay leaf powder
1 lb raw shrimp, peeled and deveined
8 oz crabmeat, canned or frozen
2 doz oysters or 1 can (8 oz) chopped clams, if desired
1 T file powder (powdered sassafras leaves, available at spice specialty stores, such as R. Hirt Jr. Co. and Rafal Spice Co., both in the Eastern Market), dissolved in ¼ c hot water
Hot cooked rice

In large Dutch oven or heatproof casserole, heat butter or margarine; add celery, onion and green pepper and cook until tender, about 15 minutes. Add okra and cook, stirring to prevent sticking, about five minutes. Add hot water, tomatoes, salt, sugar, garlic powder, allspice and bay leaf powder or bay leaf. Bring mixture to a boil and boil 10 minutes. Add shrimp, crabmeat and oysters or clams, if desired. Bring mixture to a boil again and immediately stir in file powder that has been dissolved in hot water. Serve over hot cooked rice. Makes six to eight servings.

FISH and SEAFOOD

Fish Cakes with Two Sauces

1 lb firm white-fleshed fish
1 t lemon juice
2 c mashed potatoes
1 T butter
1 small onion, finely chopped
⅓ c finely chopped green pepper
1 egg, lightly beaten
2 T minced fresh parsley
¼ t basil, crushed
Salt and freshly ground black pepper to taste
Dash cayenne
¼ c chopped pimiento
1 egg, lightly beaten with 1 T water
¾ c dry unseasoned bread crumbs
⅓ c vegetable oil for cooking
Pink Hollandaise or Egg-Dill Sauce (recipes follow)

In large skillet, poach fish in water just to cover, which has been acidulated with the lemon juice, about two to three minutes or until fish is opaque. Remove with slotted spatula and drain on paper towels. Remove and discard skin and carefully remove any bones. Flake fish into large bowl and mix with mashed potatoes.

In small saucepan, melt butter; add onion and green pepper and cook until soft, about five minutes. Add onion mixture to fish/potato mixture; add egg, parsley, basil, salt and pepper to taste and cayenne. Fold in chopped pimiento and shape mixture into six flat cakes. Dip cakes in egg wash, then in bread crumbs, coating cakes evenly all over. Let stand 15 minutes to set coating.

In large skillet, heat vegetable oil; add fish cakes and cook until golden brown on both sides, about four minutes a side. Serve with Pink Hollandaise or Egg-Dill Sauce (recipes follow). Makes six servings.

Pink Hollandaise

- 2 egg yolks
- 1 T lemon juice
- ⅛ t salt
- Dash cayenne
- 8 T unsalted butter
- 1 T boiling water
- 1 T tomato paste
- 1 T finely chopped capers

In top of enameled double-boiler or in non-metal, heat-resistant bowl that fits on top of deep saucepan, combine egg yolks, lemon juice, salt and cayenne. Heat on top of — not touching — simmering water; add butter, one tablespoon at a time, stirring with wire whisk, until all butter is melted and mixture is thickened. Add boiling water and cook until mixture rethickens to the consistency of thick custard. Remove from heat and stir in tomato paste, stirring until tomato is thoroughly incorporated. Stir in capers. Makes about 1½ cups Pink Hollandaise.

Egg-Dill Sauce

- 2 T butter
- 2 T finely chopped green onion
- 2 T flour
- 1½ c milk
- Salt and white pepper to taste
- 2 chopped hard cooked eggs
- 1 T chopped parsley
- 1 t dill weed
- Pinch tarragon

In medium saucepan, melt butter; add green onion and cook, stirring frequently, about three minutes, until onion is soft. Stir in flour; cook, stirring frequently, until mixture is bubbly, about two minutes. Gradually add milk, whisking constantly with wire whisk, and bring to a boil. Let boil one to two minutes. Add salt and white pepper. Stir in eggs, parsley, dill weed and tarragon. Makes about 1¾ cup Egg-Dill Sauce.

SERVES 6

Fish in a Bag

- 1 lb raw shrimp, shelled and deveined
- 2 small lobster tails
- 8 oz Alaskan king crabmeat
- 2 lbs boned Icelandic cod or red snapper fillets
- 5 T butter
- 5 T flour
- 3¾ c milk
- ¼ c Madeira or sherry wine
- 3 scallions, chopped, including green tops
- ¼ t garlic powder
- ¼ t rosemary, crumbled
- ¼ t thyme
- ¼ t dill weed
- Dash white pepper
- Salt to taste, if desired
- 12 brown paper lunch bags
- 1 c melted butter
- Paprika
- Chopped fresh parsley
- Parsley sprigs and lemon wedges for garnish

Drop shrimp in boiling water to cover. Remove pan from heat immediately and let stand one minute. Drain partially cooked shrimp and set aside to cool.

Drop lobster tails in boiling water to cover. Return to boil and cook two minutes; drain and cool. Remove lobster meat from shell and cut into ¾-inch chunks; set aside.

Place crabmeat in small sieve; press down to remove excess water. Set aside to drain thoroughly.

Cut fish fillets into six portions; set aside to drain on paper towels.

In large saucepan, melt butter. Stir in flour and cook about two minutes, until bubbly and thick. Add milk all at once and stir briskly with wire whisk; continue to cook, stirring constantly, until sauce thickens and boils. Stir in Madeira or sherry, scallions, garlic powder, rosemary, thyme, dill weed, pepper and salt, if desired. Taste for seasoning. Add prepared shrimp, lobster and crabmeat; set aside.

Open lunch bags and make six double bags; cut off about three inches from the top of each of the bags, making them shorter and easier to handle. Dip cod portions in the melted butter and place one portion in each of the six bags. Place about one cup of the prepared seafood mixture on top of each portion. Sprinkle with paprika and parsley. Place bags on cookie sheet and roll up tops; secure with large paper clip. Brush outside of bags thoroughly with melted butter so that entire surface is coated. Bake at 375 degrees 20 to 30 minutes. Snip off tops of bags and discard; place bags on individual dinner plates and garnish with parsley sprigs and lemon wedges. Makes six servings.

MAKES 2 DOZEN

Gefilte Fish

3½ lbs whitefish, skinned and boned
1½ lbs pickerel, skinned and boned
3 eggs
1 onion, grated
1 small carrot, grated
4 to 5 T plus ½ c sugar, divided
2 T salt, divided
1 t pepper, divided
2 qts plus ½ c cold water, divided
Bones and heads from fish
1 carrot
1 medium onion
Parsley for garnish
Horseradish, preferably freshly grated

Using food processor or meat grinder, grind whitefish and pickerel together. Place fish in large bowl of electric mixer; add eggs, grated onion and carrot, four to five tablespoons of the sugar, one tablespoon of the salt and ½ teaspoon of the pepper. Beat about 10 minutes, until mixture forms rubbery mass. Slowly add ½ cup of the cold water and continue beating five minutes. Cover bowl and let mixture stand in refrigerator two hours.

Place remaining two quarts (more if necessary) cold water in large kettle or pot, filling it halfway to the top. Add fish heads and bones leftover from filleting fish, carrot and onion. Stir in remaining ½ cup sugar, one tablespoon salt and ½ teaspoon pepper. With wet hands, form fish mixture into balls or ovals, using ⅓ to ½ cup for each ball. Place fish balls in kettle and bring to a boil. Reduce heat to medium and simmer about two hours. Drain and cool on serving platter garnished with parsley. Serve at room temperature, or chilled if desired, with plenty of horseradish, preferably freshly grated. Makes about two dozen fish balls.

**SERVES 10 TO 12
AS APPETIZER**

Gravlax (Salmon Marinated with Dill)

    Fresh salmon, middle cut, about 3 lbs
    Large bunch fresh dill
4 T sea salt
1½ T superfine sugar
2 T crushed white peppercorns
    Swedish flat bread or Danish rye
    Gravlaxsas (recipe follows)

Have the piece of salmon cleaned, scaled, deboned and bisected lengthways. Place one of the pieces skin side down in a glass or enamel dish large enough to hold salmon without folding. Place the dill, chopped if necessary, on top. In small bowl, combine sea salt, sugar and peppercorns; mix thoroughly. Sprinkle mixture on top of the dilled fish. Place on top the remaining piece of salmon, skin side up. Place a platter or wooden board larger than the area of the salmon on top of the fish and weight it down. Place entire assemblage in refrigerator for 36 to 72 hours, depending on the degree of saltiness desired. Turn over the fish every 12 hours or so and baste (including inside surfaces) with the juices that accumulate.

To serve, scrape off the dill and the salt mixture. Pat the fish dry and slice thinly at an angle as you would smoked salmon. Serve with Swedish flat bread or Danish rye, thinly sliced, and accompany with a bowl of Gravlaxsas (recipe follows). Makes 10 to 12 appetizer servings.

MAKES 3/4 CUP

Gravlaxsas (Mustard Sauce)

4 T Dijon-style mustard
2 T white vinegar
1 T superfine sugar
1 t dry mustard
6 T vegetable oil
3 T chopped fresh dill weed

Combine ingredients in a small bowl and mix thoroughly. Makes about ¾ cup of sauce.

SERVES 6

Harbor Casserole

    1 can (15½ oz) red or pink salmon
    1 pkg (10 oz) frozen chopped spinach
    3 T butter, divided
    1 large onion, chopped
    2 T flour
 1½ c milk
    1 chicken bouillon cube, crumbled
    2 t Worcestershire sauce
    1 t Dijon-style mustard
    1 t marjoram, crumbled
   ¼ t salt
    3 c shredded sharp cheddar cheese, divided
   ½ c sour cream
 2½ c uncooked small-shell macaroni
    1 egg, lightly beaten
    2 T grated Parmesan cheese
      Paprika
      Butter, if desired

Drain salmon and set aside. Cook spinach according to package directions and drain thoroughly, set aside.

In medium saucepan, melt one tablespoon of the butter; add onion and cook until soft. Add remaining two tablespoons butter; stir in flour and cook, stirring constantly, one minute. Gradually stir in milk. Continue to stir, and add chicken bouillon cube, Worcestershire sauce, mustard, marjoram and salt. Cook over low heat until mixture thickens. Remove from heat and stir in half the cheddar cheese, stirring until melted; set aside. In medium bowl, combine reserved salmon, reserved spinach, sour cream and one cup of the cheese sauce; set aside.

Cook macaroni according to package instructions, cooking only until al dente, about six to eight minutes. Drain well and toss with egg.

Spoon half the salmon mixture into a lightly greased 2-qt. casserole. Top with half the macaroni. Repeat layers, ending with macaroni on top. Spoon remaining cheese sauce over macaroni. Sprinkle with remaining half of the cheddar cheese, the Parmesan cheese and paprika. For crisper topping, dot with butter, if desired. Bake at 350 degrees 35 to 40 minutes, until bubbly and top is browned. Cool in pan 10 minutes before serving. Makes six generous servings.

SERVES 8

Red Snapper with Tomato Sauce and Olives (Huachinango Veracruzano)

- 1 or 2 jalapeno chilies
- ¼ c plus 2T olive or vegetable oil, divided
- 2 medium onions, chopped
- 1 large clove garlic, minced
- 1 can (15 oz) tomato sauce
- 1 T lime or lemon juice
- 2 t salt, divided
- ½ t sugar
- ⅛ t cinnamon
- ⅛ t ground cloves
- ¼ t pepper, divided
- ¼ c flour
- 2 lbs red snapper fillets, cut into serving pieces
- ¼ c sliced pimiento-stuffed olives
  Chopped parsley

Remove stems, seeds and membranes from chilies; cut into thin strips or dice finely and set aside. In large skillet, heat two tablespoons of the oil. Add onions and garlic and cook until tender, about five minutes. Add prepared chilies, tomato sauce, lime or lemon juice, one teaspoon of the salt, sugar, cinnamon, cloves and ⅛ teaspoon of the pepper. Heat to boiling; reduce heat and simmer, uncovered, five minutes. Keep warm.

Mix flour, the remaining teaspoon salt and the remaining ⅛ teaspoon pepper. Coat fish pieces with the mixture. In large heavy skillet, heat remaining ¼ cup oil. Cook coated fish pieces over medium heat until golden brown on both sides, about four minutes per side. Remove to serving platter and cover with prepared sauce. Sprinkle with olives and chopped parsley. Makes eight servings.

SERVES 6 TO 8

Salmon Mousse with Cucumber Sauce

      1 can (10¾ oz) tomato soup
      1 pkg (8 oz) cream cheese
      2 pkgs (¼ oz each) unflavored gelatin
      ½ c cold water
      1 c mayonnaise
      1 can (15½ oz) pink salmon, or 2 c poached and flaked fresh
         salmon
      1 c chopped celery
      1 c chopped green pepper
      1 medium onion, chopped
      2 T minced, fresh parsley
      2 drops liquid hot pepper sauce
      ¼ t marjoram
      ¼ t thyme
         Pinch tarragon
         Salt and pepper, to taste
         Lettuce leaves
         Cucumber Sauce (recipe follows)

Place soup and cheese in top of double boiler and heat, stirring, until cheese has melted. Soften gelatin in the cold water and add to hot soup mixture, stirring until dissolved and thoroughly combined. Remove from heat and cool to lukewarm. Add mayonnaise, salmon, celery, green pepper, onion, parsley, pepper sauce, marjoram, thyme, tarragon, salt and pepper. Stir until all ingredients are thoroughly mixed; pour into a well-greased two-quart mold. Chill at least six hours or overnight in the refrigerator. Unmold on a bed of lettuce leaves and serve with Cucumber Sauce (recipe follows). Makes six to eight servings.

Cucumber Sauce

      1 c sour cream
      1 c finely chopped cucumber, seeds removed
      2 T fresh lemon juice
      1 T dill seed
      1 T grated onion
      1 t prepared mustard
      1 t salt
         Dash garlic powder

In medium bowl, combine sour cream, cucumber, lemon juice, dill seed, onion, mustard, salt and garlic powder. Stir until well mixed, and turn into serving bowl. Makes about 1¾ cups sauce.

Shrimp with Lobster Sauce

1 lb fresh or frozen peeled, deveined raw shrimp
¼ c peanut or vegetable oil, divided
1 T rice wine or pale dry sherry
1 t minced garlic
2 T fermented black beans (available at Oriental markets), chopped
¼ lb lean pork, chopped or ground
1 T soy sauce
1 t salt
¼ t sugar
⅛ t freshly ground black pepper
1 large scallion, including green top, finely chopped
1 c chicken stock
2 T cornstarch, dissolved in 3 T cold chicken stock
2 eggs, lightly beaten
Hot cooked rice

Before starting, arrange all prepared ingredients next to cooking surface. Rinse shrimp and pat dry; butterfly if desired. Heat wok over high heat about 30 seconds; add two tablespoons of the oil and heat until almost smoking. Add prepared shrimp and stir-fry just until shrimp turns pink; add wine or sherry, stir and remove mixture to plate. Add remaining oil to wok; add garlic and black beans and stir-fry a few seconds. Add pork; stir-fry two to three minutes, until pork loses its pink color. Stir in soy sauce, salt, sugar, pepper, scallion and reserved shrimp mixture. Add chicken stock, cover wok and bring mixture to boil. Stir cornstarch mixture and add to wok. Stir until mixture thickens and becomes clear. Pour in eggs in a thin stream, stirring and lifting ingredients so eggs merge and cook in ribbons. Transfer to serving dish and serve at once with hot cooked rice. Makes two to four servings as a main dish, four to six servings as part of a larger meal.

**MAKES 4
TO 5 CUPS**

Squid Vinaigrette

    3 lbs fresh or frozen squid (available at Italian specialty
      stores and some supermarkets)
      Pinch each of oregano, thyme and basil
    ⅓ to ½ c lemon juice
    ½ c olive oil
    2 T wine vinegar
    1 to 2 cloves garlic, crushed
    1 T prepared Dijon-type mustard
    ½ t salt
    ¼ t freshly ground black pepper
    ¼ t dried basil
    ¼ t dried thyme
    ¼ t dried tarragon
    ¼ t dried oregano
    ⅓ c finely chopped celery
    ⅓ c finely chopped scallions
    ¼ c finely chopped green olives
      Parsley sprigs for garnish, if desired

If frozen squid are used, thaw in cool water. Place squid on flat cutting board. With one hand firmly grasp the body or mantle; with the other hand pull off head and tentacles. The viscera of the squid will pull out with the head. Cut off tentacles just below the eye and reserve. Discard rest of head and viscera. Split body lengthwise so that it unfolds into a triangular flat piece. Lay body out, spotted skin side down. Scrape away and discard any remaining jelly-like inner matter. Lift out the semi-transparent "quill" or cartilage and discard. Turn body over and, starting at one end, pull off purple-spotted skin. It usually will come off easily but not always in one piece. Cut body into strips, about ½x2 inches. Place squid strips and tentacles in sieve or colander and rinse thoroughly. Drain.

Place prepared squid in skillet and sprinkle with pinch of oregano, thyme and basil. Pour over enough boiling water to just cover squid. Return to boil; reduce to simmer and cook four to five minutes. Do not overcook or squid will be tough. The water will turn a purplish color. Drain squid into sieve or colander and run cold water over to stop cooking process. When drained, turn squid into medium bowl and toss with the lemon juice; set aside in refrigerator.

In small bowl, combine olive oil, vinegar, garlic, mustard, salt, pepper, basil, thyme, tarragon and oregano; with wire whisk, beat until well mixed and creamy. Pour over prepared squid and toss to coat. Add celery, scallions and green olives; toss again until thoroughly mixed and coated. Let stand in refrigerator several hours before serving to improve flavor. Makes about four to five cups appetizer. Serve with crackers.

SERVES 4

Sichuan Fish

1 t soy sauce
1 t salt
½ T plus ½ t cornstarch, divided
¼ t black pepper
¼ t sesame oil
1 lb pollock, cut into serving pieces
3 T catsup
2 T water
1 small hot chili pepper, seeded and finely chopped
½ T sugar
1 t sesame seed
3 c cooking oil
1 small onion, coarsely chopped
6 green onions, cut into 3-inch lengths
6 thin slices fresh ginger
1 to 1½ c cooked diced peas and carrots
1 T peanut oil

In shallow dish, combine soy sauce, salt, ½ tablespoon of the cornstarch, black pepper and sesame oil; mix well. With sharp knife, score fish pieces on both sides and place in prepared marinade, turning so that fish is well coated. Let stand 20 minutes.

Meanwhile, in small bowl, combine catsup, water, chili pepper, sugar, sesame seed and remaining teaspoon cornstarch; mix thoroughly and set aside.

In wok or medium skillet, heat cooking oil to about 370 degrees on a thermometer for candy or deep frying or until a drop of water sputters on surface of oil. Add marinated fish and small chopped onion and stir-fry one minute. Remove fish and onion with slotted spoon and set aside on platter. Pour off all but one tablespoon of the cooking oil; add green onion and ginger and stir fry until mixture is aromatic, about 1½ minutes. Add prepared catsup mixture and stir-fry five seconds. Add fish and onions and stir-fry another minute, taking care not to break up fish pieces. Add peas and carrots and stir-fry just until heated. Sprinkle with peanut oil and serve at once. Makes four servings.

VEGETABLES

VEGETABLES

SERVES 4

Creamed Radishes

> 2 bunches, or one 16-oz package, large, round red radishes
> 1 c whipping cream
> 2 T unsalted butter
> 1 T finely chopped fresh parsley
> ¼ t salt
> ⅛ t pepper

Carefully cut a thin peel from the radishes so no red remains on them. Boil in salted water to cover until nearly tender, about 10 to 15 minutes. Drain thoroughly. Replace in saucepan and shake over low heat until completely dry. Pour cream over radishes and simmer over low heat until cream thickens and has the consistency of cream sauce. Stir in butter, parsley, salt and pepper. Makes four servings.

SERVES 4

Mary Grime's Curried Cauliflower

> 5 cloves garlic
> 1 inch square piece of ginger, grated
> 1 t salt
> ¼ t paprika
> ¼ t chili powder
> 1 t turmeric
> 2 to 3 T lemon juice
> 3 T vegetable oil
> 1 large cauliflower, washed, and cut into bite-size pieces
> ½ c water
> ½ t ground black pepper
> ½ t ground coriander
> ¼ t ground cardamom
> Pinch ground cloves
> ⅛ t ground cinnamon
> 2 c yogurt
> Salt, pepper and cayenne to taste
> 1 t ground cumin

Mash together garlic, ginger, salt, paprika, chili powder, turmeric and lemon juice to make runny paste. Heat vegetable oil in heavy pan, add paste and stir until it bubbles. Add cauliflower and stir until coated. Cover, add water, and cook until tender, about 15 minutes. Combine pepper, coriander, cardamom, cloves and cinnamon, and sprinkle over cauliflower before serving. Serve with yogurt, seasoned with salt, pepper and cayenne to taste and cumin. Makes four servings.

SERVES 2 TO 4

Eggplant with Spicy Meat Sauce

```
 1  medium eggplant
    Vegetable oil for frying
¼   c water
 1  t cornstarch
1½  T dry white wine
1½  T soy sauce
 1  T vinegar
 1  t sugar
½   t powdered ginger or finely minced fresh ginger
¼   t salt
½   c water
 2  T ground pork or beef
½   t cayenne pepper or dried red pepper flakes
½   t garlic powder
¼   c finely chopped green onion
¼   t sesame oil
    Hot cooked rice
```

Peel eggplant and cut into finger-size pieces. Fry in vegetable oil until golden brown on all sides. With slotted spoon, remove from pan and set aside on absorbent paper to drain.

In small bowl, mix together ¼ cup water and cornstarch. Add wine, soy sauce, vinegar, sugar, ginger and salt; stir mixture until smooth. Set aside.

In wok or deep-sided skillet, over high heat, heat ½ cup water until boiling. Add ground pork or beef and cook one minute. Add reserved cornstarch mixture, reserved eggplant, cayenne pepper or red pepper flakes, garlic powder, onion and sesame oil. Stir-fry over medium heat until eggplant becomes slightly mushy and sauce is thick. Serve with hot cooked rice. Makes two to four servings.

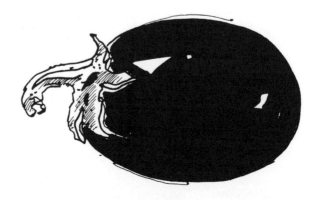

SERVES 8

Fresh Carrot Ring with Broccoli and Hollandaise Sauce

- 6 T butter or margarine
- ½ c chopped onion
- 6 T flour
- 1 c milk
- 2 c pureed cooked carrots
- ¼ c grated Parmesan cheese
- 1 t monosodium glutamate (optional)
- ½ t salt
- ¼ t ground nutmeg
- ⅛ t pepper
- 6 eggs, separated
- 3 c cooked broccoli flowerettes
  Hollandaise Sauce (recipe follows)

In large saucepan, melt butter or margarine. Add onion and cook until soft, about five minutes. Stir in flour; cook one minute. Remove from heat and gradually stir in milk. Return to heat and cook, stirring constantly, until mixture thickens. Stir in carrots, Parmesan cheese, monosodium glutamate, salt, nutmeg and pepper. Remove from heat and set aside. In small bowl, beat egg yolks; add to carrot mixture and return to heat. Cook five minutes, stirring constantly, until mixture thickens slightly. Remove from heat and cool five minuter. Meanwhile, beat egg whites until stiff peaks form. Fold into carrot mixture. Spoon mixture into well greased 6½- or 8-cup ring mold. Set mold in larger baking pan filled with water halfway up the sides of the mold. Bake at 325 degrees 1½ hours or until firm. Remove from oven and set mold on wire rack to cool slightly, about 20 minutes, before unmolding. Unmold on heated serving plate. Arrange hot broccoli flowerettes in center of carrot ring. Serve with Hollandaise Sauce (recipe follows). Makes eight servings.

Hollandaise Sauce

- 2 egg yolks
- 2 T fresh lemon juice
- ¼ t salt
  Dash cayenne pepper
- ½ c butter softened

In earthenware or Pyrex bowl, combine egg yolks, lemon juice, salt and cayenne pepper. Place over bottom of double-boiler that contains about two inches of simmering water (do not let the bottom of the bowl touch the water). Add butter gradually, stirring constantly with whisk, until mixture thickens and becomes the consistency of custard. Remove from heat and keep warm on back of stove top — near, but not on, a burner. Sauce will keep several hours, until serving time. Makes about ⅔ cup.

171

SERVES 6 TO 8

German Red Cabbage

3 slices bacon, diced
1 medium onion, chopped
1 medium head red cabbage, sliced very thin
3 medium apples, cored, pared and diced
1 T lemon juice
1 T brown sugar
3 T vinegar
⅓ c red wine
1 t caraway seed
2 t cornstarch

In Dutch oven or deep skillet, fry bacon until crisp. Remove with slotted spoon and drain on paper; reserve for later use. In bacon fat, fry onion until translucent. Meanwhile, soak cabbage in water 15 minutes. Transfer cabbage and water that clings to it to pan with onions. Sprinkle apples with lemon juice and add to pan. Add brown sugar, two tablespoons of the vinegar, wine and caraway seeds. Mix well and simmer, tightly covered, about 45 minutes or until slightly thickened and tender, stirring occasionally. Dissolve cornstarch in remaining vinegar and add to cabbage, stirring until thick. Makes six to eight servings.

SERVES 6

Helen Scur's Italian Eggplant Parmigiana

    2 medium-sized eggplant, about 1¼ pounds each, washed
       and stemmed
       Salt
    2 T olive oil
    1 c chopped onion
    1 can (6 oz) tomato paste
 2¼ c water
    1 t crumbled basil
  ½ t crumbled oregano
    1 t salt
  ¼ t pepper
       Olive or vegetable oil for frying
       Flour
    3 eggs, beaten
  ¾ lb sliced mozzarella cheese
    1 c grated Parmesan cheese

Cut unpeeled eggplant crosswise into ¼-inch slices and sprinkle with salt. Place in colander and let stand 30 minutes.

In medium skillet, heat two tablespoons olive oil; add onion and cook until soft, about five minutes. Add tomato paste and stir in water, basil, oregano, salt and pepper. Cook slowly about 20 minutes, stirring often. Remove from heat.

In large, heavy skillet, heat about ¼ cup of the olive or vegetable oil. Dry eggplant slices in paper towels. Dust each slice with flour, then dip into beaten egg. Fry slices until golden on both sides; drain on paper towels. Add more oil as needed.

Spread a small amount of prepared tomato sauce in bottom of 2½-quart baking dish. Arrange layer of cooked eggplant on top and cover with layer of mozzarella cheese. Sprinkle with Parmesan cheese. Repeat layers until all ingredients have been used, ending with Parmesan cheese. Bake, uncovered, at 350 degrees 30 minutes, or until golden brown on top and bubbling.

SERVES 6 TO 8

Marj Harwood's Squash

Butternut squash to equal 4 c (about 1 small squash)
6 T olive oil or butter, divided
1 c chopped onions
3 scallions, chopped
3 cloves, garlic, crushed
2¼ c fresh corn, cut off the cob
1½ c mixed chopped green, red and banana peppers, combined according to taste
1 small tomato, sliced
2 t ground cumin
1 t coriander
1 t chili powder
¼ t cayenne pepper
Salt and pepper to taste
2 eggs
8 oz grated cheddar or Monterey Jack cheese

Split squash lengthwise and remove seeds and stringy pulp. Place cut side down on greased cookie sheet and bake at 350 degrees 30 minutes, or until fork tender. Set aside to cool. When cool, remove skin and lightly mash enough to measure four cups.

Meanwhile, in large skillet, heat three tablespoons of the butter or oil. Add onions, scallions and garlic and cook, stirring, over high heat about 30 seconds. Add corn, mixed peppers and tomato and stir-fry one minute. Pour mixture into greased 2-qt. casserole and set aside. To same skillet, add remaining three tablespoons oil or butter and heat. When oil or butter is bubbling, add cumin, coriander, chili powder, cayenne and salt and pepper to taste. Stir-fry 15 seconds; pour spice mixture into casserole with vegetables. Add prepared reserved squash and unbeaten eggs and stir gently to combine all ingredients. Sprinkle cheese on top and bake, uncovered, at 350 degrees 35 minutes. If necessary, run casserole under broiler for several minutes to brown cheese. Makes six to eight servings.

SERVES 6 TO 8

Mushrooms and Artichokes in Wild Rice Ring

  1 can (8½ oz drained) whole artichoke hearts, juice retained
 12 oz fresh mushrooms
  5 T butter or margarine, divided
  3 T flour
1½ c chicken broth
  1 t paprika
  1 t lemon juice
½ t grated lemon peel
½ t salt
    Pinch freshly ground black pepper
6½ c boiling chicken broth
⅓ c uncooked wild rice
1⅓ c uncooked long grain white rice
½ c butter or margarine, melted

Drain artichokes, retaining ¾ cup of the liquid. Cut artichokes into quarters and set aside on paper towels to drain thoroughly.

Rinse, pat dry and cut mushrooms in halves (quarter large mushrooms). In large skillet, melt three tablespoons of the butter or margarine. Add mushrooms and cook over medium-high heat until lightly browned, about five minutes. Remove with slotted spoon and set aside.

In small skillet, melt remaining two tablespoons butter or margarine; mix in flour and cook until bubbly, about one minute. Gradually stir in chicken broth and liquid reserved from the artichokes. Cook, stirring constantly, until sauce is thickened, about three minutes. Stir in paprika, lemon juice, lemon peel, salt and pepper. Add reserved mushrooms and artichokes. Continue cooking until vegetables are hot throughout; keep warm while preparing rice ring or cool and reheat later.

In medium saucepan, combine boiling chicken broth and wild rice. Cover and simmer 25 minutes, stirring occasionally. Add white rice, cover and cook another 20 minutes, stirring frequently. Drain, if necessary (most of the broth should be absorbed by this time) and add melted butter or margarine. Spoon into greased 5-cup ring mold and press down firmly with back of spoon. Set aside for two or three minutes. Unmold onto serving platter and fill with prepared hot mushroom mixture. Serve extra filling in serving bowl. Makes six to eight servings.

SERVES 4 TO 6

Ratatouille

1 medium onion
1 medium green pepper
1 medium red pepper
1 medium zucchini
2 medium yellow squash
1 small eggplant
½ c olive oil
4 cloves garlic, chopped
1 T basil
1 t tarragon
1 t oregano
4 tomatoes
   Grated Gruyere cheese, to taste

Chop onion, green and red peppers, zucchini, yellow squash and eggplant into bite-sized pieces. In large skillet, cook onion and garlic in olive oil until translucent; remove with slotted spoon and set aside on plate. Next, cook green and red pepper in oil remaining in skillet until soft; remove with slotted spoon. Repeat the procedure with the zucchini and yellow squash. Cook the eggplant last, adding oil if necessary. All vegetables should be sautéed until cooked but still slightly crunchy. Return all cooked vegetables to the skillet; add basil, tarragon and oregano and toss with olive oil remaining in skillet.

Peel, seed and puree tomatoes. Add tomato puree to sauce pan just before serving and heat ratatouille. Spoon into individual ramekins and sprinkle with grated Gruyere cheese. Place under the broiler for just long enough to melt the cheese. Makes four to six servings.

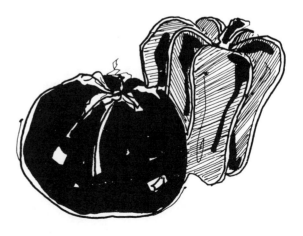

VEGETABLES

Sauerkraut

- **2 lbs sauerkraut (bulk is better than canned)**
- **2 T goose fat, lard or chicken fat**
- **1 medium onion, chopped**
  Water or chicken stock
- **1 t caraway seed**
- **1 goose thigh, duck neck or ham hock for flavoring**
- **1 small apple, peeled, cored and chopped, if desired**
- **1 small potato, peeled and finely grated**
- **2 t flour**

Drain sauerkraut thoroughly. Set juice aside and rinse sauerkraut under cold running water; set aside to drain.

Meanwhile, in small skillet, heat goose fat, lard or chicken fat; add onion and cook until translucent but not browned, about five minutes. Transfer to large heavy pot or Dutch oven. Add drained sauerkraut and enough water or chicken stock to cover. Mix well and add caraway seed and goose thigh, duck neck or ham hock. Bring to a boil, reduce heat and simmer, uncovered, about 30 to 40 minutes. If desired, add chopped apple during last 15 minutes of cooking.

In small bowl, combine grated potato and flour; mix well and add to sauerkraut, stirring vigorously. Let cook about two minutes, until potato is soft, stirring frequently. Remove meat and discard. Makes about six servings.

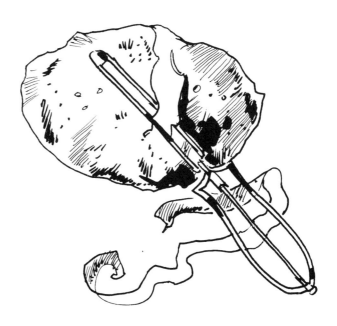

SERVES 4 TO 6

Spaghetti Squash Carbonara

> 1 lb spaghetti squash, 4 to 4½ lbs, split lengthwise, seeds and stringy pulp removed
> 4 slices bacon, diced
> 4 T butter
> ½ lb mushrooms, thinly sliced
> 3 T olive oil
> 1 c prosciutto or boiled ham, cut into matchstick strips
> 2 eggs, beaten
> 4 T Parmesan cheese
> Salt and freshly ground pepper, to taste
> Additional Parmesan cheese, if desired

Place prepared squash, cut side down, in baking dish; pour about ½-inch water in bottom of dish to prevent scorching. Bake at 350 degrees, about 50 to 60 minutes, until fork tender. Pour off water and keep squash warm while preparing sauce.

In large skillet, cook bacon until browned but not crisp; remove with slotted spoon and set aside on plate. Drain bacon fat from pan; add two tablespoons of butter and heat. Add mushrooms and cook over high heat until lightly browned. Remove with slotted spoon and set aside with bacon. Add remaining butter and olive oil to skillet and heat. Add prosciutto or ham; cook five minutes, until ham is shrivelled but not browned. Return bacon and mushrooms to skillet and heat.

With long fork, scrape pulp from squash into large serving bowl — the pulp will fall out in long strands like spaghetti. Immediately pour eggs over squash and toss so eggs will partially cook on the strands. Add prepared ham mixture and Parmesan cheese and toss until well mixed. Season to taste with salt and pepper and serve immediately with slotted spoon. (A certain amount of water from the squash will collect in the bottom of the dish.) Pass a dish of additional Parmesan cheese, if desired. Makes four to six servings.

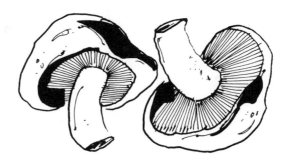

SERVES 3 TO 4

Sze-Chuan's Spicy Broccoli with Shredded Pork or Beef

    1 medium bunch broccoli
    2 oz shredded pork or beef (recipe may be made without
       meat if desired)
       Vegetable oil for frying
  ¾ c water, divided
    1 T cornstarch
1½ T white wine
1½ T soy sauce
    1 T vinegar
    1 t sugar
  ½ t fresh ginger, finely minced, or powdered ginger
    1 T vegetable oil
  ¼ c finely chopped green onion
  ½ t dried red pepper flakes or cayenne pepper
  ½ t garlic powder
  ¼ t sesame oil
       Hot cooked rice

Separate broccoli into finger-size flowerets. Combine with shredded pork or beef, if desired, and set aside. Heat vegetable oil in wok or large skillet; stir-fry broccoli-meat mixture about two minutes. Remove with slotted spoon and set aside to drain on paper towel.

In small bowl, combine ¼ cup of the water, cornstarch, wine, soy sauce, vinegar, sugar and ginger. Stir mixture until well combined; set aside.

In large skillet or wok, heat the one tablespoon vegetable oil. Add onion, red pepper flakes or cayenne pepper and garlic powder; stir once and add reserved broccoli mixture. Add remaining ½ cup water and simmer, stirring often, over medium heat until broccoli is crisp-tender. Add reserved cornstarch-wine mixture; cook, stirring constantly, until sauce is thickened and clear. Add sesame oil and serve at once with hot cooked rice. Makes three to four servings.

VEGETABLES

Tomato Pudding

    1 can (16 oz) peeled tomatoes, drained and diced
    1 c cubed bread
    ⅔ c brown sugar
    ½ c melted butter

In 8- or 9-inch square baking pan, distribute diced tomatoes and bread cubes. Sprinkle with brown sugar and pour butter over all. Bake at 350 for 50 to 60 minutes, until lightly browned and bubbly. Makes three to four servings.

Vegetables a la Grecque

    ½ c olive, peanut or corn oil
    ⅓ c white wine vinegar
    ⅓ c dry white wine or vermouth
    1 t salt
    ½ t black pepper, freshly ground
    1 bay leaf
    1 or 2 garlic cloves
    1 t dried thyme, tarragon, oregano or basil
    Dash hot red pepper sauce
    ½ lb green beans, ends trimmed and halved
    ½ lb small young carrots, scrubbed and cut into 2-inch lengths
    ½ lb mushroom caps, rinsed thoroughly
    Salt, if desired

In large shallow pan or deep skillet, combine oil, vinegar, wine, salt, pepper, bay leaf, garlic, dried herb of choice and hot red pepper sauce. Bring mixture to a boil slowly and add beans. Cook over medium heat until beans are barely tender, about seven minutes; remove with slotted spoon and transfer to refrigerator container. Return liquid to boil and add carrots; cook until barely tender, about eight minutes. Remove with slotted spoon and add to beans in refrigerator dish. Return liquid to boil and add mushroom caps; cook for about two minutes, remove with slotted spoon and add to beans and carrots. Pour liquid over vegetables and bring to room temperature. Add salt, if desired. Refrigerate until well chilled. Drain vegetables and serve well chilled. Strain liquid and save for use with other vegetables. Makes four to six servings.

SERVES 4 TO 6

Whipped Turnips and Sweet Potatoes

  1 lb turnips, peeled and sliced
  1 lb sweet potatoes, peeled and sliced
  2 T butter
  ½ t salt
  ¼ t allspice
     Milk, optional
     Sliced green onion tops or chives
     Additional butter

In covered pan, cook turnips and sweet potatoes in small amount of salted water until tender, about 15 minutes; drain. Place hot vegetables, butter, salt and allspice in processor or mixer bowl and puree. If needed, add a small amount of milk to make mixture fluffy. Top with onion tops or chives and additional butter. Serves four to six.

SERVES 6

Yataklete Kilkil (Fresh Vegetables with Garlic and Ginger)

- 6 small red potatoes, peeled
- 3 medium carrots, scraped, halved lengthwise and cut into 2-inch lengths
- ½ lb fresh green beans, stemmed and cut into 2-inch lengths
- ¼ c vegetable oil
- 2 medium onions, peeled, quartered and layers separated
- 1 green pepper, seeded and cut into 2-inch strips
- 2 hot chili peppers, seeds removed and discarded, finely chopped
- 1 T finely minced garlic
- 2 t powdered ginger
- 1 t salt
- ½ t white pepper
- 6 scallions, cut in half lengthwise, then cut into 2-inch strips

In large pot, put potatoes, carrots and beans and enough lightly salted water to just cover completely. Bring to a boil and cook, uncovered, 5 minutes over high heat. Drain vegetables in colander under cold running water to stop cooking process. Set aside to drain completely.

In large pot or Dutch oven, heat vegetable oil; add onions, green pepper and chilies and cook, stirring frequently, about five minutes, until vegetables are soft but not browned. Add garlic, ginger, salt and white pepper and stir-fry two minutes. Add prepared potatoes, carrots and beans and scallions, stirring until each vegetable is coated with oil. Reduce heat to low, partially cover pot and cook until vegetables are tender-crisp, about 15 minutes, stirring occasionally to prevent scorching. Serve at once. Makes about six servings.

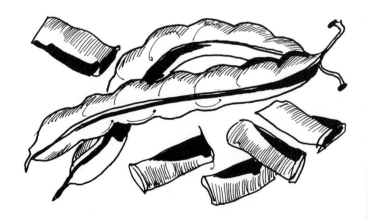

VEGETABLES

SERVES 6

Burundi Beans

½ lb dried black-eyed peas
2 qts cold water
¼ c peanut oil
1 large onion, peeled and chopped
1 clove garlic, minced
1½ t salt
1 t crushed, dried red pepper flakes

Wash peas in cold water and drain. Place peas and cold water in large pot and bring to a boil; reduce heat and simmer 30 to 40 minutes, until peas are just tender. Drain and set aside.

In large skillet, heat peanut oil; add onions and garlic and cook until translucent, about five minutes, stirring occasionally. Add drained peas, salt and red pepper. Cook and stir five minutes, until peas are heated throughout. Serve hot or cold. Makes about six servings.

SERVES 10

Curried Beans

1 lb dry navy beans
6 c water
1 t salt
2 medium, yellow Delicious apples, peeled and diced
½ c golden seedless raisins
1 medium onion, chopped
⅓ c sweet pickle relish
⅔ c packed brown sugar
1 T prepared Dijon-type mustard
1 to 2 t curry powder

In large bowl or pot, combine beans, water and salt; let stand overnight.

The next day, simmer beans and soaking water two hours, adding more water as needed to keep the beans covered. Drain beans, reserving liquid. Combine beans with apples, raisins, onion, relish, brown sugar, mustard and curry powder. Mix thoroughly and turn into baking dish or casserole. Add enough of the reserved bean liquid to just cover beans. Bake at 300 degrees about 1½ hours, adding a little more bean liquid if necessary. Makes about 10 servings.

VEGETABLES

SERVES 10

Durgin Park's Boston Baked Beans

    2 lbs pea beans or small navy beans
    1 t baking soda
    1 lb salt pork
    1 medium onion, peeled
    8 T sugar
    ⅔ c molasses
    2 t dry mustard
    4 t salt
    ½ t pepper
    2 c hot water

In large bowl, soak beans overnight in cold water to cover by two inches. The next day, drain beans and pour into large kettle or pot. Cover with fresh water and baking soda. Bring to a boil, skimming froth from surface; parboil 10 minutes. Drain beans in colander, running cold water through them; set aside.

Dice salt pork into 1-inch cubes; place half the cubes in bottom of 2-quart bean pot with whole onion. Pour drained beans into pot and place remaining salt pork cubes on top. In small bowl, combine sugar, molasses, mustard, salt, pepper and hot water; mix thoroughly and pour over beans. Cook, uncovered, at 300 degrees 5½ to six hours. Add more water from time to time to keep the liquid just at the pot level of the beans. Do not add too much water at a time and do not let the liquid level go below that of the beans. Serve very hot. Makes 10 full servings.

SERVES 6 TO 8

Ginger Baked Beans

    1 large can (52 or 55 oz) pork and beans
    1 large onion, chopped
    1 medium green bell pepper, chopped
    1 large tomato, seeds removed, chopped
    1 c brown sugar
    1 c Vernors

In large-holed colander, drain most liquid from pork and beans. Pour beans into baking dish and add onion, green pepper and tomato; mix gently. In small bowl, combine brown sugar and Vernors and stir until sugar is dissolved. Pour evenly over bean mixture and bake at 350 degrees about 35 minutes, until bubbly. Makes six to eight servings.

SERVES 8

Hoppin' John

1 lb dried black-eyed peas
3 pts cold water
½ lb salt pork or smoked bacon, cut in thirds
1 t hot red pepper sauce
1 small bay leaf
  Dash garlic powder
2 T bacon fat or lard
2 medium onions
1 c uncooked rice
  Salt and pepper to taste

In large bowl, cover peas with the cold water and soak overnight. The next day, transfer peas and soaking water to large pot or Dutch oven; add salt pork or bacon, hot red pepper sauce, bay leaf and garlic powder. Simmer mixture about one hour. Meanwhile, in medium skillet, heat bacon fat or lard. Add onions and cook until soft, about five minutes; add to peas. Add rice and additional boiling water, if necessary. Cook until rice is tender and water is absorbed, about 20 to 25 minutes, stirring occasionally. Taste for seasoning and add salt and pepper to taste. Makes eight servings.

Bill Weinert's Twice Baked Potatoes

Butter or margarine
5 large Idaho baking potatoes
12 strips bacon, cut into ½-inch pieces
1 container (24 oz) sour cream
6 green onions, chopped, including green tops
⅓ c grated Parmesan cheese
⅓ c grated Romano cheese
2 to 3 t garlic powder
Salt and pepper to taste
1 c grated cheddar cheese
Butter or margarine
Paprika

Wash potatoes thoroughly, pat dry and rub with butter or margarine. Bake at 350 degrees 1¼ hours.

Meanwhile, in medium skillet, cook bacon pieces until browned and crisp; drain on paper towel.

When potatoes are done, cool slightly, cut in half lengthwise and carefully scoop pulp into medium bowl, taking care not to tear skins. Set skins aside. Mash potato pulp until smooth; add sour cream until desired consistency is reached. Mixture should not be too thin. Add drained bacon pieces, onion, Parmesan and Romano cheeses and garlic powder, salt and pepper to taste. Spoon mixture back into potato shells, heaping in center. Sprinkle evenly with cheddar cheese and push dab of butter or margarine into center of each potato half. Dust halves with paprika and bake at 350 degrees about 20 minutes, until heated through and cheese is melted. Makes 10 servings.

VEGETABLES

Peruvian Spicy Potatoes

2 T vegetable oil
1 medium onion, chopped
2 cloves garlic
2 T tomato sauce
1 t hot pepper (jalapeno or green chili), minced
½ t oregano, crushed
½ t salt
¼ t pepper
1 c water
4 large potatoes, peeled and cut into small cubes
¼ c evaporated skimmed milk
1 T fresh parsley, minced

In heavy skillet, heat oil and fry onion and garlic until soft, about five minutes. Stir occasionally to prevent browning. Add tomato sauce, hot pepper, oregano, salt, pepper and water. Stir to mix well. Add potatoes and cook over low heat until potatoes are tender, about 30 minutes. Just before serving, add milk, mix well and garnish with parsley. Makes six servings.

Potato Kugel

5 lbs Idaho potatoes, peeled
3 large onions, finely chopped
6 eggs, beaten
1 c cooking oil, divided
2 T salt
1 T sugar
½ T pepper

Using food processor or grater, grate potatoes and transfer to large bowl. Add finely chopped or grated onions, eggs, ½ cup of the oil, salt, sugar and pepper; mix thoroughly.

Add remaining ½ cup oil to large 9x13-inch baking pan and heat. Pour potato mixture into heated oil and bake, uncovered, at 350 degrees 1½ to two hours, until potatoes are well browned on top. Makes about 10 servings.

VEGETABLES

SERVES 4

Tijuana Stuffed Potatoes

  2 **large potatoes, baked**
  2 **T butter or margarine**
  ½ **c diced chorizo or pepperoni sausage**
  1 **small tomato, seeded and finely chopped**
  ⅓ **c finely chopped onion**
  ¼ **c chopped canned green chilies**
  1 **T taco seasoning**
    Salt and pepper to taste
  1 **c shredded Monterey Jack cheese**

While still warm, halve potatoes lengthwise and scoop pulp into medium bowl, leaving potato shells unbroken. With fork, mash potatoes and butter or margarine coarsely, leaving small lumps. Add sausage, tomato, onion, chilies, taco seasoning and salt and pepper to taste. Heap mixture into potato shells, mounding in center. Sprinkle cheese evenly over top of potato shell. Bake at 400 degrees five minutes, until heated throughout. Run under broiler just until cheese is lightly browned, bubbly. Makes four servings.

188

BREADS

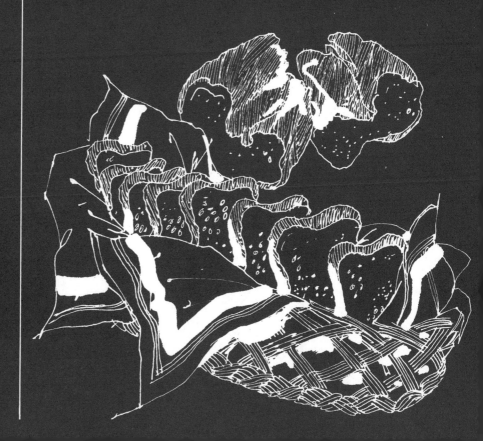

MAKES 2 LOAVES

Beer Bread

    1 pkg (¼ oz) active dry yeast
    1 t sugar
    ¼ c warm water
    1¼ c warm beer
    2¼ c bread flour (available at most supermarkets)
    1⅓ c flour
    2 t salt
       Cornmeal
    1 large egg
    ½ t salt

In small bowl, mix yeast, sugar and warm water; let stand 10 minutes, until foamy. In small saucepan, heat beer just until warm.

Meanwhile, in large bowl or in bowl of food processor, combine bread flour, flour and two teaspoons salt; mix well or process two seconds. Beating with wooden spoon, or with processor running, add yeast mixture and beer. Process 10 seconds or beat until well combined. (Dough will be elastic and sticky.) Transfer dough to well-greased bowl, rotating to oil all surfaces of the dough. Cover bowl with damp cloth and let dough rise in warm place until doubled in bulk, about 60 to 90 minutes.

Punch down dough and turn out onto heavily floured work surface. Knead in enough extra flour to render dough easy to handle and no longer sticky. Divide dough in half and roll each half into a rectangle. Starting at the long side, roll each rectangle into a long oblong loaf. Pinch ends together tightly and seam and put loaves in well-oiled double French bread pan that has been sprinkled with cornmeal. Cover loaves with damp cloth and let rise in warm place until almost doubled in bulk, about 45 minutes.

In small bowl, beat together egg and ½ teaspoon salt. Make several slashes in the tops of the loaves, and brush tops with egg mixture. Bake at 425 degrees until loaves are deeply browned and sound hollow when rapped with knuckles. Cool 10 minutes on wire rack. Remove from pans and wrap tightly in foil. Cool completely and freeze.

To serve: Place frozen wrapped loaves in pre-heated 350-degree oven and bake 20 minutes, until soft and heated through. Makes two French-style loaves.

MAKES 1 LOAF

Blueberry Nut Bread

3 c flour
½ c sugar
3 t baking powder
1 t salt
1 c milk
2 eggs, lightly beaten
2 T vegetable oil
1 t grated lemon or orange rind or ½ t nutmeg
1 c chopped nuts
1 c blueberries

In large bowl, sift together flour, sugar, baking powder and salt; set aside. In small bowl, combine milk, eggs, vegetable oil and grated lemon or orange rind or nutmeg; beat until well mixed. Add milk mixture to dry ingredients, mixing just until moist. Stir in nuts; carefully fold in blueberries. Spoon mixture into greased and floured 9x5-inch loaf pan. Let stand at room temperature 20 minutes. Bake at 350 1¼ to 1½ hours, or until loaf tests done. Cool in pan on wire rack about 30 minutes. Remove loaf from pan and cool on rack completely. Wrap tightly in plastic wrap. Makes one loaf.

BREADS

MAKES 2 LOAVES

Bonanza Bread

       1 c sifted flour
       1 c whole wheat flour
      ⅔ c non-fat dry milk powder
      ½ c brown sugar, firmly packed
      ½ c raisins
      ½ c chopped dry roasted peanuts
      ⅓ c wheat germ
      ¼ c chopped walnuts
       2 t baking powder
      ½ t baking soda
      ½ t salt
       3 eggs
      ¾ c orange juice
      ½ c vegetable oil
      ½ c molasses
       2 medium bananas, mashed
      ⅓ c chopped dried apricots

Combine flour, whole wheat flour, milk powder, brown sugar, raisins, peanuts, wheat germ, walnuts, baking powder, soda and salt. Blend thoroughly with fork. Whirl eggs in blender until foamy. Add orange juice, oil and molasses, whirling after each addition. Add bananas and apricots; whirl just to blend. Pour mixture into bowl with dry ingredients. Stir just until all flour is moistened. Pour into two 9x5x3-inch cake pans. Bake in 325-degree oven one hour or until center is firm. Cool slightly in pan on wire rack, then remove from pan and cool completely. Wrap tightly and store overnight to mellow flavors. Makes two loaves.

MAKES 1 LOAF

Carol Walsh's Cheese Bread

       2 c flour
       3 t baking powder
      ½ t salt
      ½ t baking soda
       1 c grated sharp cheddar cheese
       1 T caraway seed
       2 eggs
       1 c buttermilk

Grease bottom and sides of 9x5x3-inch loaf pan. Line bottom with wax paper; grease paper. Set pan aside. In medium bowl, stir together flour, baking powder, salt and baking soda. Stir in grated cheese and caraway seeds. Set aside. In large bowl, beat eggs until ivory color; add buttermilk and beat to combine. Add reserved flour mixture and stir until moistened but still lumpy. Turn batter into prepared pan; bake at 350 degrees 35 to 40 minutes or until bread tests done. Makes one loaf.

BREADS

Cracked Wheat Bread

¾ c water
¾ c bulgar (cracked wheat)
4 c flour
1 c whole wheat flour
2 pkgs (¼ oz each) active dry yeast
1 T salt
1½ c apple juice
¼ c honey
3 T butter or margarine

In small saucepan over medium heat, heat water and bulgar to boiling point. Reduce heat and cook until water has been absorbed, about two to three minutes. Set aside to cool.

In medium bowl, combine regular and whole wheat flours; mix well and set aside. In large bowl of electric mixer, combine dry yeast, salt and 1½ cups of prepared two-flour mixture; set aside.

In medium saucepan, combine apple juice, honey and butter or margarine; heat until very warm (120 to 130 degrees). Butter or margarine does not need to melt completely. With mixer at low speed, gradually beat apple juice mixture into flour/yeast mixture just until blended. Increase mixer speed to medium and beat two minutes, scraping bowl frequently. Gradually beat in one cup of the remaining two-flour mixture to make a thick batter; beat another two minutes, scraping sides of bowl occasionally. With wooden spoon, stir in cooled bulgar and two more cups of the remaining two-flour mixture to make a medium-soft dough. Turn out onto lightly floured working surface and knead dough no less than 10 minutes, working in the remaining ½ cup flour mixture as needed. The dough should be smooth and elastic. Shape dough into a ball and place in large, generously oiled bowl, turning once to coat entire surface of dough. Cover with towel and let stand in warm place until doubled in bulk, about 1½ to two hours.

Punch down dough and divide into two equal parts; cover with bowl and let rest 15 minutes for easier shaping.

Grease two 8½x4½-inch medium loaf pans; set aside. On floured surface, pat out each dough piece into oval about five inches wide. Pick up dough and shake gently, stretching it out to a strip about 15 inches long. Fold ends over so they slightly overlap in center and press together to seal. Starting with long edge of dough, roll up jelly roll fashion, pressing out air as you roll; pinch edges together to seal. Place dough, seam side down, in prepared pan. Repeat process with remaining dough piece. Cover with towel and let stand in warm place until doubled in bulk, about one to 1½ hours. Bake at 400 degrees 30 to 35 minutes, until brown on top and loaves sound hollow when tapped lightly with fingers. Cool 10 minutes in pans on wire rack. Remove from pans and cool completely on wire rack. Wrap tightly in plastic wrap when cool; loaves may be frozen wrapped again in foil or freezer wrap. Makes two medium loaves.

MAKES 2 LOAVES

English Muffin Loaves

5½ to 6 c flour, divided
2 pkgs (¼ oz each) active dry yeast
1 T sugar
2 t salt
¼ t baking soda
2 c milk
½ c water
   Cornmeal

In large bowl, combine three cups of the flour, yeast, sugar, salt and baking soda; set aside. In medium saucepan, combine milk and water and heat until very warm (120 to 130 degrees). Add to flour mixture gradually, beating constantly; beat until batter is smooth. Gradually add enough of the remaining flour to make a very stiff batter. Set aside.

Prepare two 8½x4½-inch loaf pans by greasing lightly and sprinkling with cornmeal. Divided prepared batter in half and place equal amounts in each pan; sprinkle tops with additional cornmeal. Cover pans with slightly damp cloth and let stand in warm place until almost doubled in bulk, about one to 1½ hours. Bake at 400 degrees 25 minutes, until tops of loaves are lightly browned and loaves sound hollow when rapped with knuckles. Remove from pans at once and let cool on wire rack. Makes two English Muffin Loaves.

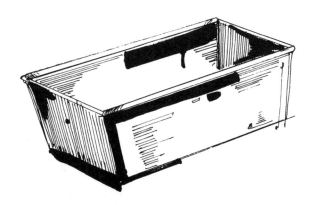

MAKES 4 LOAVES

Mexican Hot Pepper Bread

- 5 to 6 c flour, divided
- 4 c cornflakes, crushed to fine crumbs, or 1 cup commercial cornflake crumbs
- 1 T sugar
- 1 T salt
- 2 pkgs (¼ oz each) active dry yeast
- 1½ c milk
- ½ c vegetable oil
- 2 eggs
- ½ c grated sharp cheddar cheese
- ½ c finely chopped onions
- ¼ to ½ c finely chopped hot chili peppers
- 2 T butter or margarine, melted

In large bowl of electric mixer, stir together two cups of flour, cornflake crumbs, sugar, salt and yeast; set aside.

In small saucepan, combine milk and oil. Cook over low heat until very warm, about 120 degrees. Remove from heat and add, very gradually, to flour mixture, beating until well combined. Add eggs and beat on medium speed two minutes. Stir in cheese, onions and hot peppers. By hand, or using a wooden spoon, stir in enough of the remaining flour to make a stiff dough. Turn out onto a well-floured surface, cover with dish towel and let rise in warm place until doubled in bulk, about 1½ hours.

Punch down dough and divide into four portions. Roll each side into a 7x10-inch rectangle. Roll up loaves from long side and place on lightly greased baking pans or French bread pans. Cover and let rise again until almost doubled in bulk. Make diagonal slits across top of loaves. Bake at 400 degrees 15 to 20 minutes, until golden brown on top. Remove from oven and brush with melted butter or margarine. Serve immediately or cool on wire racks, wrap tightly in foil and freeze. Makes four large loaves of bread.

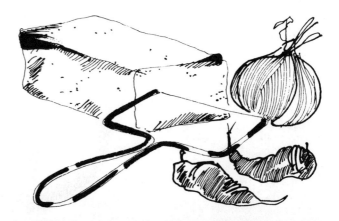

SERVES 10 TO 12

Monkey Bread

    2 pkgs (¼ oz each) active dry yeast
    ¼ c warm water
    ¾ c plus 1 t sugar, divided
    1 c milk, scalded
    1 c butter, softened
    1 t salt
    3 eggs
    6 c flour
    ½ c butter, melted

In small bowl, dissolve yeast in warm water. Add one teaspoon of the sugar and stir thoroughly; set aside.

In large bowl of electric mixer, combine hot milk, softened butter, remaining ¾ cup of sugar and salt. Cool to lukewarm. Add eggs and reserved yeast mixture; beat thoroughly. Add two cups of the flour and beat until well combined. With wooden spoon, stir in enough of the remaining flour to make a soft dough. Turn out into well-floured surface; knead until smooth and elastic, about five to 10 minutes, adding more flour if necessary to prevent sticking. Place dough in well-greased bowl, turning to coat entire surface of dough. Cover with cloth and let rise in warm place until doubled in bulk, about two hours.

Punch down dough and turn out on lightly floured surface; let rest 10 minutes. Pinch off pieces of dough about the size of golf balls; roll each piece in melted butter and layer in well-greased 3-qt. ring mold or angel food cake pan. When mold is filled, press dough balls down gently to make surface fairly even. Drizzle any remaining melted butter on top. Cover with cloth and let rise until doubled in bulk, about 30 to 45 minutes.

Bake at 350 degrees 40 to 45 minutes. (To prevent top from browning too much, cover with foil after bread has baked 25 minutes.) Remove form oven and let cook in pan five to 10 minutes. Invert onto serving dish. Serve warm. Let each guest pick off a piece of the bread (it will separate naturally into roll-size pieces). Makes 10 to 12 servings.

MAKES 2 LOAVES

Portuguese Sweet Bread (Pao doce)

¼ c instant mashed potato granules
⅔ c boiling water
⅔ c sugar
¼ c instant non-fat dry milk
½ c butter or margarine
2 pkgs (¼ oz each) active dry yeast
⅓ c warm water (about 110 degrees)
4½ to 5½ c flour, divided
3 eggs
1 t salt
½ t vanilla
¼ t lemon extract
1 egg, beaten
Granulated sugar, if desired

In medium saucepan, beat instant potato granules into boiling water until smooth. Stir in sugar, dry milk and butter until butter is melted and mixture uniform. Set aside to cool to 110 degrees.

Meanwhile, in large bowl of electric mixer, dissolve yeast in the warm water. Blend in cooled potato/butter mixture. Add two cups of the flour and beat until well blended. Stir in eggs, salt, vanilla and lemon extract; beat until smooth and blended. Beat in another 1½ cups of the flour until a thick batter is formed. By hand, beat in enough of the remaining flour to make semi-stiff dough. Turn out onto floured surface and knead at least 10 minutes or up to 20 minutes, adding more flour as needed, until a smooth, satiny dough is formed which no longer sticks to the working surface. Form dough into flat ball and place in large oiled bowl, turning once to coat entire surface. Cover loosely with kitchen towel and let rise in warm place until doubled in bulk, one to two hours.

Punch dough down and knead briefly to release any air pockets. Let rest, covered with towel, 10 minutes. For loaves, divide dough in two.

To make coiled loaves, roll each half into 30-inch long rope. Coil each rope into greased 10-inch pie pan, starting at outside edge of pan and ending at center, twisting rope slightly as you coil.

To make round loaves, shape each half into flattened round, about eight inches in diameter. Place in two greased 9-inch pie pans.

To make braided loaves, cut dough into six equal parts and roll each into a 14-inch rope. For each loaf, lay three ropes side by side on greased baking sheet; braid loosely and pinch ends together, turning under loaf.

BREADS

To make coiled buns, divide dough into 12 equal parts; roll each part into 12-inch long rope. On greased baking sheets, coil and twist each rope as described for coiled loaves to make 2½- to 3-inch buns. Place at least two inches apart on baking sheet.

Cover loaves or buns with kitchen towel and let rise in warm place until almost doubled in bulk, about 30 minutes for buns and about 45 minutes for loaves. Brush tops with beaten egg and sprinkle with granulated sugar, if desired. Bake at 350 degrees until golden brown, 20 to 25 minutes for buns, and 25 to 30 minutes for loaves. Cool on wire racks. Serve warm or cooled. Makes two loaves or 12 buns.

May be frozen, wrapped tightly in foil. To serve, defrost at room temperature. Place on baking sheet, loosely covered with foil and bake at 350 degrees 10 minutes for buns and about 20 minutes for loaves.

MAKES 2 LOAVES

Zucchini Walnut Bread

    1 c raisins
    3 c white flour, divided
    1 t baking soda
    1 t salt
    ¾ t baking powder
    1 T cinnamon
    4 eggs
    2 c sugar
    1 c vegetable oil
    2 c grated, unpeeled zucchini (about 2 or 3 medium)
    2 t grated lemon peel
    1 c chopped walnuts

Rinse raisins, drain and mix with two tablespoons of the flour. Sift remaining flour with baking soda, salt, baking powder and cinnamon. Beat eggs and gradually beat in sugar, then oil. With rubber spatula, blend in dry ingredients alternately with grated zucchini. When thoroughly mixed, stir in raisins, lemon peel and nuts. Turn into two greased and floured 9x5x3-inch pans. Bake at 350 degrees about 55 minutes, or until top springs back when lightly touched. Cool in pans about 10 minutes, then turn out on wire racks to cool.

SERVES 12 TO 15

Marjory Kurzmann's Pull-Apart Coffee Cake

½ c warm water (105 to 115 degrees)
2 pkgs (¼ oz each) active dry yeast
1½ c lukewarm milk
8 to 9 c flour, divided
1 c butter or margarine, softened
1¾ c sugar, divided
4 eggs
1 t salt
½ c finely chopped nuts
1 t cinnamon
½ c melted butter
Raisins

In small bowl, soften yeast in warm water; add milk and mix in one cup of the flour, stirring with wooden spoon until mixture is smooth. Set aside, about 15 minutes, until mixture starts to bubble.

Meanwhile, cream together softened butter or margarine and one cup of the sugar. Add eggs one at a time, beating well after each addition; add salt and mix well. Add remaining flour one cup at a time, alternating with prepared yeast mixture, until a soft dough is formed. Turn out onto well-floured surface and knead, adding more flour as needed to prevent sticking, until dough is smooth and satiny, about 10 minutes. Divide dough in half; store half in covered bowl in refrigerator and use within three or four days for making second coffee cake or other sweet rolls.

Divide remaining dough into 36 to 40 equal pieces about the size of a walnut; set aside. In small bowl, combine remaining ¾ cup sugar, nuts and cinnamon, mix well. Dip each dough piece in melted butter, then roll in sugar-nut mixture. Make layer of dough balls in bottom of well-greased 10-inch tube pan and sprinkle generously with raisins. Repeat process for a second layer of dough balls; sprinkle with additional raisins. Make third layer if necessary, keeping dough balls as level as possible. Cover with clean towel and let rise in warm place until almost doubled in bulk, about 45 minutes to 1½ hours. Bake at 375 degrees 35 to 40 minutes, until golden brown. Remove from oven and immediately invert onto serving plate. Cool slightly on wire rack. Serve warm or cold. To serve, pull apart with fingers.

SERVES 12 TO 15

Sour Cream Coffee Cake

    1 c butter or margarine
    2 c sugar, divided
    3 eggs
    1 t vanilla
  2⅔ c flour
  1½ t baking powder
    1 t baking soda
    ¼ t salt
    1 c sour cream
    1 c chopped nuts
    1 t cinnamon

In large bowl, cream butter or margarine with one cup of the sugar until light and fluffy. Add eggs, one at a time, beating well after each addition. Add vanilla. In medium bowl, combine flour, baking powder, baking soda and salt. Add dry ingredients to egg mixture alternately with sour cream; beat until thoroughly mixed. In medium bowl, combine remaining cup of sugar, nuts and cinnamon; set aside.

Spread one-half of the prepared batter evenly on bottom of greased 13x9x2-inch baking pan. Sprinkle evenly with one-half nut mixture. Spread remaining half batter on top. (The easiest way is to drop batter by small spoonfuls evenly on top of nut mixture, then smoothing it out with lightly greased spatula). Sprinkle evenly with remaining half of nut mixture. Bake at 350 degrees 35 to 40 minutes, until golden brown and puffed. Makes 12 to 15 servings.

MAKES 18

Apple-Oatmeal Muffins

1 c plus 2 T quick-cooking rolled oats
1 c buttermilk
1 t vanilla
1 c minus 2 T flour
1 T baking powder
1 t salt
½ t baking soda
½ t cinnamon
½ t nutmeg
½ c coarsely chopped walnuts
1 large tart apple, unpeeled, cored and coarsely chopped
1 c firmly packed brown sugar
1 large egg, slightly beaten
¼ c butter, melted
Cinnamon, if desired

In large bowl, combine oats, buttermilk and vanilla; set aside. In medium bowl, combine flour, baking powder, salt, baking soda, cinnamon, nutmeg, nuts and apple. Add brown sugar, egg and melted butter and stir until well mixed, about one minute. Add mixture to dry ingredients, mixing only until flour disappears. Spoon mixture into well greased muffin tins, filling cups two-thirds full. Bake at 400 degrees, with oven rack in the middle of the oven, about 18 to 20 minutes, or until muffins are puffed and brown around the edges. Remove from pan and sprinkle with cinnamon, if desired. Serve warm. Makes 18 muffins.

BREADS

MAKES 16 TO 18

Bagels

2 pkgs (¼ oz each) active dry yeast
2 c warm water (about 110 degrees)
3 T sugar
3 t salt
5 to 5½ c all purpose flour, unsifted, divided
3 qts water with 1 T sugar
Cornmeal
1 egg yolk beaten with 1 T water

In large bowl, dissolve yeast in water. Stir in sugar and salt; gradually add four cups of the flour. Beat well to make smooth batter. Mix in about 1½ cups more flour to make a stiff dough. Turn out on floured surface and knead until smooth and elastic, about 10 to 15 minutes. Add more flour if necessary to keep dough from sticking to surface. (Dough should be firmer than most yeast breads.) Turn dough over in well-greased bowl; cover with towel and let rise until doubled in bulk, about 60 to 90 minutes.

Punch dough down, knead lightly to release the air and divide in 16 to 18 equal pieces. To shape, knead each piece into a round ball. Holding ball with both hands, poke thumbs through center. With one thumb in the hole, work around edge of dough, shaping it into doughnut form about 2½ inches across. Place bagels on floured surface, cover with towel and let rise about 20 minutes.

Meanwhile, in 5-qt. pot, bring the water with sugar to a gentle boil. Lightly grease baking sheets and sprinkle with cornmeal; set aside. Gently lift one bagel at a time and slide into boiling water. Boil five or six bagels at a time for five minutes, turning often with spatula. Lift out with slotted spatula and drain briefly on towel. Place bagels on prepared baking sheets. Brush bagels with egg yolk mixture and bake at 400 degrees 25 to 30 minutes, until well browned and crusty. Cool on rack. Makes 16 to 18 bagels.

Crumpets

1 c milk
4 T unsalted butter
½ c water
2 pkg (¼ oz each) active dry yeast
2 t sugar
3⅓ c flour
1½ t salt
1 t baking soda dissolved in 6 T warm water
Butter and marmalade, if desired

In small saucepan, scald milk with butter. Pour mixture into large bowl and add water; cool to lukewarm. Add yeast and sugar; stir until dissolved. Let mixture stand about 15 to 20 minutes, until foamy. With wooden spoon, stir in flour and salt, scraping sides of bowl, until a thick dough is formed. Cover loosely and let stand in warm place until doubled in bulk, about one hour. Stir in baking soda mixture until well combined.

Grease 3-inch muffin rings (or use 7 oz tins, such as tuna tins, with tops and bottoms removed) and arrange them in greased heavy skillet. Heat skillet and rings over moderate heat. Spoon ¼ cup of the batter into each ring, spreading batter out to the edges of ring with fingers or spatula. Cook crumpets about two minutes, until golden brown on one side. Release rings with tip of knife and lift off crumpets. Turn crumpets and cook on other side about three minutes, until golden brown. Continue to make crumpets in same manner with remaining batter. Serve warm at once, or if desired, split, toast and serve with butter and marmalade. Makes about 18 crumpets.

MAKES 8 TO 12

Popovers

1 c all-purpose flour
1 c milk
1 T butter, melted
¼ t salt
2 eggs

Preheat oven to 450 degrees. Lightly grease baking cups or baking pan with butter. In a bowl combine flour, milk, butter, and salt. Beat just until smooth. Add eggs, one at a time. Don't overbeat. Fill the buttered baking cups two-thirds full. Place in oven. After 15 minutes, without opening the oven door, reduce oven temperature to 350 degrees and bake 20 minutes longer. A good test for doneness is to check the sides of the popovers for firmness. If you like the interior of the popover to be especially dry, prick each popover with a fork to let steam escape. Then let stand in the turned-off oven, door slightly ajar, for eight to 10 minutes. Makes 12 popovers baked in ⅓-cup sized pans, 10 popovers baked in ½-cup sized pans, or eight to nine baked in five- or six-ounce oven-proof glass cups.

MAKES 12

Sister Barbara Ann's Beer Muffins

4 c Bisquick
5 T sugar
1 can or bottle (12 oz) beer, chilled

In large bowl, combine Bisquick and sugar; mix well. Gradually add beer and stir until well combined. Divide batter equally in well-greased 12-count muffin tin. Bake at 350 degrees 40 to 45 minutes, or until muffins are large and puffy and lightly browned on top. Makes 12 muffins.

Tiny Orange Muffins

1 c butter or margarine
1 c sugar
2 eggs
1 t baking soda
1 c buttermilk
2 c flour
Grated rind of 2 oranges
½ c golden raisins
Juice of 2 oranges
1 c brown sugar

In large bowl of electric mixer, cream together butter or margarine and sugar; add eggs and beat until well mixed. Dissolve the baking soda in the buttermilk; add buttermilk mixture alternately with the flour to egg mixture. Add orange rind and raisins. Fill well-buttered tiny tart tins three-quarters full and bake at 400 degrees 15 minutes. Remove from tins immediately and keep warm on serving plate. In small bowl, mix orange juice and brown sugar and pour a teaspoonful of the mixture over each warm muffin. Serve warm. Makes 48 tiny muffins.

Our story about Herman, the sourdough starter, generated more response from readers than any other food story we have ever published. Herman spread like wildfire. Most people got Herman from a friend, along with instructions for feeding him, and recipes for using him. If you follow the instructions, at the end of ten days, you'll have two cups of Herman to use for baking, a cup to give to a friend, and another cup to start the process all over again.

Herman Starter

2 c all-purpose flour
2 c warm water
1 pkg (¼ oz) active dry yeast

In glass or plastic bowl, mix flour, water and yeast with wooden spoon. (Do not use metal container or spoon.) Let stand overnight in a warm place. In the morning, feed Herman one batch of Herman Food (recipe follows.) You'll feed him another batch of Herman Food on the fifth day and another batch on the 10th day, when the process starts again.

Herman Food

    1 c flour
    1 c milk
    ½ c sugar

Mix flour, milk and sugar; makes one batch of Herman Food.

Mix Herman Food with Herman Starter (the mixture will be lumpy). Cover bowl loosely with plastic wrap and store mixture in refrigerator. Stir daily. On the fifth day, feed Herman again with another batch of Herman Food. On the 10th day, use two cups of the Herman mixture for cooking, give one cup to a friend, feed the remaining cup with another batch of Herman Food and return to refrigerator to start the process again.

SERVES 12

Herman Coffee Cake

    1 c brown sugar
    ½ c chopped nuts
    ¼ c margarine, softened
    2 c plus 1 T flour, divided
    1 T plus 1 t cinnamon, divided
    2 c Herman
    1 c sugar
    ⅔ c vegetable oil
    2 eggs
    2 t baking powder
    ½ t salt
    ½ t baking soda
    1 c raisins
    1 c drained, crushed fruit (pineapple, peaches, etc.)

To make topping: In medium bowl, combine brown sugar, nuts, margarine, one tablespoon of the flour and one tablespoon of the cinnamon. Mix until well blended; set aside.

To make cake: In large bowl, combine the remaining two cups of flour, remaining one teaspoon cinnamon, Herman, sugar, vegetable oil, eggs, baking powder, salt and baking soda. Beat until well combined. Fold in raisins and crushed fruit. Pour into well-greased and floured Bundt pan, large ring mold or 9x13-inch baking pan. Top with reserved topping. Bake at 350 degrees 50 to 60 minutes, until cake tests done. Makes about 12 servings.

SERVES 12 TO 15

Hawaiian Herman Cake

- 1½ c brown sugar
- 2 t cinnamon
- ¼ t ginger
- ½ c chopped walnuts
- ¼ c chopped macadamia nuts
- ½ c bread crumbs
- 1 c sugar
- ½ c butter
- ½ c vegetable shortening
- 2 eggs
- 1 t vanilla
- 3 c flour
- 2 t baking powder
- ½ t salt
- 1 c Herman
- 1 can (8½ oz) crushed pineapple, well-drained
- ¼ c rum
- ½ c melted butter

In medium bowl, combine brown sugar, cinnamon, ginger, walnuts, macadamia nuts and bread crumbs; mix well and set aside.

In large bowl of electric mixer, cream together sugar, butter and vegetable shortening. Add eggs and vanilla and beat until light and fluffy. Add flour, baking powder, salt and Herman; beat until smooth. Spoon half the batter into a well-greased and floured 9x13-inch baking pan. Spoon half the reserved brown sugar mixture over the batter and sprinkle with pineapple. Smooth the remaining batter over the top and sprinkle with the remaining brown sugar mixture. Sprinkle with rum and pour melted butter over all. Bake at 375 degrees 25 to 30 minutes, until cake is puffed and browned. Cool several minutes before serving, but serve warm. Makes about 12 to 15 servings.

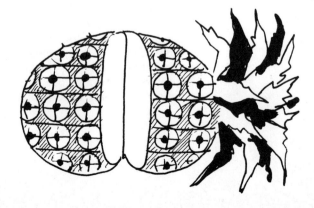

DESSERTS and PIES

Buechel.

SERVES 12 TO 15

Apple Pie '63

½ lb light candy caramels (about 28-30)
½ c evaporated milk
3 c sifted flour
¼ c sugar
1½ t salt
½ c butter, chilled
2 eggs, divided
¼ c vegetable oil
¼ c cold water
6 c pared, sliced apples
1⅓ c sugar, divided
⅓ c flour
2 t grated lemon rind
2 to 4 T lemon juice
1 pkg (8 oz) cream cheese, softened
⅓ c chopped walnuts

In top of double boiler, melt caramels and evaporated milk together, stirring occasionally, until smooth. Keep warm over hot water.

Sift together three cups sifted flour, ¼ cup sugar and salt into mixing bowl; cut or process in butter, until mixture resembles gravel. In small bowl, blend one of the eggs with vegetable oil and water until smooth and creamy; add to flour mixture and stir just until mixture holds together. (The pastry may be wrapped in plastic wrap and refrigerated for one hour to make it easier to roll.)

Meanwhile, in medium bowl, combine apples, one cup sugar, ⅓ cup flour, lemon rind and lemon juice. (Apples may be sliced right into the lemon juice in bowl, tossing occasionally, to prevent discoloring). Toss so that apples are coated; set aside. (*Note:* In the fall when apples are juicier, cook filling until thickened before turning into pie shell.)

On ungreased 18x14-inch sheet of heavy duty foil, roll out pastry into a 12x17-inch rectangle; fold edge of pastry to form standing rim. Fold foil up around pastry to make pan. Place on cookie sheet. (Or press dough evenly on bottom and sides of ungreased 18x14-inch jelly roll pan, fluting dough around edges.) Fill dough evenly with prepared apple filling; set aside.

In small bowl, combine cream cheese with remaining egg and remaining ⅓ cup of sugar; beat until smooth. Set aside.

Drizzle warm caramel mixture in diagonal strips across apple filling. Spoon cream cheese topping between caramel strips. Sprinkle entire pie with chopped nuts and bake at 375 degrees 30 to 35 minutes, until pastry is lightly browned. Serve warm or cold, cut into squares. Makes 12 to 15 servings.

DESSERTS and PIES

SERVES 8

Banana Cream Pie

¾ c sugar
½ c flour
¼ t salt
3 c milk
3 egg yolks, lightly beaten
2 T butter
1 t vanilla
2 ripe bananas

Prepare a Basic Pie Dough and pre-bake for 12 to 15 minutes according to dough recipe instructions. In a large saucepan, combine sugar, flour, salt and milk. Stir continuously over moderate heat until mixture thickens. When thickened, stir in egg yolks and heat for one more minute. Remove from heat, stir in butter and vanilla, let cool for about 15 minutes. Peel and slice bananas and line bottom of crust with banana slices. Top with cream filling and refrigerate until ready to serve. Makes one pie.

SERVES 2

Bananas Foster

2 T butter
4 T light brown sugar
2 firm, ripe bananas, cut in half lengthwise
⅛ t cinnamon
2 oz rum, warmed
Vanilla ice cream

In medium skillet or chafing dish, melt butter. Add brown sugar and stir until melted. Add bananas; sprinkle with cinnamon. Cook, basting with sugar syrup, until soft, five to seven minutes. Pour warmed rum over bananas and ignite. Cook, basting with flaming sauce, until flame extinguishes. Serve over vanilla ice cream. Makes two servings.

DESSERTS and PIES

MAKES THE EQUIV.
OF 12, 3¼ OZ. BOXES
COMMERCIAL
PUDDING MIX

Basic Pudding Mix

8 c nonfat dry milk powder
4 c sugar
3 c cornstarch
1 t salt

In large bowl, combine milk powder, sugar, cornstarch and salt; mix thoroughly, making sure cornstarch is blended in well. Store in tightly covered container or individual one-cup packages. This recipe makes the equivalent of 12 3¼-oz. size commercial pudding mixes.

Vanilla Pudding: Add 1 t vanilla and 1 T margarine before removing from heat.

Coconut Pudding: Add ½ c coconut to Vanilla Pudding.

Lemon Pudding: Add 1 T fresh lemon juice, 1 T butter and about ½ t grated lemon rind.

Banana Pudding: Add 1 or 2 mashed bananas to cooled pudding.

Butterscotch Pudding: Use dark brown sugar in place of white sugar in basic pudding mix recipe.

SERVES 4

Chocolate Pudding

1 c prepared Basic Pudding Mix
2 c boiling water
3 T unsweetened cocoa
1 egg, if desired
¼ t almond extract

In medium saucepan, combine pudding mix with boiling water, stirring constantly. Add cocoa and one egg, if desired for a richer pudding. Cook over low heat, stirring, until mixture thickens. Remove from heat and stir in almond extract. Cool slightly and pour into serving dishes or sherbet glasses. Chill until firm. Makes four servings.

DESSERTS and PIES

SERVES 8

Carol Haskins' Caramel-Nut Apple Pie

1½ c heavy cream, unwhipped
¾ c firmly packed brown sugar
⅓ c butter
1 oz sweet chocolate
1 c chopped mixed nuts
1 deep-dish apple pie, baked and cooled

In medium-size, heavy saucepan or skillet, combine cream, brown sugar, butter and chocolate. Bring mixture to a boil and cook over medium heat until mixture darkens and lightly coats a spoon, about 10 to 15 minutes. Remove from heat and stir in nuts. Set aside to cool slightly. Invert cooled pie onto serving dish and spoon caramel-nut mixture over the top so it runs down the sides. Chill thoroughly before serving. Makes about eight servings.

SERVES 6

Cherry Bread Pudding

1 can (21 oz) prepared cherry pie filling
6 slices white bread, crusts removed, cubed
¼ c butter or margarine, melted
1 T lemon juice
1 c milk
3 eggs
⅓ c sugar
½ t almond extract
cinnamon
1 c heavy cream, whipped with 2 T sugar and ½ t cinnamon

Spoon cherry pie filling evenly on bottom of shallow 1½-qt. casserole. Arrange bread cubes on top. Drizzle melted butter or margarine over bread and sprinkle with lemon juice.

In small bowl, combine milk, eggs, sugar and almond extract; beat until well mixed and pour over bread cubes. Press bread cubes down into milk mixture to coat thoroughly. Sprinkle with cinnamon. Microwave at medium (50 percent) 18 to 20 minutes, rotating four times, until bread/custard is lightly set in center. Remove and let stand five minutes. Serve warm or chilled with sweetened, cinnamon flavored whipped cream. Makes about six servings.

SERVES 12

Finnish Strawberry Dessert Cake

- 4 large eggs
- 1 c sugar
- ½ c flour
- ½ c cornstarch
- 1 T baking powder
  Strawberry jam
- 1 qt strawberries, stem removed and halved
- 3 medium bananas, peeled and sliced
- 2 c heavy cream, whipped

In medium bowl of electric mixer, combine eggs and sugar; beat until fluffy. In another bowl, combine flour, cornstarch and baking powder; add slowly to egg mixture and beat until well combined. Pour batter into greased and floured 9-inch springform pan and bake at 400 degrees 20 to 25 minutes, until cake is puffed and golden brown on top. Test for doneness. Do not let top get overly browned. Remove from oven and let cool on wire rack. (The cake may fall slightly in the middle but it won't affect the result.)

After cake is completely cooled, cut in half horizontally. Put bottom half on serving plate and spread with strawberry jam. Arrange about one-third of the strawberry halves and half the banana slices on top of jam. Spread with about one cup of the whipped cream. Cover with remaining cake half and spread with strawberry jam. Arrange one-third of the strawberries and remaining half of banana slices on top. Spread top and sides of cake with remaining whipped cream or use pastry bag to pipe whipped cream up sides and around top of cake. Decorate top of cake with remaining strawberry halves. Makes about 12 servings.

SERVES 6

Flan de Naranja (Orange Flan)

¾ c sugar, divided
   Finely grated rind of 2 oranges and ½ lemon
1 c orange juice
   Juice of ½ lemon
6 eggs, separated

In heavy saucepan over low heat, melt ½ cup of the sugar. When completely melted, turn up heat and stir syrup with wooden spoon until dark golden brown. Pour caramel into flan mold or 1-qt. charlotte mold and quickly tilt mold so that caramel covers bottom and halfway up the sides. Set aside.

Set a baking pan on lowest shelf of oven and fill with enough hot water to come halfway up the sides of filled mold.

In small bowl, combine remaining ¼ cup of sugar, grated orange and lemon rinds and orange and lemon juice; stir until sugar is dissolved and set aside.

In two separate bowls: beat egg yolks until stiff and lemon colored; beat egg whites until stiff peaks form. Gradually add yolks to the whites, beating constantly. Add juice mixture, combine thoroughly and let stand until froth subsides, stirring froth down occasionally, about 20 to 30 minutes. Wait for the froth to subside before pouring into caramel-lined flan or charlotte mold. Grease lid of mold, cover and set mold in pan of hot water. Bake at 350 degrees until flan is set, about two hours. Test by inserting knife in center of mold. If blade comes out clean, flan is ready. Set aside to cool on wire rack (not refrigerator) before unmolding on serving plate. Makes about six servings.

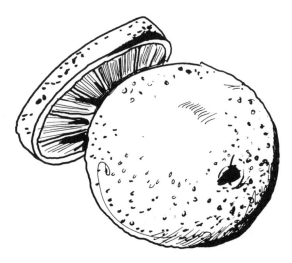

SERVES 10 TO 12

Frozen Chocolate Torte

- 6 T unsalted butter
- 1¾ c fine graham cracker crumbs
- 2 T confectioners sugar
- 2 T sweetened dry cocoa mix
- ½ c sugar
- ½ c water
- 2 eggs
- 6 oz semisweet baking chocolate, broken into small pieces
- 2 T cognac or brandy
- ¼ c chocolate-flavored liqueur
- 1 c heavy cream, whipped
- 1 c chopped pecans or toasted almonds
  Whipped cream for garnish

In medium saucepan, melt butter; add graham cracker crumbs, confectioners sugar and cocoa mix. Stir until thoroughly mixed and press onto the sides and bottom of 8-inch spring mold. Freeze until solid, about one hour.

Meanwhile, in small saucepan, combine sugar and water; heat until sugar is completely dissolved and keep warm. In food processor or blender, combine eggs and chocolate pieces. Add hot syrup and process until chocolate is melted and mixture is smooth. Add cognac or brandy and chocolate-flavored liqueur and refrigerate until thickened, about two hours. Fold thickened mixture into whipped cream and add pecans or almonds. Turn mixture into prepared crust and freeze until solid, about four hours, or up to one month, wrapped in plastic wrap.

To serve, remove from freezer, run sharp knife around edges of pan and remove sides of pan. Let stand 10 minutes before serving. Makes 10 to 12 servings.

DESSERTS and PIES

Fudge Mint Sauce

    1 c sugar
    ¾ c water
    ½ c butter
    ¼ c light corn syrup
    1 pkg (12 oz) semi-sweet real chocolate bits
    ¼ c creme de menthe (1 t peppermint extract may be
       substituted)

In medium saucepan, combine sugar, water, butter, cut into small
pieces, and corn syrup. Cook over medium heat, stirring constantly,
until mixture comes to a full boil, about five to eight minutes. Boil
three minutes. Remove from heat and immediately add chocolate;
beat with wire whisk until chocolate is melted and mixture is smooth.
Stir in creme de menthe. Cool to lukewarm and pour into containers;
seal tightly. Serve warm or cool over ice cream, cake or fresh pears.
Store in refrigerator up to two months or in freezer up to six months.
Makes four cups sauce.

Grasshopper Pie

   24 chocolate wafer cookies, finely crushed
    4 T butter, melted
    ½ c milk
   24 large marshmallows
    4 T green creme de menthe
    2 T white creme de cacao
    1 c whipping cream
       Chocolate curls

Mix together crushed cookies and butter. Press evenly into bottom
and sides of a 9-inch pie plate. Freeze at least one hour. In saucepan,
heat milk. Stir in marshmallows and heat stirring, until they melt. Let
mixture cool. Stir creme de menthe and creme de cacao into
marshmallow mixture. Beat cream until stiff. Fold whipped cream
into marshmallow mixture. Pour filling evenly into the frozen pie shell.
Decorate with chocolate curls. Freeze pie; remove from freezer 15
minutes before serving.

SERVES 8

Indian Pudding

3½ c milk, divided
 ½ c yellow cornmeal
 2 eggs
 ½ c maple syrup
 ¼ c dark molasses
 2 T melted butter
 1 t salt
 ¾ t cinnamon
 ¾ t ginger

In top of double boiler, scald three cups of the milk. In small bowl, mix remaining ½ cup milk with cornmeal; add slowly to scalded milk, stirring constantly. Cook over gently boiling water, stirring frequently, 30 minutes, until thick and creamy.

In 1½-qt. baking dish, beat eggs lightly; add syrup, molasses, butter, salt, cinnamon and ginger and mix thoroughly. Slowly stir in hot cornmeal mixture. Place dish in pan of hot water and bake at 350 degrees 60 to 70 minutes, or until knife inserted in middle comes out clean. Serve hot with vanilla ice cream or sweetened whipped cream flavored with cinnamon. Makes about eight servings.

**MAKES ONE
LARGE PAN**

International Restaurant's Pumpkin Baklava

- 6 c pumpkin, peeled and cut into small pieces, boiled 10-15 minutes, or 6 c canned pumpkin
- 2 c ground walnuts
- 2 c ground almonds
- ½ c whole wheat bread crumbs
- 2 T farina
- 3 eggs
- 3 egg whites
- 1 T cinnamon
- ⅛ t powdered cloves
- 4 T sugar
- 1 lb filo dough (available at most markets)
- ½ lb butter, melted
  Spicy syrup (recipe follows)

If using fresh pumpkin, mash pumpkin or put through food processor or food mill. Drain thoroughly.(Canned pumpkin is ready to use). Mix pumpkin, walnuts, almonds, bread crumbs and farina; stir until well blended. Add eggs, egg whites, cinnamon, cloves and sugar; thicken if necessary with more bread crumbs. Set mixture aside.

Line large baking dish, about 15x10x2½, with half the filo dough so it hangs over the edge. Butter the top sheet of the filo generously. Add prepared filling, smoothing it evenly over the dough. Layer rest of filo, one sheet at a time, buttering between each sheet. Butter top sheet generously.

Bake 1½ hours at 250 degrees. Then cut into diamond shapes and top with spice syrup to taste.

Leftover syrup may be stored in refrigerator for other uses.

Spicy Syrup

- 3 c water
- 3 c sugar
- ½ lemon, cut in wedges
- ½ orange, sliced
- ½ apple, cut into wedges
- 2 cinnamon sticks
  Pinch of cloves
- ½ t vanilla

Combine all ingredients in large heavy saucepan. Bring to a boil, reduce heat and simmer 45 minutes to one hour, until thickened and syrupy. Strain and pour evenly over baklava until the syrup is no longer absorbed by the pastry. Makes about 2½ cups of syrup.

SERVES 12

Marilyn Trent's Almond Cheesecake

1½ c graham cracker crumbs
¼ c butter, melted
2 T plus, 1¾ c sugar, divided
1 t flour
4 pkgs (8 oz each) cream cheese, softened
2 eggs, lightly beaten
1 t vanilla
1¾ t almond extract, divided
2 c sour cream
½ t fresh lemon juice
    Toasted sliced almonds for garnish, if desired

In medium bowl, combine cracker crumbs, melted butter, two tablespoons of the sugar and flour; stir until well combined and moistened. Press mixture on bottom and sides of 10-inch springform pan. Bake at 350 degrees five to seven minutes. Remove and set aside to cool.

In large bowl of electric mixer, combine cream cheese, one cup of the remaining sugar, eggs, vanilla and one teaspoon of the almond extract. Beat at low speed until mixture is smooth and silky. Pour into cooled prepared crust. Bake at 350 degrees until middle of cheesecake is set. This will take from 30 to 50 minutes depending on the performance of your oven. Test for doneness with knife or broom straw inserted in the middle of the cake. Remove cheesecake from oven when done. Leave oven on.

Meanwhile, in medium bowl, combine sour cream, remaining ¾ cup sugar, remaining ¾ teaspoon almond extract and lemon juice; beat until smooth. Using rubber spatula, spread mixture on top of cheesecake to within ½ inch of the edge. Return cheesecake to oven and bake at 350 degrees eight minutes. Remove cake and cool completely on wire rack. Refrigerate overnight. Just before servings, remove sides of springform pan and set cake on serving platter. Garnish with toasted sliced almonds, if desired. Makes about 12 servings.

SERVES 16

Jim Britt's Fresh Fruit Flan

   5 egg yolks
   ⅓ c sugar
   ⅓ c cornstarch
   2 c half and half
   2 c flour
   ¾ c sugar
     Pinch salt
     Grated peel of 1 lemon
   2 eggs, beaten
  10 T butter
     Currant jelly or raspberry jam
     Strawberries, blueberries, grapes, raspberries, sliced
     kiwi fruit, blackberries, sectioned oranges, sliced
     bananas, nectarines, melon balls, pineapple
     Melted currant jelly or apricot jam (sieved)

To make pastry cream: In small bowl, combine egg yolks, sugar and cornstarch; beat until well mixed. In small saucepan, scald half and half; remove from heat and stir about ¾ cup into egg mixture, stirring briskly. Combine egg-half and half mixture with hot half and half and cook, stirring constantly and vigorously until mixture thickens and bubbles. Remove from heat, cover top of mixture with circle of wax paper and chill.

To make pastry: In large bowl, or in bowl of food processor with metal blade, combine flour, sugar, salt and lemon peel. Work in butter. If using food processor, chill butter and add in tablespoon pieces; process mixture until it resembles pea gravel. Drizzle in eggs or add eggs through feeding tube; knead or process just until loose ball of dough is formed. The dough will be quite soft. Chill bowl until dough is firm enough to form into ball. Wrap ball in plastic wrap until well chilled — at least three hours.

On lightly floured surface, roll out dough to 11-inch circle. Press dough into fluted 9x1-inch flan ring with removable bottom. Leave about ¼-inch rim above top of pan to allow for shrinkage. Chill dough thoroughly. Cut wax paper on parchment to fit bottom and fill shell with uncooked beans or pastry weights. Bake at 400 degrees 12 minutes. Remove shell from oven; remove bean or weights and paper lining. Prick shell on bottom and sides again. Return to oven and bake six to eight minutes longer, until light brown. Remove and cool on wire rack.

DESSERTS and PIES

Fill cooled pastry shell with prepared chilled pastry cream, bring cream almost to top of shell and smoothing until even. Have choice of fruits prepared, drained and ready to make your design. Arrange whole or halved berries, sectioned or sliced larger fruits in attractive design, completely covering top of pastry cream. If you are using dark colored fruits, brush tops of fruit with melted currant jelly, covering all fruits completely. If you are using light color fruits, brush completely with melted and sieved apricot jam. Chill until serving time. Cut into wedges. Makes about 16 servings.

SERVES 8 TO 12

Kathe Bartusek's Fresh Fruit Pizza

    1 pkg (¼ oz) active dry yeast
    ¼ c warm water (110 degrees)
    ½ c milk
 1¼ c sugar, divided
    ¼ c butter or margarine
    3 or more c flour, divided
      Grated rind of ½ lemon
    2 t vanilla, divided
    1 egg
    2 egg yolks, divided
    1 lb (or 15 oz carton) ricotta cheese
    2 to 3 c dry fresh blueberries (other berries or pitted, sliced fruit may be used in season)
      Sliced almonds
      Cinnamon
    1 egg beaten with 1 t water
      Confectioners sugar

To make pizza dough: In small bowl, combine yeast and warm water, stirring until yeast is dissolved; set aside and let stand until yeast starts bubbling.

In small saucepan, combine milk, ½ cup of the sugar and butter or margarine; heat, stirring occasionally until butter is melted and sugar dissolved. Remove from heat and cool to at least 110 degrees.

In large bowl, using wooden spoon, or in large bowl of electric mixer using paddle attachment, combine and mix one cup of the flour, lemon rind, one teaspoon of the vanilla, egg and one of the egg yolks. Slowly add the yeast mixture and cooled milk mixture and beat to a smooth batter. Add another cup of the flour and beat until smooth. Add third cup of flour and mix with floured hands until dough becomes dull and non-stick in appearance and texture. Turn out on floured surface and knead four to five minutes, adding flour as needed to avoid sticking. Form dough into ball and place in well-greased bowl, turning once to coat entire surface. Cover with plastic wrap and let stand in warm place until doubled in bulk, one to 1½ hours.

Knock down dough and knead lightly to remove any air bubbles. Roll out into large circle and spread onto greased 16-inch pizza pan. Work dough into a thick rim all around pan. Cover lightly with kitchen towel and let rise 15 minutes.

Meanwhile, in medium bowl of electric mixer, combine ricotta cheese, remaining egg yolk, remaining teaspoon vanilla and remaining ¾ cup of the sugar. Beat at high speed until smooth and spread over bottom of prepared pizza crust. Sprinkle blueberries (or arrange other fruit) over cheese filling in one layer. Sprinkle with sliced almonds and cinnamon to taste. Bake at 375 degrees 10 minutes. Remove from oven and glaze rim of dough with egg-water mixture. Return to oven and bake another 20 to 25 minutes, taking care that pizza rim does not get too browned. Remove, cool slightly and sprinkle with confectioners sugar. Serve warm or cooled. Makes eight to 12 servings.

SERVES 8

Margarita Pie

- 1 env unflavored gelatin
- 1 c sugar, divided
- 1 t salt
- 4 eggs, separated
- 1 c lime juice
- ⅓ c tequila
- 2 T orange liqueur
- 2 T grated lime peel
  Baked 10-inch pie crust
  Sweetened whipped cream
  Fresh lime slices

In saucepan, combine gelatin, ½ cup of the sugar and salt; set aside. Beat egg yolks and lime juice until foamy. Stir into gelatin mixture and cook about three minutes over low heat, until gelatin is dissolved. Stir in tequila, orange liqueur and grated lime peel. Cool and refrigerate until thick but not set. Beat egg whites until foamy. Slowly add the remaining ½ cup of sugar and continue beating until stiff peaks form. Fold egg whites into chilled gelatin mixture. Turn into baked pie shell and decorate with whipped cream and lime slices. Makes eight servings.

SERVES 16

Old English Plum Pudding

- ½ lb dried currants
- ½ lb seedless raisins
- ½ lb golden raisins
- ½ lb citron, finely diced
- ¼ lb diced candled lemon peel
- ¼ lb diced candled orange peel
- ¼ lb pitted dates, chopped
- ½ c silvered blanched almonds
- 1 c plus 3 T brandy or rum
- 1 c flour
- ½ t cinnamon
- ¼ t nutmeg
- ¼ t mace
- ⅛ t ground cloves
- ⅛ t ground ginger
- ½ lb ground beef suet
- ½ c fine dry bread crumbs
- ½ t salt
- 2 large eggs
- ½ c red currant jelly
- Rum, brandy or orange juice for moistening
- Sweetened whipped cream, if desired
- Brandied Hard Sauce (recipe follows), if desired

In large ceramic or glass bowl, combine currants, raisins, citron, lemon and orange peels, dates and almonds; pour over one cup of brandy or rum and toss to coat. Cover bowl with plastic wrap and let stand, stirring occasionally, in cool place 24 hours.

Sift flour with cinnamon, nutmeg, mace, cloves and ginger; mix with suet, bread crumbs and salt. Combine flour mixture with soaked fruit mixture and toss until all ingredients are well coated and mixed. In small bowl, beat eggs until frothy; add currant jelly and beat until jelly is in small specks. Stir egg mixture into fruit mixture and mix well. Turn dough into two well-buttered, 6-cup pudding molds with lids and pack down. Cover with lids and rub butter along the seam between the lid and the mold. Tie each mold in kitchen towel soaked in water, wrung out well and dusted with flour. Place puddings in large kettle or pot and pour in boiling water just reaching the top of the molds. Do not submerge molds. Boil gently for about seven hours, replenishing the water when necessary to keep it to the level with the top of the molds. Remove molds, unwrap and let cool to room temperature on wire rack. While still slightly warm, unmold puddings and wrap in several layers of cheesecloth or other light fabric. Moisten wrapping with rum or brandy and let ripen in refrigerator three to four weeks, keeping wrappings moistened with liquor or orange juice.

When ready to serve, steam puddings 2½ to three hours by placing in

DESSERTS and PIES

sieve, colander or top of double boiler over simmering water. Turn onto serving plate and pour three tablespoons warm brandy over; keeping face away from the flame, ignite brandy and carry to the table flaming. Serve with sweetened whipped cream or Brandied Hard Sauce (recipe follows). Makes two plum puddings, about eight servings for each pudding. If well-wrapped and refrigerated, this will keep up to a year.

Brandied Hard Sauce

- ¾ c unsalted butter, softened
- 2 c sifted confectioners sugar
- 2 T, or to taste, brandy or rum

In small bowl of electric mixer, cream butter until light and fluffy. Gradually beat in sugar and brandy. Spoon into small serving dish and refrigerate until use. Makes about one cup sauce.

SERVES 8

Michigan Glazed Strawberry Pie

- 1 pkg (3 oz) cream cheese, softened
- 1 baked 9-inch pie shell
- 1 qt drained, hulled Michigan strawberries, divided
- 1½ c strawberry juice
- 1 c sugar
- 3 T cornstarch
- 1 c heavy cream

Spread softened cream cheese over bottom of prepared pie crust. Arrange half of the choicest berries on top of cream cheese, standing upright, cover with plastic wrap and refrigerate while making glaze.

Mash remaining strawberries in fine strainer, extracting juice but not pulp. Add water, if necessary, to make 1½ cups juice. In small saucepan, bring juice to a boil. Combine sugar and cornstarch and mix thoroughly; add to hot juice and beat constantly with wire whisk until mixture thickens, becomes clear and comes to a boil. Boil one minute. Cool slightly and pour evenly over strawberries in pie shell. Chill at least two hours. Just before serving, beat cream until stiff peaks form. Using pastry bag or spoon, decorate edge of pie with whipped cream and serve any remaining cream on the side. Makes eight servings.

SERVES 8 TO 10

Palm Beach Lime Mousse

1 pkg (¼ oz) unflavored gelatin
¼ c cold water
¾ c sugar, divided
⅔ c fresh lime juice (from about 6 limes)
4 egg whites
  Dash salt
1 c heavy cream, whipped
  Lime slices and grated lime peel, for garnish
  Grape clusters, for garnish

In medium saucepan, combine gelatin and water; let stand one minute to soften. Stir in ½ cup of the sugar; warm mixture over low heat to dissolve sugar and gelatin. Stir in lime juice and let mixture chill until syrupy.

Meanwhile, in medium bowl, beat egg whites and salt together until foamy. Gradually add remaining ¼ cup sugar and beat until mixture forms soft peaks. Fold in chilled gelatin mixture until well combined. Fold in whipped cream. Pour into 1½-qt. mold that has been rinsed in cold water.

Chill at least four hours or overnight. Unmold onto serving platter and garnish with lime slices, grated lime peel and grape clusters. Makes eight to 10 servings.

DESSERTS and PIES

Pete Peterson's Country Rhubarb Cobbler

- 2 c flour
- 2½ t baking powder
- ½ t salt
- ⅓ c shortening
- 1¼ c sugar, divided
- 1 t grated lemon rind
- 4 c fresh or frozen rhubarb, cut into ½-inch pieces
- 1 egg, lightly beaten
- ¼ c melted butter
- Cream or vanilla ice cream

To make pastry mix: In medium bowl or food processor, combine flour, baking powder and salt; mix or process until well blended. Process or cut in shortening until mixture is gravelly; set aside.

In large bowl, combine ⅓ cup prepared pastry mix, ¾ cup of the sugar, lemon rind; stir in rhubarb until well coated and turn mixture into well buttered 8-inch casserole or baking dish.

In medium bowl or food processor, combine 1¼ cups pastry mix, remaining ½ cup of the sugar and egg. Stir or process until mixture resembles coarse crumbs. Sprinkle evenly over top of rhubarb and drizzle melted butter evenly over top. Bake at 375 degrees 30 to 35 minutes, until top is puffed and golden brown. Serve warm with cream or vanilla ice cream. Makes about six servings.

SERVES 4 TO 6

Plum Pudding

1 lb ripe fresh plums
1 c red wine
1 c water
¼ c clear honey
¼ t salt
¼ t cinnamon
⅛ t galingale or ginger (galingale available at most East-Indian food markets)
⅛ t mace
¼ c cornstarch or rice flour dissolved in ¼ c cold water
½ t anise seed
Vanilla ice cream or sweetened whipped cream, if desired

In medium saucepan, cover plums with wine and water. Bring to a boil, cover and simmer about five to 10 minutes, until soft. Remove plums, reserving cooking liquid, and peel, discarding pits. In blender or food processor, puree plums; add honey, salt, cinnamon, galingale or ginger and mace. Stir mixture into reserved cooking liquid in saucepan. Heat over low heat; add cornstarch mixture and continue heating, stirring constantly, until mixture thickens and clarifies. Pudding should be very thick. If there are lumps, puree mixture again. Pour into serving bowl and cover at once with plastic wrap. Let cool to room temperature. Sprinkle with anise seed and rewrap. Chill overnight in refrigerator. Serve with vanilla ice cream or sweetened whipped cream, if desired. Makes four to six servings.

SERVES 20

Pumpkin Cheesecake

- 2 c graham cracker crumbs
- 7 T butter, melted
- 1⅓ c sugar
- 2½ t cinnamon, divided
- 4 pkgs (8 oz each) cream cheese, softened
- 4 large eggs, lightly beaten
- 3 egg yolks, lightly beaten
- 3 T flour
- 1 t ground cloves
- 1 t ginger
- 1 c heavy cream
- 1 T vanilla
- 1 can (16 oz) mashed pumpkin (not pumpkin pie filling)
  Whipped cream, if desired

In medium bowl, combine cracker crumbs, melted butter, ⅓ cup of the sugar and ½ teaspoon of the cinnamon; mix thoroughly and press onto the bottom and part way up the sides of a 10-inch springform pan. Place in freezer and chill for one hour before filling.

In large bowl of electric mixer, combine cream cheese, rest of sugar, eggs and yolks; beat until smooth. Add flour, cinnamon, cloves and ginger and beat until combined. Beat in cream, vanilla and pumpkin until mixed thoroughly. Pour mixture into prepared chilled pie crust. Place in pre-heated 425-degree oven and bake 15 minutes. Reduce oven temperature to 275 degrees; bake one hour, or until middle of cake is almost set. Turn oven off but leave cake in oven overnight to cool. This step is important for the cake to set completely and glaze on top.

The next day, remove cake from oven and chill if desired. Pumpkin Cheese Cake may be served warm or chilled with whipped cream, if desired. Makes about 20 servings.

SERVES 8

Pumpkin Praline Pie

2 c flour
1 c frozen unsalted butter, cut into 1 T pieces
1 egg
1 T heavy cream
1½ t salt, divided
2 c pureed fresh pumpkin (one 3½ to 4 lb pumpkin)
1 c evaporated milk
½ c light or dark corn syrup
½ c plus ⅔ c brown sugar, packed, divided
3 eggs
1½ t cinnamon
½ t ground ginger
½ t nutmeg
⅛ t ground cloves
3 T soft butter or margarine
⅔ c coarsely chopped pecans

To make pastry: In bowl or food processor with metal blade attached, combine flour, butter, egg, cream and one teaspoon of salt. Process, turning machine on and off, about 15 seconds. Continue processing until dough ball forms on blade. Remove dough and chill 30 minutes. If not using food processor, bring butter to room temperature and cut into flour and salt with two knives or pastry cutter until mixture resembles pea gravel. Then add egg and cream and stir until dough forms a ball. Chill 30 minutes. Remove from refrigerator and roll out on lightly floured surface to a rectangle approximately 8x16 inches. Fold into thirds, like an envelope and roll out to former size. Repeat process twice. Divide dough in half. Each half makes enough for one 8- or 9-inch pie shell. Roll out one half to fit 9-inch pie plate and set aside. Dough not used immediately may be frozen.

To make filling: Cut pumpkin in half lengthwise. Remove stem, seeds and stringy pulp. Place cut-side-down in baking dish and add enough water just to cover bottom of pan. Bake at 350 degrees about 40 minutes, or until skin is easily pierced with fork. Remove from oven and cool. Peel off skin and mash pulp; puree pulp in blender or food processor. Place in sieve or colander lined with cheesecloth or thin dish towel and let drain overnight in bowl in refrigerator. The next day, discard water that has collected in bottom of bowl and measure 2 cups drained puree. Refrigerate or freeze extra puree.

In large bowl of electric mixer, combine prepared pumpkin puree, evaporated milk, corn syrup, ½ cup of the brown sugar, eggs, cinnamon, remaining ½ teaspoon salt, ginger, nutmeg and cloves. Beat at medium speed until smooth and creamy, about three minutes. Pour into prepared unbaked pie shell. Bake at 425 degrees 15 minutes. Lower oven temperature to 350 degrees and bake 30 to 40 minutes longer, until knife inserted in middle of pie comes out clean. Remove from oven.

In small bowl, combine soft butter or margarine, remaining ⅔ cup brown sugar and chopped pecans. With fork, stir mixture until crumbly. Sprinkle topping over baked pie and run under broiler, about five inches from heat, until mixture begins to bubble, about one to two minutes. Remove pie and cool on wire rack. Makes six to eight servings.

SERVES 8

Pumpkin Spice Roll

    3 eggs
    1 c sugar
    ⅔ c canned, mashed pumpkin (not pumpkin pie filling)
    1 t lemon juice
    ¾ c flour
    1 t baking powder
    2 t cinnamon
    1 t ginger
    ½ t nutmeg
    ½ t salt
    ½ to ¾ c chopped walnuts
    2 pkgs (3 oz each) cream cheese, softened
    1 c sifted confectioners sugar
    ½ t vanilla
    4 T butter, softened
      Confectioners sugar, if desired
      Whipped cream, if desired

In a large bowl, use electric mixer to beat eggs until foamy and lemon colored, about five minutes. Gradually add sugar and mix well. Stir in pumpkin and lemon juice. Sift together flour, baking powder, cinnamon, ginger, nutmeg and salt; gradually fold into egg mixture. Grease jelly roll pan; line with wax paper and lightly butter paper. Pour batter evenly into prepared pan and sprinkle evenly with walnuts. Bake at 375 degrees for 15 minutes, until risen and golden brown on top. Remove from oven and turn out on kitchen towel lightly dusted with extra confectioners sugar. Be sure that the walnuted side is face down on the towel. Roll up towel lengthwise as you would a jelly roll and let cake cool.

Meanwhile, in medium bowl of electric mixer, combine cream cheese, one cup of confectioners sugar, vanilla and butter; beat until very fluffy, about five minutes. Spread on cooled cake and re-roll lengthwise into jelly roll shape. Place on serving plate, seam side down, and chill at least one hour before serving. Sprinkle with additional confectioners sugar if desired and serve with whipped cream, if desired. Makes about eight servings.

SERVES 12 TO 14

Rice Pudding

2 qts milk
¾ c uncooked rice
2 sticks cinnamon
6 eggs
3 t vanilla extract
2 t lemon extract
3 T cornstarch dissolved in ½ cup water
1½ c sugar
Powdered cinnamon

In large, heavy saucepan or pot, combine milk, rice and cinnamon sticks. Bring to a boil, reduce heat and simmer about 45 minutes, until rice is tender, stirring frequently.

Meanwhile, in medium bowl, beat eggs with vanilla and lemon extracts. Add cornstarch mixture and mix thoroughly.

Add sugar to hot rice mixture and stir until dissolved. Remove cinnamon sticks and discard. While rice mixture is still very hot, stir in prepared egg mixture and mix thoroughly. Cover pot and set aside to cool. Pudding will thicken as it cools. Spoon into individual serving dishes and sprinkle with powdered cinnamon. Makes about 12 to 14 servings.

DESSERTS and PIES

Rocky Road Pie

2½ c chocolate cookie crumbs
 8 T butter or margarine, melted
 1 qt chocolate ice cream, softened
 1 jar (7½ oz) marshmallow creme
 ¼ c water
 ⅓ c chocolate syrup, divided
 1 qt butter almond or butter pecan ice cream, softened
   Sweetened whipped cream
   Chopped toasted almonds

In medium bowl, combine cookie crumbs and melted butter or margarine; mix thoroughly and press onto bottom and part way up sides of 8- or 9-inch springform pan. Freeze until firm.

Scoop chocolate ice cream onto frozen crust and spread evenly with back of spoon; return to freezer.

Meanwhile, in small bowl of electric mixer, combine marshmallow creme and water; beat until smooth. Spoon half of marshmallow mixture onto chocolate ice cream and dribble with half of the chocolate syrup. Return to freezer until marshmallow and syrup are partially set. Spoon butter almond or pecan ice cream over top of mixture and repeat layers of remaining marshmallow creme and chocolate syrup. Freeze pie at least six hours or overnight. Before serving, remove sides of springform pan; top pie with whipped cream and sprinkle with toasted almonds. Cut into wedges to serve. Makes eight to 10 servings.

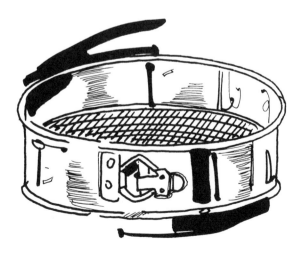

SERVES 8

Summer Pudding

14 to 16 thin slices dense homemade type bread, crusts removed
4 c raspberries, rinsed and well-drained
½ c sugar
4 T orange-flavored liqueur, divided
1 pt blueberries, rinsed and well-drained
½ c blackberries, rinsed and well-drained
1 c heavy cream
2 T confectioners sugar

Slice 12 slices of the bread in half diagonally. Trim one slice into a round to fit the bottom of a 1-qt. charlotte or round deep mold and set it into place. Arrange the triangular pieces of bread on end and overlapping around the side of the mold; set mold aside.

In medium saucepan, combine raspberries, sugar and two tablespoons of the liqueur; bring mixture just to a boil, stirring gently, and simmer about two to three minutes, until sugar is dissolved. Remove from heat and cool. Spoon one-half into prepared mold. Cover with bread cut to fit mold. Spoon remaining half raspberry mixture over bread and top with bread cut to cover mold completely. Cover top of mold with plastic wrap or wax paper. Place saucer on top and weigh saucer down with two-pound weight. Secure edges of plastic wrap or wax paper with rubber band. Refrigerate weighted pudding overnight.

To serve: Remove weight and covering; unmold pudding onto large serving plate and surround with blueberries. Carefully arrange blackberries on top of pudding. Whip heavy cream and confectioners sugar until stiff peaks form. Fold in remaining two tablespoons liqueur and spoon into serving dish. Serve with pudding. Makes about eight servings.

SERVES 14 TO 16

Susan Sheffield's Warp Drive Chocolate Pie

    1½ c finely crushed chocolate wafers
     6 T butter, melted
     1 pkg (12 oz) semisweet real chocolate bits
     5 egg yolks
     3 T Kahlua or cognac
    1½ c heavy cream

In small bowl, combine crushed wafers and melted butter. Mix thoroughly and press into bottom and sides of 10-inch Pyrex or pottery pie plate. Place in freezer for one hour.

In blender container, combine chocolate bits, egg yolks and kahlua or cognac; set aside.

In small saucepan, heat cream until it just comes to a boil. With blender going on low speed, pour hot cream into chocolate mixture. When all cream has been added, blend on high speed one minute. The heat of the cream will melt the chocolate and cook the egg yolks. Pour mixture into frozen pie shell and chill at least three hours. Do not freeze. Cut into very thin wedges to serve. Makes about 14 to 16 servings.

SERVES 10

Toffee Torte

8 chocolate-covered toffee bars (⅞ oz each)
1 qt coffee ice cream, softened
1 oz rum- or coffee-flavor liqueur
   Layer of pound cake
4 squares bittersweet chocolate (1 oz each)
⅓ c toasted slivered almonds
1 qt chocolate ice cream, softened
1 oz creme de cacao
   Crushed chocolate-covered toffee bars, for garnish

In food processor or with rolling pin, coarsely crush toffee bars. Put half the toffee in the bottom of an 8-inch springform mold; set aside. Reserve other half for later use.

In large bowl, mix coffee ice cream with rum- or coffee-flavor liqueur; spoon on top of toffee layer in springform mold and freeze to harden.

Meanwhile, prepare a layer of pound cake cut to the size of the springform mold; set aside. In small pan, over hot water, melt chocolate squares. Stir in almonds and keep warm. Remove mold from freezer; place pound cake over hardened ice cream layer and frost with chocolate-almond mixture, spreading to edges of cake. Return to freezer until chocolate hardens.

Meanwhile, mix chocolate ice cream and creme de cacao. Spoon on top of hardened chocolate layer. Sprinkle evenly with remaining half of the toffee and return to freezer.

To serve: Remove from freezer 10 minutes before serving time. Run sharp knife around edges and remove sides of mold. Pat crushed toffee around sides of torte, for garnish, to make a toffee coating. Makes about 10 servings.

COOKIES and CAKES

Canadian Butter Tarts

- 1 c flour
- ⅓ c butter or margarine, softened
- 1 pkg (3 oz) cream cheese, softened
- 1 c packed brown sugar
- 2 T melted butter
- 2 t cornstarch
- 1 large egg
- 1 T heavy cream
- 1 t lemon juice
- ⅛ t nutmeg
- ⅓ c raisins or currants, soaked in hot water until plump, drained

In medium bowl or food processor, combine flour, butter or margarine and cream cheese. Process or blend together thoroughly; press into ball, wrap in plastic wrap and refrigerate 30 minutes.

Divide dough into 12 equal parts and press each part into sides and bottom of each cup of a 12-cup fluted tart pan. Set aside.

In medium bowl, combine brown sugar, melted butter, cornstarch, egg, cream, lemon juice and nutmeg; beat until well mixed. Place about one teaspoon of the drained raisins in the bottom of each prepared pastry cup and fill about two-thirds full with the prepared brown sugar filling. Bake at 400 degrees 12 to 15 minutes, until pastry is golden brown and filling is bubbly. Remove and cool briefly on wire rack. While still warm, gently remove tarts from pan and finish cooling on rack. Makes 12 tarts.

MAKES 5 DOZEN

Cherry Winks

2¼ c flour
1 c sugar
2 t baking powder
½ t salt
¾ c shortening
2 T milk
1 t vanilla
2 eggs
1 c chopped pecans
1 c chopped dates
⅓ c chopped maraschino cherries, drained and chopped
1 c crushed cornflakes
15 maraschino cherries, cut in quarters

In large bowl of electric mixer, combine flour, sugar, baking powder, salt, shortening, milk, vanilla and eggs. Blend thoroughly. Stir in pecans, dates and chopped cherries; mix well and drop by rounded teaspoons onto ungreased cookie sheets. Sprinkle with cornflakes and top with cherry quarters. Bake at 375 degrees 10 to 12 minutes. Makes about five dozen cookies.

MAKES 4 DOZEN

Cinnamon Nut Cookies

- ½ lb unsalted butter, room temperature
- 1 c sugar
- 1 T cinnamon
- 1 t salt, divided
- 1 large egg yolk
- 1 c flour
- 1 c cake flour
- 1 large egg
- ½ c chopped walnuts

In food processor or electric mixer, combine butter, sugar, cinnamon and ½ teaspoon salt. Mix until fluffy. Add egg yolk and process or beat about 30 seconds longer. Add flour and cake flour and beat or process until just combined. Refrigerate dough one hour. Divide dough into quarters. On lightly floured surface, roll each quarter into a log about two inches in diameter. Wrap each log separately in plastic wrap and refrigerate until firm or freeze up to four months.

To serve: Sprinkle well-greased baking sheets with water, shaking off excess. Thaw dough slightly. Slice dough about ¼-inch thick and place rounds on baking sheet. Press to desired thinness with heel of your hand (this dough will not spread as it bakes). In small bowl, combine egg and remaining ½ teaspoon salt; beat until well mixed. Brush egg glaze on cookies with pastry brush. Sprinkle with walnuts, pressing nuts lightly in place with back of spoon. Bake at 350 degrees eight to 10 minutes until lightly browned. Cool on wire racks. Makes about 50 cookies.

SERVES 16

Dee Dee's Stardust Pound Cake

1⅓ c sugar
⅔ c butter, softened
3 eggs
2⅓ c cake flour, sifted
1 t baking soda
½ t salt
¾ c milk
1 T grated orange rind
1 t grated lemon rind
1 t lemon juice
Confectioners sugar

In large bowl of electric mixer, beat together sugar, butter and eggs until light and fluffy, about three minutes on high speed. Sift together flour, baking soda and salt and add to butter mixture alternately with milk, orange and lemon rinds and juice, beating at low speed and scraping sides of bowl often. Grease and flour a 2-qt. tube pan or a 9x5x3-inch loaf pan; pour in the prepared batter and bake at 350 degrees 50 to 55 minutes, or until cake tests done. Cool on wire rack 10 minutes before removing from pan. Invert onto serving platter and when completely cool, dust lightly with confectioners sugar. Cut into thin slices. (May be frozen.) Makes about 16 servings.

MAKES 4 TO 5 DOZEN

Delicate Shortbreads

1 c Butter Flavor Crisco
1¼ c flour
½ t salt
1 c confectioners sugar
2 t vanilla
2 c rolled oats
1 c semi-sweet chocolate bits

In medium bowl of electric mixer, cream shortening; add flour and salt and mix well. Stir in sugar and vanilla. Add rolled oats (see note) and blend thoroughly. Shape dough into rolls about 1½ inches in diameter, wrap in plastic wrap and chill several hours or overnight.

Slice rolls in ¼-inch slices and bake on ungreased cookie sheet at 350 degrees 12 to 15 minutes, until puffed and slightly browned. Let cool before dipping chocolate.

In small bowl over hot water, melt chocolate bits. Dip one end of each cookie into the melted chocolate and place on cookie sheet lined with waxed paper or plastic wrap. Refrigerate until chocolate is set. Store in cool place. Makes about four to five dozen cookies.

Note: If you process the oats in a food processor or blender with a few OFF and ON motions, the cookie rolls will be much easier to cut later on.

SERVES 12 TO 16

Ethel Amsler's Heritage Carrot Cake

- 1 c golden raisins
- 1 c brandy
- 1½ c sugar
- 1 c water
- 2 T butter
- 2 c grated carrots
- 1 t cinnamon
- 1 t nutmeg
- 1 t ground cloves
- 1 c chopped black walnuts
- 2½ c flour
- 2 t baking powder
- 1 t baking soda
- 1 t salt

At least two days before serving, in a medium saucepan, soak raisins in brandy overnight at room temperature. The next day, add sugar, water, butter, carrots, cinnamon, nutmeg and cloves. Bring mixture to a boil, stirring occasionally; simmer 10 minutes. Pour mixture into large bowl; cover and let stand at room temperature overnight.

The next day, add walnuts, flour, baking powder, baking soda and salt to carrot mixture. Mix thoroughly and pour into greased and floured 12-cup fluted pan or 10-inch angel-food pan. Bake at 275 degrees about 1¾ hours, until cake tests done. Cool pan upright on wire rack 15 minutes. Invert onto serving plate and cool completely. Store tightly covered. Makes 12 to 16 servings.

SERVES 12

Finnish Apple Cake

¼ c butter, softened
1 c sugar
2 large eggs
2 c sifted flour
1½ t baking powder
   Dash salt
¾ c light cream or sour cream
2 apples, peeled, cored and sliced
2 T sugar mixed with 1 t cinnamon

In medium bowl of electric mixer, cream butter and sugar together until fluffy. Add eggs, one at a time, beating well after each addition. Re-sift flour with baking powder and salt; add to batter alternately with cream or sour cream. Mix until batter is velvety and pour into well-greased 9x12-inch baking pan. Insert apple slices in rows so rounded edge stands upright in batter. Sprinkle evenly with cinnamon sugar and bake at 350 degrees about 50 minutes, or until cake is nicely browned and tests done. Cool on wire rack and serve either slightly warm or completely cooled. Makes about 12 servings.

SERVES 12

Fresh Apple Cake

- 1½ c vegetable oil
- 2 c sugar
- 3 eggs
- 3 c all-purpose flour
- 1 t baking soda
- 2 t cinnamon
- ½ t nutmeg
- ½ t mace
- ½ t salt
- 3 c apples, pared, diced and sprinkled with fresh lemon juice
- 1 c chopped walnuts
- 2 t vanilla
- Glaze (recipe follows)

Combine oil and sugar in bowl or mixer. Blend well. Add eggs, one at a time, beating after each addition. Sift together dry ingredients and add gradually, combining thoroughly. Blend in apples, nuts and vanilla. The batter will be very thick so be sure that it is well blended. Spoon into a well-greased and floured 9- to 10-inch tube pan — a ring mold or bundt pan is best — and bake for 1¼ hours at 325 degrees or until a knife or broom straw comes out clean.

Remove from oven and cool on a rack for half hour. Unmold gently on a large plate, preferable at least ½-inch larger in circumference than the cake to catch the glaze drippings. As soon as the cake is cool, spoon glaze (recipe follows) over cake.

Keeps for 2 weeks, wrapped in plastic wrap, at room temperature.

Glaze

- 3 T butter or margarine
- 3 T brown sugar
- 2 T heavy cream
- ½ t vanilla

Melt butter or margarine in heavy pan. Add other ingredients and boil rapidly for 2 minutes. Spoon over cake.

MAKES 3 LOAVES

Gum Drop Cake

- 1 c shortening, at room temperature
- 1 c sugar
- 1 c brown sugar
- 4 eggs, beaten
- 2 c applesauce
- 2 t soda
- 4 c flour, divided
- 3 c gumdrops, cut into quarters, licorice excluded
- 1 c dates, coarsely chopped
- 1 c chopped nuts
- 1 c golden raisins
- 2 t cinnamon
- 2 t nutmeg
- 2 t allspice
- 1 t salt
- 1 T vanilla

In large bowl of electric mixer, combine shortening and sugars; beat until creamy. Add eggs and beat until well combined. Mix applesauce and soda and add to bowl; beat until combined, scraping sides of bowl often. (The mixture may look curdled, but texture will disappear when flour is added.)

In medium bowl, combine ½ cup of the flour with gumdrops, dates, nuts and raisins; stir thoroughly so all ingredients are dusted with flour to prevent sticking together. Set aside.

In another bowl, combine remaining 3½ cups flour with cinnamon, nutmeg, allspice and salt; mix thoroughly.

Add flour/spice mixture to egg/sugar mixture and beat until smooth and thoroughly blended. Stir in flour/gumdrop mixture and vanilla until well distributed.

Line three 9x5x3 loaf pans with waxed paper or metal foil. Distribute batter equally into pans. Place a pan of water on bottom rack of oven. Bake at 300 degrees about two hours or until cake tests done when a silver knife is inserted in the center of the cake. Cool in pan on wire rack. Remove from pan and carefully peel off waxed paper or foil. Wrap tightly in plastic wrap to store. Cake is best stored for a week or two before serving.

COOKIES and CAKES

MAKES 4 DOZEN

Honey Crinkles

    2 c sifted flour
    2 t baking soda
    ¾ t mace
    ⅔ c cooking oil
    1 c sugar
    1 egg, unbeaten
    ¼ c honey
       Granulated sugar

Sift flour again with baking soda and mace into small bowl; set aside.

In medium bowl, using fork or electric beater, beat oil and sugar until well mixed; add egg and beat thoroughly. Stir in honey and gradually add flour mixture, beating well. Partially fill a small bowl with granulated sugar; drop teaspoons of the batter into the sugar and roll around with fingers until sugar-coated balls are formed, about the size of small walnuts. Place balls three inches apart on ungreased cookie sheets. Bake at 350 degrees 10 to 12 minutes, until flat and golden brown. Remove from oven and let rest one minute before removing with spatula to cool on wax paper. Store in airtight container to retain crispness. Makes about four dozen cookies.

MAKES 3½ DOZEN

Incredible Edibles

    ¾ c butter or margarine, melted
    2 c crushed graham cracker crumbs
    1 jar (12 oz) peanut butter
    2 c confectioners sugar
    1 pkg (12 oz) semi-sweet chocolate bits

In medium bowl, combine melted butter or margarine, graham cracker crumbs, peanut butter and sugar; beat with wooden spoon or electric beater until thoroughly mixed and crumbly. Press evenly into an ungreased 9x13-inch pan and set aside.

In top of double boiler, melt chocolate over hot, not boiling, water until smooth; spread evenly over peanut butter mixture in pan. Let stand at room temperature until chocolate hardens. When hard, cut into small squares (the cookies are very rich). Makes about 3½ dozen cookies.

COOKIES and CAKES

MAKES 2 DOZEN

Jennie Booth's Nighty-Nights

    2 large egg whites
    ⅔ c sugar
    1 generous cup real chocolate bits

Line two cookie sheets with metal foil. The foil is necessary because if the sheets have any grease at all on them, the recipe will not work.

Pre-heat oven to 325 degrees.

In small bowl of electric mixer, beat egg whites until foamy. Gradually add sugar, beating at high speed. Continue beating until meringue is very stiff. Fold in chocolate bits. Drop by teaspoonfuls onto prepared cookie sheets. Place sheets in pre-heated oven and turn off oven. Let sit in oven overnight. In the morning the confections will be crisp and dry. Makes about two dozen meringue candies.

SERVES 18

Joan Elliot's Chocolate Zucchini Cake

    1 c brown sugar
    ½ granulated sugar
    1 stick (8 T) margarine, softened
    ½ c vegetable oil
    3 eggs
    1 t vanilla
    ½ c milk mixed with ½ t vinegar
    2½ c flour
    ¼ c unsweetened cocoa
    2 t baking soda
    ½ t allspice
    ½ t cinnamon
    1½ to 2 c grated zucchini
    ½ to 1 c semi-sweet chocolate bits, if desired
    ½ to 1 c chopped nuts, if desired

In large bowl of electric mixer, combine sugars, margarine and vegetable oil. Beat until fluffy. Add eggs one at a time, beating after each addition. Add vanilla and soured milk; beat until smooth. Sift flour, cocoa, baking soda, allspice and cinnamon together and add gradually to mixture, beating until smooth. Fold in zucchini and chocolate bits and nuts, if desired, until well incorporated. Turn batter into greased and floured 9x13-inch baking pan. Bake at 325 degrees 45 to 60 minutes, or until cake tests done. Cool on wire rack and cut into squares to serve. Makes about 18 servings. Frosting is not necessary and cake may be frozen, well-wrapped.

SERVES 12 TO 18

Laurie Happ's Brownie Bars

- 1 pkg (14 oz) caramels
- ⅔ c undiluted evaporated milk, divided
- 1 pkg (18.5 oz) German chocolate cake mix
- ¾ c margarine, softened
- 1 c chopped walnuts
- 1 pkg (6 oz) semi-sweet chocolate bits

In top half of double-boiler, melt caramels and ⅓ cup of the condensed milk over hot water.

Meanwhile, in large bowl, combine cake mix, margarine, nuts and remaining ⅓ cup condensed milk; mix until all ingredients are moistened. Spoon one half of the mixture into greased and floured 9x13-inch baking pan and bake six minutes at 350 degrees.

Remove pan from oven and sprinkle evenly with chocolate bits. Spread melted caramel mixture on top of chocolate and spoon remaining cake mixture over all. Return to oven and bake 12 to 18 minutes longer at 350 degrees, until puffed and edges start to leave sides of the pan. Cool and cut into small squares.

MAKES 4 CAKES

Lucy's Fruitcake-Haters Fruitcake

    2 c butter, softened
 2½ c firmly packed light brown sugar
    1 c honey
  10 eggs
    4 c sifted flour
    2 t baking powder
    2 t cinnamon
    1 t ground allspice
  ¾ t salt
    3 lbs dried apricots, sliced
    2 lbs pecan halves
 1½ lbs pitted dates, sliced
    1 lb golden raisins
    1 c apricot nectar
  ½ c light cream
    2 T lemon juice
    1 c brandy
  ¼ c orange-flavored liqueur

In large bowl of electric mixer, cream together butter, brown sugar and honey. Add eggs one at a time, beating well after each. In another large bowl, sift together flour, baking powder, cinnamon, allspice and salt. Stir half the flour mixture into the butter mixture. In the remaining flour mixture, dredge apricots, pecans, dates and raisins. In small bowl, stir together nectar, cream and lemon juice. Add nectar mixture to batter and fold in apricot/nut mixture. Pour batter into four buttered and floured 9 x 5 x 3-inch loaf pans. Bake at 250 degrees 2½ to three hours, or until cake tester inserted in center comes out clean. Cool cakes in pans on wire racks. In small bowl, stir together brandy and orange liqueur; sprinkle each cake with one-quarter of the mixture. Let cakes stand one hour. Remove from pans, wrap tightly in foil and refrigerate at least one week. Makes four fruitcakes.

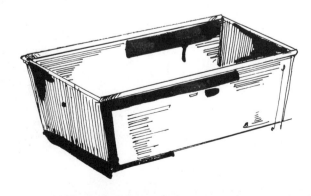

MAKES 8 TO 9 DOZEN

Marga Stya's Cranberry Christmas Cookies

½ c butter, softened
1 c sugar
¾ c brown sugar
¼ c milk
1 egg
2 T orange juice or orange-flavored liqueur
3 c flour
1 t baking powder
½ t salt
¼ t baking soda
2½ c coarsely chopped cranberries
1 c chopped walnuts

In large bowl, cream together butter and sugars until fluffy. Beat in milk, egg and orange juice or orange-flavored liqueur until well blended. Gradually add flour, baking powder, salt and baking soda; beat until thoroughly combined. Fold in cranberries and walnuts.

Drop by teaspoons on greased baking sheet and bake at 375 degrees 10 to 15 minutes, until puffed and light brown. Let rest on baking sheet a few minutes before removing with spatula. Cool completely on wire rack or wax paper. Makes eight to nine dozen cookies.

COOKIES and CAKES

MAKES 3 DOZEN

Oatmeal Cookies and Variations

      3⅓ c Homemade Oatmeal Cookie Mix
      1 egg
      3 T water
      1 t vanilla

In medium bowl combine cookie mix, egg, water and vanilla; mix well with electric beater or wooden spoon until stiff dough is formed. Drop by rounded teaspoons onto greased cookie sheet. Bake at 350 degrees 12 to 15 minutes, until light golden brown. Cool one minute on cookie sheet before removing to wire rack or waxed paper. When cooled, store in covered container. Makes about three dozen cookies.

For variations, add one of the following to each batch of oatmeal cookies:

Raisin-Spice Cookies — Add ½ cup raisins, ½ teaspoon cinnamon, ¼ teaspoon nutmeg and ⅛ teaspoon ground cloves.

Oatmeal Chippers — Add one 6-oz. package semi-sweet chocolate pieces or butterscotch pieces.

Sunny Nut Drops — Add ½ cup chopped nuts and 1 teaspoon grated orange or lemon peel.

MAKES 13⅓ CUPS MIX OR 4 BATCHES OF COOKIES

Oatmeal Cookie Mix

      2½ c flour
      2 t salt
      1 t baking soda
      2 c firmly-packed brown sugar
      1 c sugar
      1½ c vegetable shortening
      6 c (1 18-oz carton) quick or old-fashioned rolled oats

In large bowl, combine flour, salt, and soda; add brown sugar and sugar, mixing until well combined. Cut in shortening, using food processor or pastry blender, until mixture resembles gravel. Stir in oats. Store in tightly covered containers in refrigerator or in cool dry place for up to three months. Makes 13⅓ cups cookie mix, or enough for four batches of cookies.

SERVES 12

Orange Chiffon Cake

1½ c instant blending flour or cake flour
1½ c sugar
 3 t baking powder
 1 t salt
 ½ c vegetable oil
 7 eggs, separated
 ¾ c cold water
 1 t vanilla
 2 T grated orange rind
 ½ t cream of tartar
      Orange Butter Frosting (recipe follows) or confectioners sugar, if desired

In large bowl, combine flour, sugar, baking powder and salt; blend thoroughly. Make a depression in the dry ingredients and add oil, egg yolks, water, vanilla and orange rind. Beat with electric mixer or spoon until smooth. In large bowl of electric mixer, beat egg whites and cream of tartar until stiff peaks are formed. Fold flour mixture into egg white mixture gently until well combined. Pour batter into *ungreased* 10x4-inch tube or angel food cake pan. Bake at 325 degrees 55 minutes. Increase oven heat to 350 degrees and continue baking 10 to 15 minutes, until cake springs back when touched lightly. Invert pan on funnel or on pan prongs and cool completely. Carefully remove from pan and frost with Orange Butter Frosting (recipe follows) or sprinkle with confectioners sugar, if desired. Makes about 12 servings

Orange Butter Frosting

 ⅓ c butter or margarine
 3 c confectioners sugar
 ½ t grated orange rind
 2 T fresh orange juice

In medium bowl, soften butter or margarine. Add sugar and orange rind; mix until well combined and add orange juice, a little at a time, until mixture is desired spreading consistency. Makes about 1½ cups frosting.

COOKIES and CAKES

MAKES 1 CAKE

Orange-Zucchini Pound Cake

  1 c butter or margarine
  2 c brown sugar
  1 T orange rind, grated
  1 t cinnamon
  ½ t nutmeg
  ¼ t ground cloves
  4 eggs
  3 c flour
  3 t baking powder
  ½ t salt
  ½ c orange juice
  1 c zucchini, grated and lightly packed
  Confectioners sugar or frosting of choice, if desired

In large bowl of electric mixer, cream together butter or margarine, brown sugar, orange rind, cinnamon, nutmeg and cloves. Add eggs, one at a time, beating thoroughly after each addition. In medium bowl, stir together flour, baking powder and salt. Add flour mixture to egg mixture alternately with orange juice. Stir in zucchini and mix thoroughly. Pour batter into lightly greased and floured bundt pan or 10-inch tube pan. Bake at 350 degrees one hour or until cake tests done. Let rest in pan on wire rack 10 minutes; remove from pan and cool completely on wire rack. When cooled, sprinkle with confectioners sugar or frost, if desired.

MAKES 4 DOZEN

Quick Mix and Pecan Pie Squares

  2 c Bisquick or Quick Mix
  2 T granulated sugar
  ¼ c firm butter or margarine
  ½ c firmly packed brown sugar
  1 c light corn syrup
  3 T melted margarine or butter
  3 eggs
  1 t vanilla
  1 c chopped pecans

In large bowl or food processor, mix Bisquick or Quick Mix and sugar. Cut in firm butter or margarine until mixture is crumbly. Press mixture onto bottom of ungreased 13x9x2-inch baking pan. Bake at 350 degrees until light brown, about 10 to 12 minutes. Remove from oven and cool.

Meanwhile, in medium bowl, mix brown sugar, corn syrup, melted margarine or butter, eggs, vanilla and pecans; blend thoroughly. Pour mixture over cooled crust. Return to oven and bake at 350 degrees until set and light brown on top, about 25 minutes. Remove from oven and loosen edges from sides of pan while still warm. Cool completely; cut into 1½-inch squares. Store in loosely covered container. Makes about four dozen squares.

MAKES 4 DOZEN

Renee Murawski's Hungarian Nut Horns

- 1 c butter or margarine
- 2 c flour
- 1 egg yolk
- ¾ c sour cream
- ¾ c finely ground walnuts
- ¾ c sugar
- 2 t cinnamon
- Confectioners sugar

Cut margarine or butter into flour as for pie dough. Mix sour cream and egg yolk; add to flour mixture and knead on floured board until smooth. Divide dough into three balls. Wrap in waxed paper or plastic wrap and refrigerate overnight.

The next day, in small bowl, combine nuts, sugar and cinnamon. Roll out each dough ball into a 9-inch circle and sprinkle each circle with one-third of the nut mixture. Cut each circle into 16 wedges. Starting from the wide end, roll up each wedge into a crescent. Place crescents on lightly greased cookie sheet and bake at 375 degrees about 20 minutes. When cool, dust with confectioners sugar. Makes about four dozen cookies.

COOKIES and CAKES

Sharon Warner's German Sour Cream Twists

3½ c flour
1 t salt
1 c shortening, at least ⅓ butter
1 pkg (¼ oz) active dry yeast
¼ c warm water
¾ c sour cream
1 whole egg and 2 egg yolks, well beaten
1 t vanilla
1 c sugar, divided

In large mixing bowl, combine flour and salt. With two knives or pastry cutter, cut in shortening-butter mixture; set mixture aside.

Sprinkle yeast into water and stir until dissolved. Stir into reserved flour mixture with sour cream, eggs and vanilla. Mix well with hands (the dough will be sticky). Cover bowl with damp cloth and refrigerate at least two hours.

Divide dough in half. Return half to refrigerator; on well-sugared board, roll the other half into an 8x16-inch oblong. Fold ends toward center, overlapping ends. Sprinkle with ¼ cup sugar and roll out again. Repeat process, using another ¼ cup sugar. Then roll out to a rectangle about ¼-inch thick. Cut into 1x4-inch strips. Twist each strip and form into a horseshoe shape.

Remove dough from refrigerator and repeat process, using the remaining ½ cup of sugar. Put strips on ungreased cookie sheet two inches apart and bake at 375 degrees 12 to 15 minutes, until lightly browned. Remove from cookie sheet immediately and cool, upside down, on waxed paper or on wire rack. Makes about 36 twists.

SERVES 12 TO 18

Theresa Smola's Brownies

- ½ c butter, softened
- 1 c sugar
- 4 eggs
- 1 t vanilla
- 1 can (16 oz) chocolate syrup
- 1 c sifted flour
- ½ t salt
- 1 c chopped nuts
- 1 pkg (6 oz) semi-sweet chocolate bits

In large bowl, cream butter and sugar together until light and fluffy. Add eggs, vanilla and chocolate syrup; beat thoroughly. Add flour and salt and beat until blended. Stir in nuts and chocolate bits. Spread mixture in greased 9x13-inch baking pan. Bake at 350 degrees 30 to 35 minutes. Cool and cut into squares.

MAKES 4½ TO 6 DOZEN

Vanilla Wafers

    2 c sifted flour
    2 t baking powder
    ½ t salt
    ⅔ c softened butter or margarine
    1 c sugar
 1½ t vanilla
    1 extra-large egg
    ¼ c milk

Sift together flour, baking powder and salt into small bowl and set aside. In medium bowl of electric mixer, cream butter or margarine, sugar and vanilla until fluffy. Beat in egg. Add flour mixture alternately with milk and beat until well mixed. Drop by teaspoons onto ungreased cookie sheet, about 2½ inches apart. Place wet cloth over bottom of a glass and flatten dough balls to about ⅛-inch thickness. (Wring out cloth in cold water frequently to prevent it from becoming sticky.) Bake at 375 degrees about 10 minutes, or just until cookies brown at the edges. Remove from pan at once with spatula, cool and store in airtight containers. Makes 4½ to six dozen wafers.

MISCELLANEOUS

MAKES 2 LBS

Baked Caramel Corn

- 1 c (two sticks) butter or margarine
- 2 c firmly packed brown sugar
- ½ c light or dark corn syrup
- 1 t salt
- 1 t vanilla
- ½ t baking soda
- 6 qts popped corn
- 1 lb salted peanuts, if desired

In 3-qt. saucepan, melt butter or margarine; stir in brown sugar, corn syrup and salt. Bring to a boil, stirring constantly. Then boil, without stirring, five minutes over medium heat, until mixture reaches the soft-ball stage. Remove from heat and stir in vanilla. Add baking soda and stir vigorously (the mixture will foam). Gradually pour over popped corn and peanuts, if desired, stirring and mixing well. Turn into two or three large baking pans, leaving enough room to stir the mixture. Bake at 250 degrees one hour, stirring well every 15 minutes. (The caramel tends to sink to the bottom, so the mixture must be completely turned during stirring.) Remove from oven and cool completely; break mass apart. Store in air-tight containers. Makes about two pounds of caramel corn.

Bow Wow Biscuits For Dogs

2½ c whole wheat flour
½ c wheat germ
½ c non-fat powdered dry milk
½ t salt
½ t garlic powder
1 t brown sugar
8 T meat, bacon drippings or margarine
1 egg, beaten
2 T beef or chicken broth
Crumbled bacon or grated cheese, if desired
½ c or more ice water

In large bowl or food processor container, combine flour, wheat germ, dry milk, salt, garlic powder and brown sugar. Cut in, or process, meat, bacon drippings or margarine into mixture, until mixture is crumbly. Add egg and broth — through feeder tube with machine running, if a processor is used — and mix thoroughly. Add crumbled bacon or grated cheese if desired. Add ice water as needed to form mixture into a ball. If processor is used, add water through feeder tube with machine running, just until mixture leaves the side of the bowl and starts forming a ball on metal blades. Pat or roll out dough on floured surface to ½-inch thickness. Cut into bone biscuit shapes (cutters are available in many kitchen stores) or any cookie shape. Place on cookie sheet lined with foil and oiled lightly. Bake at 350 degrees 30 minutes, or until quite hard and brown at edges. Makes about 18 large biscuits.

Creamy Chocolate Fudge

3 c sugar
¾ c margarine
1 can (5⅓ oz) or ⅔ cup evaporated milk
3 pkgs (4 oz each) sweet German chocolate, broken into pieces
1 jar (7 oz) marshmallow creme
1 t vanilla
1 c chopped nuts, if desired

In heavy 2½ qt. saucepan, combine sugar, margarine and milk; bring to a full rolling boil, stirring constantly. Boil five minutes, over medium heat, stirring constantly to prevent scorching. Remove from heat and stir in chocolate pieces until melted. Add marshmallow creme and vanilla; beat until well blended. Stir in nuts, if desired, or nuts may be reserved to press into top of fudge when partially cooled. Pour mixture into well buttered 13x9 inch pan. Chill several hours until hardened. Makes about two pounds fudge.

MISCELLANEOUS

Ellis Boal's Homemade Yogurt

 2 c non-fat dry milk powder
   Cold water
 2 to 3 T plain commercial yogurt or starter from previous
   batch homemade yogurt

Pour dry milk powder into 4-cup measuring container; add water to bring level to four cups. Stir until powder is dissolved and pour into top of double boiler. Heat over simmering water until milk reaches 180 to 200 degrees on thermometer. (A candy thermometer may be used for this step.) Remove from heat and let milk cool to 120 degrees. Add starter or plain yogurt and whisk in thoroughly and pour into 1-qt. glass jar or yogurt maker container. Put top on loosely. Place jar or container into insulator container and let sit at least four hours. (Glass jar may be wrapped in towel, then placed in a bucket, if yogurt insulator container is not available.)

When yogurt has thickened, place in refrigerator to chill. Makes about one quart yogurt.

Homemade Curry Powder

 2½ oz cumin seed
  2 oz coriander seed
  2 oz turmeric seed
  2 oz fenugreek seed
 1½ oz poppy seed
 1½ oz cardamom seeds, removed from white pods
  ½ oz mustard seed
  2 oz black peppercorns
  2 oz dried chili pods
  1 oz ground cinnamon
  ½ oz powdered ginger

In heavy iron skillet, combine seeds of cumin, coriander, turmeric, fenugreek, poppy, cardamom and mustard. (If you are unable to obtain the seeds of any of these spices, use the ground spice but add any ground spice at the end of the recipe — after the seeds have been roasted and ground.) Add peppercorns and chili pods. Heat skillet over medium heat and dry-roast mixture, stirring frequently, for about 10 minutes. Be careful not to burn mixture. When done, the mixture will be lightly browned and will give off a very pungent odor. *Do not breathe in fumes from the mixture.* Turn mixture into blender container and process on grind until mixture is pulverized. Transfer to a bowl and stir in cinnamon and ginger. Store in tightly covered container. Makes 2½ cups curry powder.

MISCELLANEOUS

MAKES 1 CUP

Hot Mustard

½ c cider vinegar
½ c dry English mustard
  c brown sugar
1 egg
¼ t salt
1 T horseradish or to taste

In blender or food processor with steel blade, combine vinegar, dry mustard, brown sugar, egg and salt; blend or process until smooth. Scrape mixture into small saucepan and cook over moderate heat, whisking constantly, until thickened and smooth. Remove from heat and let stand five minutes. Stir in horseradish. Store in covered container in refrigerator. Makes one cup.

MAKES 8 TO 10 PINTS

Irene's Cucumber Relish

4 qts pickling cucumbers (about 16 to 20 large cucumbers) unpeeled
4 red bell peppers, seeded
4 green bell peppers, seeded
4 large onions
4 hot peppers, ends snipped off, unseeded
4 T salt
4 c cider vinegar
4 c sugar
2 t black pepper
2 t turmeric
1 t mustard seed
1 t celery seed
8 to 10 hot sterilized pint jars, sealing lids and screw-on caps

Using food grinder or food processor with steel blade, grind or finely chop cucumbers, red and green bell peppers, onions and hot peppers. (If using large cucumbers, remove large seeds before grinding). Place vegetable mixture in large crock or ceramic bowl and add salt; mix thoroughly and let stand overnight.

The next day drain vegetables thoroughly by squeezing out moisture with hands or in thin kitchen towel. Place vegetables in large pot or saucepan; add vinegar, sugar, pepper, turmeric, mustard seed and celery seed. Mix thoroughly and bring to a boil; lower heat and simmer mixture 40 to 45 minutes, stirring frequently. Ladle relish into hot sterilized jars, filling jars to ¼ inch of the top. Cap and seal immediately; adjust seals when cool. Makes eight to 10 pints relish.

MAKES 4 8 OZ. JARS

Jalapeno Pepper Jelly

    3   large green peppers
    2   to 3 fresh or canned jalapeno peppers, seeds removed
    4   c sugar
    ¾   c white vinegar
    2   or 3 drops liquid hot pepper sauce
    3   oz liquid pectin (1 3-oz envelope)
    2   drops green food coloring

In blender or food processor, puree green peppers. Drain well, pressing down in strainer; reserve 1½ cups of pureed green pepper. Puree jalapeno peppers in blender or food processor, reserving two to three teaspoonfuls of pulp. (When handling jalapeno peppers, *take care not to touch your face or eyes;* wash your hands with soap and water after contact with the peppers.)

In medium-sized, heavy saucepan, combine green pepper puree and jalapeno pepper puree, sugar and vinegar. Bring mixture to full boil over high heat. Boil, at full boil, three minutes. Remove from heat; add hot pepper sauce, pectin and food coloring. Stir until well blended and return to high heat; boil one minute. Remove from heat and immediately pour into hot sterilized eight-ounce jelly jars. Seal or top with melted paraffin. Makes four eight-ounce jars of jelly.

MAKES 6 CUPS

Mother Johnson's Irish Cream

    1   can (14 oz) sweetened condensed milk
    2   c half & half
    2   c 80 proof Canadian whisky
    1   t instant coffee granules
    2   oz coffee liqueur

In a large bottle or jug, combine evaporated milk, half & half, whisky, instant coffee and coffee liqueur. Mix well, and chill before serving.

MISCELLANEOUS

MAKES 5 6 OZ. JARS

Pumpkin Butter

- 1 can (29 oz) pureed pumpkin (do not use pumpkin pie filling) or 1½ lbs fresh pumpkin, ground
- 2¼ c firmly packed light brown sugar
- 1 lemon, ground, juice and rind
- ½ T ground ginger
- ½ T cinnamon
- ¼ t allspice
- ½ c water

If you are using fresh pumpkin: In large bowl, combine pumpkin, sugar, ground lemon, ginger, cinnamon and allspice. Let stand at room temperature overnight. In the morning, transfer to heavy saucepan, add water and bring to a boil, reduce heat and simmer gently, stirring frequently, 40 to 60 minutes, until thickened and soft.

If using canned pumpkin: Combine all ingredients in medium, heavy saucepan, and bring to a boil. Reduce heat and simmer, stirring frequently, until slightly thickened and darkened, about 20 minutes.

Pour mixture into hot, sterile 6-oz. jelly jars, leaving ½-inch head space, and seal. Process in boiling water bath 10 minutes. Cool and adjust seals. Makes five 6-oz. jars Pumpkin Butter.

MAKES 1/2 LB.

Sally Lieberman's Microwave Peanut Brittle

- 1 c sugar
- ½ c light corn syrup
- 1 c salted peanuts
- 1 t butter
- 1 t vanilla
- 1 t baking soda

Generously butter a cookie sheet and have ready next to microwave oven. In 2-qt. bowl, suitable for microwave cooking, combine sugar and corn syrup; stir until well mixed. Microwave on high four minutes. Remove from oven and add peanuts; stir until well mixed. Be very careful not to get hot syrup on hands. Microwave on high four minutes. Remove from oven and add butter and vanilla; stir until well mixed. Microwave 1½ to 2 minutes. Remove from oven and add baking soda. Gently stir until mixture is light and foamy. Pour immediately into prepared cookie sheet and spread out with buttered spatula. This step must be done quickly or brittle will start to harden in bowl.

Cool for 30 minutes to an hour. Break into pieces. Makes about ½ pound peanut brittle.

MISCELLANEOUS

MAKES 1½ CUPS

Sauce Aioli

- 1 slice white bread, about ¾-inch thick
- 3 T milk
- 4 large cloves garlic, mashed
- 2 egg yolks at room temperature
- ½ t salt
- ¼ t white pepper
- 1 c olive oil, divided
- 2 T lemon juice
  Additional salt and white pepper, if desired
  Cream, if desired

Trim crusts from bread and discard. In small bowl, crumble bread, stir in milk and let soak 10 minutes. Squeeze out excess moisture from bread and discard; place bread in bowl of electric mixer. Add garlic. At high speed, beat in egg yolks, salt and white pepper. Continue beating until very thick, about one minute. Add ⅓ cup of the olive oil, drop by drop, beating constantly at high speed until oil is completely absorbed. Add the remaining oil, in thin steady stream, beating at high speed until oil is completely absorbed and mixture has the consistency of mayonnaise. Add lemon juice and additional salt and white pepper, if desired. Thin sauce with cream, if desired. Makes about 1½ cups sauce; excellent with roast chicken or steamed vegetables or as a dip.

MAKES 36

Spiced Apple Rings

- 12 medium-size red Delicious apples
- 1 c sugar
- 8 c water
- 4 t red food coloring
- 1 t allspice
- 1 t mace
- 1 t whole cloves (about 30)
- ¼ c red cinnamon candies, if desired

Peel and core apples; cut into slices about ⅜-inch thick. (To prevent discoloration, immediately rest apple rings in a solution of one quart of water mixed with one to two tablespoons lemon juice.)

In large saucepan or skillet, combine sugar, water and food coloring. Tie allspice, mace and cloves in spice bag and add to pan. Add cinnamon candies, if desired. Bring mixture to a boil and add apple rings. Cook over medium heat, turning rings often, until apples are tender but firm, about seven to 10 minutes. Remove from heat; remove spice bag. Submerge apple rings in syrup with a weighted plate and refrigerate overnight. Freeze or store covered with the syrup. Makes about 36 apple rings.

Sweetened Condensed Milk

MAKES 14 OZ.
(equivalent of one can)

1 c instant non-fat dry milk powder
⅔ c sugar
3 T melted butter
⅓ c boiling water

In blender, combine dry milk powder and sugar. Pour in melted butter and, with machine running, add boiling water. Blend, scraping sides of blender, until mixture is smooth and thick. Store in covered container in refrigerator until used. Makes 14 oz. or equivalent of one can.

Two-Day Refrigerator Pickles

MAKES 4 PINTS

12 pickling cucumbers, about five inches long
4 to 6 sprigs of fresh dill per jar
1 qt water
¾ c vinegar
3 oz coarse salt, about ⅓ cup
4 cloves garlic, thinly sliced

Scrub cucumbers thoroughly and cut off ends and discard; pack into four sterilized pint jars with dill sprigs. (Cucumbers may be cut in half to facilitate tight packing.) In medium saucepan, combine water, vinegar, salt and garlic slices. Bring to a boil and cook five minutes over high heat. Remove from heat and let brine cool completely. Pour brine over pickles to within ¼ inch of the top of the jars. Seal and refrigerate immediately. The pickles will be ready to eat in two days. Makes four pints.